Code-switching

D0907415

It is quite commonplace for bilingual speakers to use two or more languages, dialects or varieties in the same conversation, without any apparent effort. This phenomenon, known as code-switching, has become a major focus of attention in linguistics. This concise and original study explores how, when and where code-switching occurs. Drawing on a diverse range of examples from medieval manuscripts to rap music, novels to advertisements, emails to political speeches, and above all everyday conversation, it argues that code-switching can only be properly understood if we study it from a variety of perspectives. It shows how sociolinguistic, psycholinguistic, grammatical and developmental aspects of code-switching are all interdependent, and findings in each area are crucial to others. Breaking down barriers across the discipline of linguistics, this pioneering book confronts fundamental questions about what a "native language" is, and whether languages can be meaningfully studied independently from individuals who use them.

PENELOPE GARDNER-CHLOROS is Senior Lecturer in the Department of Applied Linguistics and Communication, Birkbeck, University of London. Her publications include *Language Selection and Switching in Strasbourg* (1991) and *Vernacular Literacy: a Re-evaluation* (with Tabouret-Keller, Le Page and Varro, 1997). She is a founding member of the LIDES group, which has set up the first database of bilingual texts. She has published widely on code-switching and on her other field of interest, Terms of Address, in sociolinguistic journals and books.

Code-switching

Penelope Gardner-Chloros

Birkbeck College, University of London

CAMBRIDGE
UNIVERSITY PRESS

CAMBRIDGE UNIVERSITY PRESS
Cambridge, New York, Melbourne, Madrid, Cape Town, Singapore, São Paulo, Delhi
Delhi, Tokyo, Mexico City

Cambridge University Press
The Edinburgh Building, Cambridge CB2 8RU, UK

Published in the United States of America by Cambridge University Press, New York

www.cambridge.org
Information on this title: www.cambridge.org/9780521681131

First published 2009
Reprinted 2011

Printed in the United Kingdom at the University Press, Cambridge

A catalogue record for this publication is available from the British Library

Library of Congress Cataloging-in-Publication Data
Gardner-Chloros, Penelope.
Code-switching / Penelope Gardner-Chloros.
   p.   cm.
Includes bibliographical references and index.
ISBN 978-0-521-86264-6
1. Code switching (Linguistics)   I. Title.
P115.3.G36   2009
306.44–dc22

                                                                        2009006833

ISBN 978-0-521-86264-6 hardback
ISBN 978-0-521-68113-1 paperback

To Alexander, Nicholas, Zoe and Philip

John Godfrey Saxe's (1816–1887) version of the famous Indian legend

It was six men of Indostan
To learning much inclined
Who went to see the elephant
(Though all of them were blind),
That each by observation
Might satisfy his mind

The First approached the Elephant
And happening to fall
Against his broad and sturdy side
At once began to bawl:
"God bless me! but the Elephant
Is very like a wall!"

The Second, feeling of the tusk
Cried "Ho! What have we here,
So very round and smooth and sharp
To me tis mighty clear
This wonder of an Elephant
Is very like a spear!"

The Third approached the animal
And happening to take
The squirming trunk within his hands
Thus boldly up he spake:
"I see" quoth he, "the Elephant
Is very like a snake!"

The Fourth reached out an eager hand
And felt about the knee
"What most this wondrous beast is like
Is mighty plain," quoth he;
"Tis clear enough the Elephant
Is very like a tree!"

The Fifth, who chanced to touch the ear,
Said: "E'en the blindest man

Can tell what this resembles most;
Deny the fact who can,
This marvel of an Elephant
Is very like a fan!"

The Sixth no sooner had begun
About the beast to grope
Than, seizing on the swinging tail
That fell within his scope
"I see," quoth he, "the Elephant
Is very like a rope!"

And so these men of Indostan
Disputed loud and long
Each in his opinion
Exceeding stiff and strong,
Though each was partly in the right
And all were in the wrong!

This rendition of Saxe's poem is compiled from two sources: Don Fabun (1968), *Communications, the Transfer of Meaning*, New York: Macmillan, p. 13 and John Godfrey Saxe (1963), *The Blind Men and the Elephant; John Godfrey Saxe's version of the famous Indian legend. Pictures by Paul Galdone*, New York: Whittlesey House; a letter to me from McGraw-Hill (dated 15 August 1998) states that the text for this edition appears to be in the public domain, but the illustrations are not. Note that the text from each of these two sources differs from my version with respect to one line, and they are different lines. I have not seen the original first edition, but this is my best guess of it. Incidentally, the original parable originated in China sometime during the Han dynasty (202 BC–220 AD) as:"Three Blind Men and an Elephant".

Contents

Acknowledgements

I would like to express my warmest thanks to those – whether named here or not – who have either helped me, or provided general support and inspiration over the period of gestation – more elephantine than human – of this book.

Two distinguished scholars of Bilingualism, Andrée Tabouret-Keller and Michel Blanc, have been a source of ideas, advice, encouragement and friendship throughout the process. This book would not have seen the light without them. My debt to Bob Le Page, now sadly missed, is also considerable. Together with Andrée, and inspired by the unfocused linguistic landscapes of Jamaica and Belize, he is responsible for the fundamental question which underlies many of the puzzles in this book: "What is a language?" His legacy lives on in many of today's most significant linguists. I also owe the greatest thanks to Li Wei, one of the foremost experts on Bilingualism, who has provided support of many kinds and commented repeatedly on the manuscript as it developed.

My colleagues at Birkbeck have allowed various periods of leave devoted to writing this book and provided much fruitful discussion and advice. Malcolm Edwards gave concrete help beyond the call of duty and deserves a large part of the credit for Chapter 5, which is partly based on work we did together; his wicked sense of humour and wit have brightened up the daily grind for a number of years. Itesh Sachdev, now at SOAS, and Jean-Marc Dewaele also provided valuable advice and support. Ken Mackley in Birkbeck Library was a bibliographical hero and showed that humans still have the edge on Google.

Other colleagues have helped in numerous ways. Apart from working with me on various aspects of code-switching, Jenny Cheshire has been a first-class colleague and friend throughout. My LIPPS colleagues have played a major role, as should be clear from the book: Mark Sebba and Melissa Moyer first and foremost, but Roeland van Hout, Eva Eppler, Jeanine Treffers-Daller, Pieter Muysken, Ad Backus, Jacomine Nortier and others involved in the LIPPS enterprise are all deserving of thanks. Mark Sebba also read and commented usefully on the manuscript. Lisa McEntee-Atalianis and Katerina Finnis provided active collaboration and assistance but also companionship, without which doing research would be lonely indeed. For help in sourcing, translating and understanding the significance of the illustrations, I am most grateful to Darren Aoki, Tamar Drukker, Tony Hunt, Shahrzad Mahootian, Andrew Mason and Ian Short.

No book on code-switching can fail to acknowledge a debt to Carol Myers-Scotton, who has done so much to put code-switching on the map, and who has always been a generous correspondent. I have also benefited from advice from Jeff MacSwan. Others who deserve thanks include Peter Auer, Michael Clyne, Adam Jaworski and François Grosjean. My students at Birkbeck, particularly on the MA Applied Linguistics and MA Bilingualism, have provided many insights on, and examples of, code-switching. Needless to say, the responsibility for all errors, misinterpretations and omissions is mine alone.

My thanks also to Helen Barton and Jodie Barnes at Cambridge University Press, Adrian Stenton for his editorial work, and the Guggenheim Foundation, Venice for the right to reproduce the cover picture, especially Mr. Silvio Veronese.

Finally, this book was produced with inspiration – and no small measure of distraction – from its (plurilingual) dedicatees . My heartfelt thanks go to Piers, for defending my fundamental human right to be excused, many times, from domestic duties and to be provided with tea and sympathy as required.

Transcription conventions

(1) Making the examples easy for English-speaking readers to follow has been given priority over consistency of presentation in different instances, and the use of non-Latin alphabets has been avoided. Extracts from data discussed by others have been presented as they originally presented them, e.g. examples from Auer, Li Wei and Sebba follow the Atkinson and Heritage (1984) conventions.

(2) A word-for-word (or morpheme-for-morpheme) gloss is sometimes given below the examples, as well as a free translation below that; at other times there is a free translation only. This depends partly on what type of point is being made about the switch, and partly, where the example is taken from someone else's work, on whether a gloss was provided in the original source.

(3) CS has been picked out by the use of bold script for one of the languages involved (and corresponding use of fonts in the translation below). Where there is a third language involved this appears in bold italics. The implied decisions about which words belong to which language are often somewhat arbitrary and should be taken only as a general indication.

(4) In the examples from data collected in Strasbourg, the spelling of Alsatian is based on a system derived from German spelling (Matzen, 1980), the purpose of which is to provide a standardized spelling system for the Strasbourg dialect.

(5) In Greek/GCD examples, Greek has been transcribed into a semi-phonetic Roman script, retaining the Greek letters $/\chi/$, $/\delta/$ and $/\gamma/$ which sound the same as those in the IPA (International Phonetic Alphabet). Other sounds follow English spelling: $/\theta/$ is represented as 'th' and $/\int/$ as sh. The phonetic symbol $/j/$ is left as an i (e.g. [ja] = ia) so as to avoid confusion with the English letter j.

1 Introduction

1.1 What is code-switching?

In Alsace, in eastern France, French is commonly mixed with the local dialect, Alsatian, which is a variety of German (or more precisely Alemannic). At a family gathering in Strasbourg on New Year's Eve, a discussion starts regarding the poor quality of Alsatian butchers compared to those in the rest of France. One of the guests, Mr Eder,[1] a jovial middle-aged man and a prolific talker, holds forth:

Example 1

1 MR EDER: **du bekommsch do e fätze** ... je sais pas dans quelle graisse
  you get some sort of scraps ... in goodness knows what sort of fat

2 ... avec quoi: avec **de de de was weiss denn de teiffel**
  ... with what: with the the the the devil knows what

3 **noh geh i anne un! putz diss ding**
  then I have to go and clean the thing up

4 parce que lorsque tu as un morceau de viande **im ... im teller**
  because when you have a piece of meat   on ... on your plate

5 **un noochher hesch eso gschnuddels un muesch abschniede diss ganze ding gell.**
  and then you find you have a sort of mess and you have to cut the whole thing off you see

6 **oder e so hoch fett uf'm ding ... diss haw i halt schliesslich a nitt gere gell?**
  or fat this high on top of it ... I really don't like that at all you see

(Gardner-Chloros, 1991:124)

Mr Eder is a fluent speaker of both French and the Alsatian dialect. His apparent hesitations, represented by dots or repetitions, are found in stretches *within* the same language (L2, L4, L6) just as often as *between* stretches in different languages – their purpose is dramatic effect. No rhyme or reason appears to govern the points at which he passes from one language to the other. This form of expression in bilinguals has been called "mixed discourse" – to say that there are two separate languages is more or less meaningless from the participants' point of view. In L2, he also uses a "bridge", i.e. a word which could come from

---

[1] All proper names have been changed.

either language, to facilitate the switch: *de*, which can be a partitive in French or a definite article in Alsatian.

Example 2

A second generation Greek Cypriot teenager, brought up and living in London, Olga, told this story about why her father emigrated to England. The interviewer spoke the Greek Cypriot Dialect so as to encourage Olga to use that variety.

1 INTERVIEWER: **iati irthan stin Anglia?**
why did they come to England?

2 OLGA: this is a long story [laughs]. **Itun mesa se ena mikro χorio, tin E..[name]**
They were in a little village, E..[name].

3 **ke o pateras mu – afto mu ipen o pateras mu. δen eksero ... an ine sosto**
and my father – this is what my father told me. I don't know... if it's right.

4 **Mu ipe pos mian niχta emethisen ke pien ke epiasen mian... pos tin lene**
he told me.. that one night they got drunk ... and they went and caught a ... what's its name.

5 INTERVIEWER: **boris   na to pis sta anglika.**
You can say it in English.

6 OLGA: chicken chicken. Chicken [laughing] **pu enan γitonon....**
which (belonged) to a neighbour.

7 **ke ton ivrasi ke ipen pola. Endrapiken pola.**
and they found him and said a lot (had a big discussion). He was very ashamed.

8 **ke mu lei   ia afton ton skopon irten   stin Anglia.**
and he tells me (that it is) for that purpose [sic] *he came to England.*
(Gardner-Chloros, unpublished data)

In common with many other second/third generation London Greek Cypriots, Olga is much more at ease speaking English. She hesitates and searches for her words when she has to speak Greek. In L2, she plays for time by saying, "This is a long story" in English. Later, she cannot find the simple everyday word 'chicken' in Greek (L4), a fact which is indirectly commented upon by the interviewer (L5), and there are several other signs of her difficulties with Greek, such as her omission of the verb 'belonged' in L6. Mixing the two languages *is* the normal way to talk in her community, but speaking to a purely Greek-speaking interlocutor clearly taxes her competence in Greek.

In Example 3, it may seem to the observer that a single variety is being used, but those familiar with in-group communication in this community would recognize that speakers are in fact alternating between different varieties.

This extract is from Sebba's *London Jamaican* (1993). Two London teenage boys of Jamaican parents, Andrew and Barry, are discussing an incident involving another young man, which occurred while Andrew was serving in a shop. Although Andrew's entire description may appear to be in a variety of London English, the passages in bold are in fact in Creole. In some cases, as in the word *Lucozade* (L5), it is only the pronunciation which identifies the word as Creole (and so obviously we are taking the researcher's word that this is what happens). In other cases (e.g. the words in bold in L11), other features also tell us that this is Creole. The passage in L19–20 in capitals is described as being in a near-RP "posh" voice.[2]

Example 3

1 ANDREW: yeah man, I was on the till on Saturday (1.2) and this this black man **come** in (1.0) and (0.6) you know our shop, right, (0.6) they u:m (0.2) give (.) refund on (0.3) Lucozade bottles (0.4)

  BARRY: m:

5 ANDREW: a black man **come in an' 'im b(h)u::y** a bottle (.) of **Lucozade** while 'e was in the shop [an'

  BARRY: [free p- e's e got free pee off is it?

  ANDREW: yeah

  BARRY: small ones or big ones?

10 ANDREW: big ones and 'e drank the bottle in fron% of us an then ask(d) for the money back (see man) **me want me money now**

  BARRY: [heheh

  ANDREW: he goes (pnk) (I'm on) the till guy (.) hhh (I jus) (0.6) I jus' look round at 'im (0.6) I said well you can't 'ave it (1.9)

15 I said I 'ave to open the till (w) wait till the next customer comes (1.0) **'now! open it now and give me the money'** (1.0)

  I said I can't (0.8) the man **just thump 'is fist down** an' (screw up dis for me) (.) (s no man) the manager just comes (.)

  WOULD YOU LEAVE THE SHOP

20 BEFORE I CALL THE SECURITY: hh the man **jus' take the bottle an' fling it at me an'** (I) jus' catch it at the (ground)

  (Sebba, 1993:119–120)

Sebba suggests that code-switching is used here to "animate" the narrative by providing different "voices" for the participants in the incident which is described. Although both the customer and the narrator might be expected to speak the same variety, either London English or Creole, Andrew reserves Creole mainly to quote the customer and to describe his actions (L17 and 20–21).

These examples show that the behaviour of bilinguals can only be properly understood with some insider knowledge of the community and the circumstances

---

[2] RP is "Received Pronunciation". Pauses are indicated as in the original, as are brackets showing overlapping speech.

where it is displayed. First, the speakers' *competence* in the relevant varieties may or may not be a determining factor in their choices. Second, an observer may or may not be able to distinguish which shifts in accent, vocabulary or syntax are in some way significant for the participants in the conversation.

1.2   Why study code-switching?

Such varied combinations of two or more linguistic varieties occur in countless bilingual societies and communities, and are known as code-switching (CS).[3] It refers to the use of several languages or dialects in the same conversation or sentence by bilingual people. It affects practically everyone who is in contact with more than one language or dialect, to a greater or lesser extent. Numerous local names designate such mixed talk: Tex-Mex, Franglais, BBC Grenglish, Chinglish, Spanglish, Tuti Futi, etc. In some earlier periods of history, CS was equally common in writing (see the papers in Trotter, 2002). Apart from CS, there are a number of other possible linguistic outcomes of language contact including borrowing, convergence, pidginization, language death, etc. CS has been found to occur alongside most of these, though it does not necessarily do so. The various manifestations of contact are grouped here under the heading of *language interaction*.

1.2.1   Code-switching as a window on speech and language

The study of *why* and *how* people code-switch provides insights about many aspects of language as well as speech. This applies not only to how language and languages are organized in the brain (the mechanisms of switching as such are discussed in Chapter 6). At a functional level, bilinguals often switch varieties in order to communicate something beyond the superficial meaning of their words. Monolinguals can do this also, by switching between dialects, registers, levels of formality, intonations etc. (Bell, 1984; Coupland, 1985; Labov, 1971; Kerswill, 1994).[4] "I can do *aught* when you're with me, I can do anything", said a male speaker in his sixties from Sheffield in a Radio 4 interview, talking to his wife in an aside. *Aught* is Northern dialect, which he then repeats in Standard English, *anything*. Such a switch serves at least two functions: by using a dialect word, he emphasizes the fact that he is talking to his wife rather than the interviewer. At the same time, he reinforces his

---

[3] Code-switching is sometimes found in the literature written as two separate words, sometimes with a hyphen and sometimes as one word. Diachronically speaking, the move from two words to hyphenated words to a single word reflects the semantic acceptability and integration of the concept. I have stuck here with the intermediate solution, hyphenation.

[4] Register variation is a cover term for "the full range of language varieties associated with differences in communicative situation" (Biber & Finegan, 1993:316).

closeness to her by referring to their common heritage. This is despite the fact that such a switch is less obvious to an observer than a change of language. The associations of different varieties are sometimes consciously manipulated, as in the case of advertisements, which often use CS into English to sell their products (Chapter 4): see the German McDonald's advertisement in Box 1.

The characteristic ways in which bilinguals combine their languages in a particular community constitute a way of expressing their group identity – like a characteristic accent. Both the languages themselves *and* the sociolinguistic environment play a role in the patterns which emerge. Comparing CS across different communities and different language combinations can help reveal the *relative* role of linguistic and sociolinguistic factors – an important issue in Linguistics. *Within* particular societies, sub-groups can be identified by their characteristic CS patterns, as monolinguals can by discourse styles and registers. CS therefore helps us to understand identity formation and expression in bilinguals (Tabouret-Keller, 1997; Sebba and Wootton, 1998).

Third, switching between languages provides crucial material for our understanding of how language is both comprehended (processed) in the brain, and produced. What are the clues in the words and sentences we pronounce which allow others to decode our meaning, and which we assemble in order to put across that meaning? When we observe how this is done with two or more languages, some of those features are thrown into sharper relief.

Fourth, by analysing code-switched speech, we can find out which combinations of words or morphemes from different languages can easily be combined and which are more resistant, or perhaps even impossible. Since grammar consists of the rules regarding such combinations, CS acts as a signpost, pointing at where the difficult issues may arise, and paving the way towards a better understanding of grammar. Romaine, for example, has pointed out that code-switching research can help us to understand a key issue in Linguistics: the division of labour between grammar and lexicon (1995). Grammar specialists interested in CS try to discover whether the grammatical rules of the two varieties in contact are sufficient to explain the patterns in mixed language speech, or whether mixed codes have additional rules of their own.

All in all, CS is informative about language at a number of different levels. There are also good reasons to study it in its own right.

1.2.2   *Studying code-switching for its own sake*

It seems sensible that linguists should derive their data and evidence from the most typical speakers rather than from more exceptional ones. Numerous linguists have pointed out that most of the world is plurilingual. If you add together people who live in multilingual areas of the world (Africa, India, Singapore, Creole-speaking areas such as the Caribbean or Papua New

Box 1 Code-switching in advertising

Advertisements are a very common locus for CS, and examples can be found from round the world where English is combined with the local language in order to evoke a cosmopolitan – or American – lifestyle. This advertisement appeared as part of a code-switched series for McDonald's in Germany in the early 2000s. Note the use of many "bivalent" words (*croissant, warm, so, in*), reinforcing the other similarities between German and English; the use of German-style lower-case 'a' for the adjective *american*; and the use of the masculine pronoun *he*, as in German, to designate the ham.

McCroissant:
The american Antwort auf Croissant.

The lecker warm Croissant. Geschnitten in two Teile, this is very praktisch. So is genug Platz for weitere leckere things.

The first leckere thing: The Käse. A little bit angeschmolzen and this is very bequem for the Schinken. He can not fall out of the Croissant.

The second leckere thing: The Schinken. Saftig and in praktische stripes geschnitten.

Translation

McCroissant: the American **answer to Croissant**.

The **delicious warm**/warm **Croissant**.

Cut in/in two **parts**, this is very **practical. So**/so is **enough room** for **further delicious** things.

The first **delicious** thing: the **cheese**. A little bit **melted** and this is very **comfortable** for the **ham**. He [sic] can not fall out of the **Croissant**.

The second **delicious** thing: the **ham**. **Juicy** and cut **in**/in **practical** stripes [sic].

Guinea, etc.); people who speak a regional language or dialect on top of a national language (from Basques to Chechens); and migrants and their descendants (Greeks in Australia, Punjabis in Britain, Spanish speakers in the USA, etc.), you are left with small islands of monolingualism in a multilingual sea. This is without counting people who learn a second/third language beyond a basic level at school (e.g. the Dutch or Scandinavians); those who have a different language for literacy from the one they speak (e.g. Gujerati and Punjabi speakers whose language of literacy is Hindi); those who become bilingual through changes in personal circumstances; and those whose mother tongue is not considered adequate for formal purposes (i.e. in diglossia) and who therefore have to master another variety in order to take part in official life (e.g. Flemish speakers in Belgium, speakers of dialectal Arabic in various Arab countries) (Baker and Prys Jones, 1998). Plurilingualism is still the norm in spite of the fact that a large number of the world's languages are under imminent threat of extinction owing to economic and globalizing forces (Crystal, 2000).

Most of these plurilingual speakers mix their languages in various ways in their daily lives. CS has been studied from Mexico to Kenya and from Finland to Australia – one of the main problems in writing this book has been the difficulty of doing justice to the profusion of work which has been done. In line with the eclectic approach to CS adopted here, a balance has been attempted between giving up-to-date, accessible references and older/less accessible, but seminal ones.

1.3   A common-sense approach

The approach to CS adopted here can be described as "common sense" or as pragmatic with a small "p". "Pragmatic" research on CS with a large "p" – discussed in Chapter 4 – focuses on the conversational functions of CS and its effects on conversational participants (Auer, 1998b). CS is presented here in a rounded manner, looking at work carried out from the Sociolinguistic, Psycholinguistic, Grammatical and Acquisitional perspectives as well as the Pragmatic. CS is taken at face value, rather than with a particular theory as the point of departure. It is important that CS be considered as the multifaceted phenomenon it is, rather than purely as a means of testing theoretical positions.

So far, research on CS has been fragmented within various sub-disciplines, yet there are considerable advantages in considering it as a whole. There is an analogy with the poem at the beginning of this book, which recounts an old anecdote about six blind men feeling different parts of an elephant, and being unable to gain an overall view as to what it was. The terminological discussion below (see 1.5) illustrates how little agreement there is about CS, its definition and limits. Until greater concensus emerges, we should continue to look at it from as many different angles as possible.

One reason for this is that each of the sub-disciplines in Linguistics uses different methodological approaches. Sociolinguists seek to record "natural" conversations but are subject to the Observer's Paradox; theoretical linguists use fallible intuitions as to which sentences are correct/acceptable; psycholinguists' experiments test isolable – but incomplete – skills. None of these methods on its own can provide a complete picture of behaviour as complex as CS.

Moreover, assumptions underlying tried and tested methodological paradigms are often insufficiently discussed in Linguistics. For example, variationist descriptions of CS are still current in the grammatical field (Poplack, 2000). These are based on the assumption that if we can account for the majority of cases of CS, then we are justified in ignoring the minority of cases which do not fit in, and which are dismissed as aberrations. But one of the most famous philosophers of science, Popper (1959), considered that a proposition which was not falsified by counter-evidence was not scientific. Although there have been a number of alternative proposals since then as to what constitutes proper scientific enquiry, Popper's test remains one of the most rigorous. At what point do counter-examples to a paradigm which has been put forward make it necessary to revise it? There has so far been a lack of discussion of this problem with regard to CS, despite the fact that several scholars have argued that, in the present state of knowledge, we should be trying to formulate grammatical tendencies rather than absolute rules (Jacobson, 1998b; Muysken, 2000). As Radford (1996:81) wrote: "Many advances in our understanding of adult syntax have come from probing the syntax of structures ... which any computer corpus would show to be extremely 'rare' ... 'Every example counts!'" Tracy has also pointed out, "What one counts as an exception is not just defined by some quantitative feature but by the fact that it lies in conflict with our theory" (1995:198).

Another example from the grammatical field is the widespread belief that all bilingual utterances have an underlying "Matrix Language", i.e. a grammatical template which can usually be identified with a particular language, such as Russian, and that CS consists in grafting material from another identifiable language, such as Spanish, onto such a base. This belief has been around at least since Weinreich wrote that "Each utterance is in a definite language" (1953:7). Such a belief makes the grammatical description of mixed language utterances much simpler, but fails to address the more fundamental question of what we mean by a language in the first place.

Le Page's view is that one of the principal tasks for linguists is to explain the formation of the concept of a homogeneous "language": "We set out how we saw such a concept evolving from observation of discourse, through the stereotypes denoted by such language-owning names as 'English' or 'French', to that of the most highly abstract and focused Chomskyan 'grammar'; and how actual linguistic behaviour was influenced by the stereotypes as progressively it was named, formalized, standardized, institutionalized, and totemized by a society" (1997:31–32). "Languages" are often treated as if they were discrete, identifiable and internally consistent wholes, and we forget how historically recent and culturally selective such a view is (see Chapter 2).

The study of CS should force us to think "outside the box": to review methodologies, theoretical approaches and assumptions, often developed in a monolingual context, and see how they stand the test of being applied to the speech of bilinguals. A common sense approach involves recognizing exactly what are the limits to our ability to generalize at any given stage of the enquiry.

1.4   The study of code-switching

For a long time, CS was scarcely noticed by linguists writing about language contact. Milroy and Muysken (1995), who describe it as "perhaps the central issue in bilingualism research", point out that research on CS was slow to start compared with, say, research on borrowing or what used to be termed *interference*. In the seminal *Languages in Contact* (1953), Weinreich referred to the "transfer of words" from one language to another by bilinguals, but dismissed this as a "mere oversight" (1953:73–74). Haugen, writing at around the same time, also apparently overlooked the significance of CS, and wrote that: "The introduction of elements from one language into the other means merely an alteration of the second language, not a mixture of the two" (1950:211).

Over the last forty-odd years, there has been an explosion of interest in CS. CS had remained more or less "invisible" in research on bilingualism until the work of Gumperz and his associates in the 1960s and early 1970s (Gumperz, 1964, 1967; Gumperz and Wilson, 1971; Blom and Gumperz, 1972). Thereafter the subject took off – and there has been no sign of a downturn – as people realized that CS was not an isolated, quirky phenomenon but a widespread way of speaking. But research in this field is complicated by the multilayered significance of CS. Each new case which is documented can be looked at from multiple perspectives, so from the outset, a certain depth of engagement with the data is necessary.

Furthermore, by definition, studying CS implies dealing with several languages. Grasping the significance of a transcription where the reader or researcher is not familiar with one or both of the languages involved can be off-putting. This problem should be somewhat reduced in the future by various technical developments of use to the linguistic researcher, such as standardized transcription and coding systems, sound–text linking, and the possibility of collaborating on and sharing data over the Internet. Proposals for a system appropriate for CS are summarized in the Appendix (LIPPS Group, 2000; Gardner-Chloros, Moyer and Sebba, 2007). Because of the huge interest in CS on the one hand, and the difficulties of studying it on the other, a lot of work has crystallized around a few main approaches:

(1) *Sociolinguistic/ethnographic descriptions of CS situations.* These represent the majority of studies of CS. Although by their nature, they remain fairly fragmented, many important insights are derived from linking the manifestations of CS to aspects of the sociolinguistic situation (Chapter 3).

(2) *Pragmatic/conversation analytic approaches.* These rely on identifying the meanings brought about by CS in conversations, for example through following, or avoiding, the language choices of interlocutors (preference organization). This use of CS complements the exploitation of contrasting connotations of the two varieties (e.g. we-code/they-code). Such tactics may be used in the same conversation (e.g. Milroy and Gordon, 2003; McCormick, 2002) (Chapter 4).

(3) *Grammatical analyses of samples of CS and the search for underlying rules, models and explanations to explain the patterns found.* These have developed largely as a separate tradition from the sociolinguistic and the pragmatic. Although some authors have identified connections which deserve to be investigated (Muysken, 2000; Myers-Scotton, 1993b), this has not been a primary focus in the research so far (Chapter 5).

Each of these approaches is the subject of one chapter, as is the place of CS in language contact (Chapter 2); the implications of psycholinguistic work on bilinguals for our understanding of CS (Chapter 6); and CS in children and other learners (Chapter 7). The chapter pattern reflects the main research output and traditions, but within each chapter it is emphasized that there are no strict divisions between the questions which should be addressed in CS research – on the contrary, a major purpose of this book is to encourage the formulation of more holistic insights and research.

1.5   The vexed question of terminology

In the introduction to a volume on CS, Eastman wrote: "Efforts to distinguish code-switching, code-mixing and borrowing are doomed" (1992:1). Little has occurred since then to lighten this pessimistic view: terminology has been endlessly discussed in the CS literature without any real commonality of practice being achieved. Several good descriptions are, however, available of how the most important terms have been used in this field (Milroy and Muysken, 1995; Li Wei, 2000; Hamers and Blanc, 2000; Clyne, 2003), the key issues being described in sections 1.5.1 and 1.5.2.

1.5.1   *A misleading term?*

CS is not an entity which exists out there in the objective world, but a construct which linguists have developed to help them describe their data. It is therefore pointless to argue about what CS *is*, because, to paraphrase Humpty Dumpty, the word CS can mean whatever we want it to mean.

Janički (1990) drew attention to the dangers of *essentialism* in sociolinguistics, illustrated by the use of "left to right" rather than "right to left" definitions. A "left to right" definition states that such and such a word (which is, as it were, on the left-hand side of the page as you write) *is* this, that or the other, for instance that CS *is* the alternate use of two languages in conversation – as if this were an objective or immutable truth. Instead, he claims, sociolinguists should make use of "right to left" definitions, e.g. "We will call the alternation of two languages in conversation code-switching", where the term which we are defining is on the right-hand side. This makes the definition into a *working* definition rather than suggesting that we are imparting an essential truth. This advice is helpful given the confusing fact that each researcher provides different definitions of the relevant terms. This matters less if we consider definitions merely as a research tool with which to describe data.

Ideally, we would of course like to move forward, as researchers, speaking the same theoretical language. It would be preferable if the most salient phenomena which we observe had a name, which was not seriously misleading as to their nature. Unfortunately, both halves of the term CS *are* misleading. "Code" was originally taken from the field of communication technology (Fries and Pike, 1949; Fano, 1950; Jakobson, Fant and Halle, 1952). What was meant there has nothing to do with language: "code-switching" refers instead to a mechanism for the unambiguous transduction of signals between systems (for the history of the term, see Alvarez-Cáccamo, 1998; Benson, 2001; Tabouret-Keller, 1995). Nowadays *code* is understood as a neutral umbrella term for languages, dialects, styles/registers, etc., and partly usurps the place of the more usual "catch-all" term *variety* to cover the different sub-divisions of "language". Benson describes work on CS as we understand it now, carried out in the early years of the twentieth century, as "forgotten", because scholars have been insufficiently interested in the history of their field.

"Switching" appears transparent enough, in that it refers to *alternation* between the different varieties which people speak.[5] In the early psycholinguistic studies of bilingualism in the 1950s and 1960s, psychologists assumed that something similar to flicking an electric switch went on when bilinguals changed languages. More sophisticated models followed, in which, for example, a different switch mechanism was said to control input (listening and understanding) from that which controlled output (speaking) (see Chapter 6). But accumulated evidence from the mixed speech of bilinguals has led to the *transition* between the two varieties being seen as more and more complex and

---

[5] In French the term *alternance codique* is used, in German *Kodewechseln*, in Dutch *Kodewesseling* – however in all these, the English *code-switching* is often used instead.

less and less clear-cut. Clear-cut changes, such as the term "switching" implies, *may* occur in bilingual and bidialectal speech but they are only one of many possibilities (see Chapter 6).

1.5.2   *What does code-switching cover?*

Milroy and Muysken (1995) wrote in the introduction to *One Speaker, Two Languages*, that, "The field of CS research is replete with a confusing range of terms descriptive of various aspects of the phenomenon. Sometimes the referential scope of a set of these terms overlaps and sometimes particular terms are used in different ways by different writers" (p. 12). The same problem was outlined in Clyne (1987:740–741). He pinpointed the crucial distinction between those who consider CS to be "fuzzy-edged", i.e. on a continuum with respect to borrowing, syntactic merging, etc., and those who consider it as the one form of language contact which does *not* involve convergence of the two systems. More recently, Clyne has suggested that we should reserve *code-switching* for transference of individual lexical items through to whole stretches of speech, but that we should adopt a different term – he suggests "transversion" – for cases where the speaker "crosses over" completely into the other language (2003:75). In his survey of grammatical studies of CS, Muysken (2000) reserves the term CS for one of the three types of language mixture which he describes: *alternation*. He uses *code-mixing* for the other types, *insertion* and *congruent lexicalization* (see Chapter 5).

Haugen (1956), one of the first to write about CS, distinguished between *code-switching* on the one hand, in which the character of the contributing varieties is said to be preserved, and *interference* and *integration* on the other. This distinction was in large measure taken over by Poplack and Sankoff (1984) and Poplack (1988). They, however, used the term *borrowing* or *nonce borrowing* for instances of juxtaposition which do show some measure of convergence, be it morphological, phonological or syntactic. Others have argued that there is no clear line between CS and borrowing (Gardner-Chloros, 1987; Myers-Scotton, 1992; Thomason, 2001; Treffers-Daller, 1994) and that the two are on a *diachronic* continuum: loans start off as code-switches and then gradually become established as loans (see further discussion in Chapter 2). Yet another point of view is that speakers need to be evaluated individually in order to decide whether a particular morpheme is a one-off occurrence, a conscious code-switch or a loan. "What appears to be a nonce borrowing, or an occasional code-switch, for one speaker, could be an established morpheme for another speaker" (Aikhenvald, 2002:197).

A frequently made distinction is between *code-switching* and *code-mixing*, though here too, the line has been drawn in different ways. Some have reserved *code-switching* for cases where the two codes maintain their monolingual characteristics and used *code-mixing* for those where there is some convergence between the two (e.g. Muysken, 2000). Confusion arises, however, because the two processes often co-exist within the same stretch of discourse as well as overlapping at the conceptual level (Hamers and Blanc, 2000). Sridhar and Sridhar (1980) and Bokamba (1988) use *code-mixing* for alternation within the sentence and *code-switching* for alternations going beyond the sentence borders. Meisel (1989) employs *code-mixing* for the fusion of two grammatical systems, whereas he describes *code-switching* as the pragmatic skill of selecting the language according to the interlocutor, topic, context, etc.

Further variations can be found. In social psychology, CS refers to *language choices* in a bilingual setting (Sachdev and Bourhis, 1990). Meeuwis and Blommaert (1998) point out that CS itself can be a variety on its own, with the same functions and effects as those usually attributed to "languages". Finally, as here, CS may be used as a general term covering all outcomes of contact between two varieties, whether or not there is evidence of convergence. Such an approach is justified in that convergence can occur at many different levels and it is not in practice always possible to decide where it occurred and where it has not (Neufeld, 1976; Pfaff, 1979).

Also, of the various terms which have been used, CS is the one which has gained the widest currency. This has led to a situation where the study of CS is sometimes a victim of the success of the *term* CS. The term encourages people to think of language contact in terms of discrete alternation between two self-contained systems, and to neglect the connections between that type of occurrence and others where convergence occurs. Examples of the latter include loanwords, pidgins, mixed languages, etc., and the concept is crucial to understanding the historical development of languages, e.g. English as the product of Anglo-Saxon, Norman, Latin and other influences. The "new orthodoxy" of believing that CS is made up of alternation between discrete systems has, for some researchers, taken over from the "old orthodoxy" of ideal speaker/hearers in homogeneous communities (Gardner-Chloros, 1995).

1.6   Studies of code-switching

Substantial chapters or sections have been devoted to CS in the principal volumes on bilingualism and language contact, e.g. Romaine's *Bilingualism* (1995), Coulmas's *Handbook of Sociolinguistics* (1997), Hamers and Blanc's *Bilinguality and Bilingualism* (2000), Thomason (2001), Clyne (2003) and Li Wei (2000). Various edited collections and special issues of journals have been devoted to different aspects of CS (Heller, 1988a; Eastman, 1992; Milroy and Muysken, 1995; Auer, 1998b; Jacobson, 1998a, 2001; Dolitsky, 2000, Li Wei, 2005), as well as a large number of academic papers. A search of titles in the

Language and Linguistic Behaviour Abstracts on the term *code-switching* just for the last five years produces several hundred titles. To this, we can add several full-length monographic case-studies of bilingual situations where CS is the main focus (Agnihotri, 1987; Backus, 1992; Bentahila, 1983; Gardner-Chloros, 1991; Gibbons, 1987; Halmari, 1997; Haust, 1995; Heath, 1989; Myers-Scotton, 1993a; Nivens, 2002; Nortier, 1990; Treffers-Daller, 1994; McCormick, 2002; Zentella, 1997), covering a variety of language combinations. Two books have been devoted to the grammatical aspects of CS (Myers-Scotton, 1993b; Muysken, 2000), as well as a further volume by Myers-Scotton to developing her grammatical theory in the broader context of language contact (2002a). CS is now a prolific area of research, and the subject of many doctoral and master's theses worldwide. It figures prominently in the principal journals on bilingualism, notably the *International Journal of Bilingualism* and *Bilingualism, Language and Cognition*.

With a few exceptions, notably the European Science Foundation Network on Code-switching and Language Contact (1988–91), which produced three volumes of papers,[6] and the biennial series of Symposia on Bilingualism started by Li Wei in 1999, the field has, in general, been marked by a lack of coordination and dialogue between researchers. A project is now underway to set up a database of CS texts for researchers to share and to provide material for comparisons (LIPPS Group, 2000). As was pointed out in a paper describing the aims of this project, "The great majority of ... studies involve the collection of new sets of data by individual researchers; so while there is a lot of often painstakingly collected data around, it seems likely that the endless collection of more data for analysis will no longer constitute the most productive application of research efforts" (Gardner-Chloros, Moyer, Sebba and van Hout, 1999).

1.7   Speakers' insights

Ethnographic research on CS involving field-work in various communities and the gathering of different types of data – attitude studies and interviews as well as recordings – provides various insights into CS from the speakers themselves. Some of these insights merit particular attention:

(1) Bilingual subjects sometimes spontaneously provide an explanation as to why CS occurs: *laziness*. This explanation is not only offered by speakers who claim *not* to switch themselves, but also by self-confessed code-switchers. CS is seen as an easy way out when people cannot be bothered to search for the words they need in a single language. As laziness is not generally considered a virtue, this interpretation obviously

---

[6] The volumes themselves are no longer available, but led to the publication of Milroy and Muysken (1995).

depends on believing that it is in some way "wrong" to mix languages. Irrespective of such normative attitudes, it is of interest, from a psycholinguistic and from other perspectives, to consider whether code-switching involves less or more effort than monolingual speech.

(2) Regular code-switchers often claim to *disapprove* of CS when specifically asked. Surprisingly few systematic studies of attitudes to CS have been carried out (see Chapter 3), but where they have, they have generally confirmed that people are not proud of it. Approval of CS tends to coincide with a laid-back attitude towards authority; for example within the same community it tends to be more common in younger rather than older generations (McCormick, 2002; Gardner-Chloros, McEntee-Atalianis and Finnis, 2005). But contrary to some popular belief, it is not certain that CS is used more by uneducated people than by educated ones – in several cases, the opposite has been shown (Timm, 1978; Haust, 1995).

(3) Although people who live in bilingual communities are, generally, aware of the existence of CS and of the fact that they themselves sometimes switch, their level of awareness of their *own* CS behaviour seems to lag far behind their practice. When recordings of code-switched conversations are played to the subjects involved, for example so as to enlist their help with the transcription, they frequently express surprise and/or embarrassment on discovering the extent of their own mixing.

To sum up, CS is:

(1) thought to be an easy or lazy option;
(2) generally disapproved of, even by those who practise it;
(3) below the full consciousness of those who use it.

Such insights from speakers can be useful for formulating research hypotheses. For example, let us look briefly at the first point, whether CS is really the easiest option. Sociolinguistic studies do show that people code-switch more, and more within the clause, when they are at ease, in *informal* situations (Gardner-Chloros, 1991:186; see also Chapter 3). Dewaele (2001) also found that second language learners code-switch more in informal than in formal interviews. But does this mean it is actually *easier* to switch than not to switch? The answer depends on a variety of factors. Where the speaker is a balanced bilingual – i.e. someone who can speak either variety equally competently, CS may be used deliberately as a *compromise* strategy, when addressing others of varying competences and preferences. It might not then be the *easiest* solution, but merely the most expedient. At a psycholinguistic level, the position is also less than clear. *Inhibiting* one of the languages – i.e. preventing it from coming to the surface – does apparently require some kind of effort (or "resource"), but the joint *activation* of two varieties does so as well (Green, 1986/2000). The mental effort required for the simultaneous, or rapid successive activation of two competing systems translates into extra split seconds of time which are required in both the receptive and productive modes (see Chapter 6). The jury must therefore remain out on whether CS is always the solution requiring least effort. For the speaker in Example 2 above, it is clear that the least effort would have involved speaking monolingual English.

What the speakers' own views about CS do point to, is a dissociation between how they *use* their linguistic competence (which is dictated by expediency, pragmatic considerations, habit and a variety of other sub-conscious motivations), and what they *know* or *think they know* about it (which includes their overt attitudes, purism, etc., as well as their *representation* of how they speak). The underlying competence of the bilingual is a poly-idiolectal personal amalgam, influenced only indirectly by linguistic attitudes, which are usually shared with others in the community. This "multilayered" aspect of language within the individual is consonant with Le Page's remarks regarding the different senses of a "language" (see above).

1.8   Further types of code-switching

1.8.1   Tri-/plurilinguals

Until recently, descriptions of bilingual speech and, more generally, much of the research on bilingualism tended to mention only in passing and in a fairly speculative manner how findings might differ in the case of trilinguals, and speakers of more than three languages. Instead of bilingualism being seen as one possible case of *plurilingualism* or *multilingualism* (which, in theory, appears logical), the term "bilinguals" is often used to subsume "plurilinguals" (e.g. Sachdev and Bourhis, 2001:407). Speakers of three or more languages are by no means rare in the world, still less so if one considers competence in several varieties such as different dialects as well as those who speak distinct "languages". They have only recently begun to be considered more systematically (Hoffmann, 2001; Cenoz, Hufeisen and Jessner, 2001).

Example 4
I have **canné** *todo*
fail*ed everything*   (Baetens Beardsmore and Anselmi, 1991: 416)

This example involves *quadri*lingual components: pronoun subject and auxiliary in English (*I have*), main verb stem in Italian (*cannare* 'to fail'), French verb ending (*-é* for past participle) and pronoun direct object in Spanish (*todo* 'everything'). Lest this be thought exceptional, Clyne (2003) shows how, on the contrary, the fact of switching once actually *creates* the possibility of further switching: instead of going back to the variety used before the switch, trilingual speakers often take a different "branch" on "exiting" from it and switch to a third language, as in Example 5.

Example 5
[G = German, E = English, D = Dutch]
Ich muss ab und zu in einem [G] **dictionary** [E] ***KIJKEN*** [D]
*I have to every now and then in a **dictionary** look+*INF
'I have to look in the dictionary every now and then'
(Clyne 2003:163)

Clyne suggests that it is because the word *dictionary* is a lexical transfer in the speaker's German as well as in their Dutch that a "transversion" to Dutch is facilitated for the main verb, *kijken* 'to look'.

Baetens Beardsmore has further shown that, in complex multilingual societies such as SE Asia or Africa, relative dominance in the different languages in a speaker's repertoire may not coincide with chronological order of learning. A second language may be the source of interference or CS into the third, the first learned language being restricted to intimate family life. Although determinants of transfer are the same however many languages are involved, "an interweaving of linguistic and extra-linguistic variables decide which of the languages serves as the source of the transfer" (1986:82). These examples provide a small idea of the many further questions – mainly unexplored – which arise in relation to CS with more than two varieties.

1.8.2   Second language learners

While there is a considerable body of research about the learning processes of second language (L2) learners (Mitchell and Miles, 2004), as yet, relatively little has been written about their CS, discussed in Chapter 7 (Poulisse and Bongaerts, 1994; Dewaele, 2001). Since even "native" bilinguals are rarely balanced in their competence in the two varieties, there seems little reason in principle to draw a clear line between them and L2 learners, and it is to be hoped that, in the future, further systematic comparisons will be made of learners' CS with that of "native" bilinguals. Late acquisition of the L2 appears to make less difference to a speaker's CS than the extent to which they belong to a code-switching community. This is demonstrated in the case of members of immigrant groups, whose CS can be just as intense as that of native plurilinguals.

There remains much to be learned about CS involving different types of plurilingual speaker, and there may be many insights to come from such studies which will affect our understanding of CS as a whole. The same applies to CS between different modalities (e.g. between oral and sign languages) and doubtless to switching between other, non-linguistic forms of behaviour (Chapter 8).

1.9   Conclusion

CS is a growth area in linguistics, since it provides insights not only about plurilingualism – which concerns the majority of speakers in the world – but also about language itself, from several different perspectives. This has yet to be recognised by some linguists of a theoretical persuasion – or monolinguistic orientation – who treat the questions posed by plurilingualism as marginal to linguistics. In *The Twitter Machine*, Smith remarks: "It is obvious that different communities exhibit variation in their speech: people in Paris speak French while those in Washington speak English and those in Montreal cope with both; it is equally clear that children don't speak the same way as their grandparents, that males and females are not necessarily identical in their linguistic abilities, and so on. In short, any social parameter whatsoever may be the locus of some linguistic difference. Unfortunately, nothing of interest to linguistic theory follows from this" (1989:180).

It is nothing new for theoretical linguists to express lack of interest in performance. But of all aspects of performance, CS may be the one where the notion of "acceptability" is hardest to maintain, as it challenges the whole notion of the "native speaker". Code-switchers upset the notion of performance errors by contravening and rewriting the expected rules. The ideal speaker-listener is an elusive figure indeed in many bilingual communities.

Linguists who do study bilingual performance, in a sociolinguistic context for example, have shown how CS contributes in various ways to an understanding of how the individual is articulated with the social. They too have to be aware of the limitations imposed by continuing to use well-worn methodological approaches and failing to consider whether such approaches address the right questions. Studies of language and gender provide a good example of the dangers inherent in doing this – it is thanks to the imaginative use of different methodologies that it is now clear that gender as such is only an intervening variable, and not an explanation in itself, for many differences in performance between women and men (Coates, 1993; Eckert, 1989).

Conversation analysts specify that they only consider as CS those transitions in one speaker's discourse which can be shown to have some identifiable impact on the conversation. Researchers looking at CS from other perspectives have not, on the whole, specified so clearly their method for pinpointing the object of study. Is it sufficient for an observer to identify two different entities, or must the distinction be based on insider – even idiolectal – knowledge? CS research has not solved these problems, but it does confront us with them very starkly. If we can find ways of tackling these issues, this will be useful for many other aspects of linguistic research as well as for CS.

As we have seen, a central question is what implicit definition of "language" we are applying. This goes beyond the question of the best methods of analysis for analysing bilingual speech and raises a philosophical problem. The notions of *focusing* and *diffusion*, developed by Le Page (1989; 1997) and Le Page and Tabouret-Keller (1985), drew inspiration from the creole-speaking areas where much of their research was carried out, but were intended to have a general application. CS gives us both material and incentive to carry forward Le Page's challenge to settings where "diffuseness" still operates, if less obviously than in creole areas.

If we can rise to both sorts of challenges discussed here, the methodological and the ideological, then enhancing our understanding of CS will have a variety of repercussions in linguistics. As we will see, so far such breakthroughs have come more from grass-roots descriptions of actual data than from the top-down application of theoretical frameworks developed in more idealized settings. It is for this reason that a "common sense" approach is advocated.

2   Code-switching and language contact

2.1   Introduction

This chapter describes the place of CS in language contact, including its relationship with borrowing, pidginization, convergence and language shift. All of these are instances of change, but the time-scale in which such change occurs can vary widely. CS occurs in contact situations of many types and relates in complex ways to the processes of change at work in those situations.

CS occurs among immigrant communities, regional minorities and native multilingual groups alike. Gumperz and Hernandez wrote that it could be found "each time minority language groups come into contact with majority language groups under conditions of rapid social change" (1969:2). Others (e.g. Giacolone Ramat 1995) have on the contrary described it as a feature of stable bilingualism in communities where most speakers can speak both languages. There are descriptions of contact situations in which it receives little or no prominence (e.g. Jones, 1998, with respect to Wales; Spolsky and Cooper, 1991, on Jerusalem), but this does not necessarily mean it does not occur in those settings. Instead it may be because other instances of contact or restructuring are the primary focus, or because the data collection techniques do not centre on the informal conversational modes where CS occurs. In Section 2.2, the extent to which CS brings about language change, or is symptomatic or independent of it, is considered.

Sociolinguists have treated CS mainly as a spoken genre, and as such it undoubtedly has a long history (see Stolt (1964) on German–Latin CS in Luther's "table-talk"). But CS is also found in written texts from various historical periods (Montes-Alcala, 1998; Sebba, 2005). Examples include Latin–Greek in Cicero's letters to his friend Atticus (see Box 5), French–Italian in a thirteenth-century Coptic phrasebook and a fourteenth-century Venetian manuscript of the Song of Roland (Aslanov 2000); German–Latin in the work of a seventeenth-century linguist, Schottelius (McLelland, 2004); English–French CS in a variety of Medieval English texts (Trotter, 2002) (see Box 3); through to literary works such as Chicano poetry (Valdes-Fallis 1977) and novels where spoken CS is represented, such as Tolstoy's *War and Peace* (see Timm, 1978), Eco's *The Name of the Rose* (where Salvatore speaks a multilingual jargon), and through to contemporary novelists such as Zadie Smith (English–Creole in *White Teeth*) and John Markovitch (Spanish–Quechua in *The Dancer Upstairs*). Script-switching is also found, as when Jan van Eyck wrote 'Als ich kann' in German ('as (well as) I can') above his self-portrait in a turban, but in Greek letters: 'αλς ιχ χάν', perhaps to indicate his erudition.[1] Angermeyer (2005) has described script alternation in Russian–American advertising, as a way of signalling a bilingual identity. A Hassidic newsletter distributed in North London, Hakohol, includes code-switches from Yiddish and Hebrew, the latter in Hebrew script (see Box 6). The lifestyle magazine *Latina* for American women of Hispanic descent is full of Spanish–English CS, which Mahootian (2005) describes as a reflection of community norms, but also as challenging relations of power and dominance between the older Hispanics, the monolingual English-speaking community and the younger Hispanic generation (see Box 2). It is also symptomatic of certain types of written discourse taking on the informality of conversation, as in the email and texting practices of many young people of mixed heritage (Hinrichs, 2006). There is even a "mini-genre" of "bivalent" texts, dating from the sixteenth to eighteenth centuries, composed so that they could be read simultaneously in Latin and various Romance languages, notably Spanish – a way of "punning" with linguistic affiliation rather than with meaning (Woolard and Genovese, 2007).

2.2   Code-switching as a symptom of different/opposite tendencies

CS arises in a variety of different contexts, as a symptom of quite opposite developments, from accommodation to divergence and from language main-tenance to language shift. It reflects social differences and tendencies *within* the same society and language combination (Bentahila and Davies, 1991; Li Wei, 1998a; Treffers-Daller, 1998), just as it reflects those *between* different societies and different language combinations (Poplack, 1988; McClure, 1998). Ideally, CS should be seen as part of a "bigger picture" including other forms of register variation (Halmari and Smith, 1994).

2.2.1   *Convergence v. preserving distinctiveness*

An important question regarding the place of CS in language contact is to what extent it is a mechanism for bringing the varieties closer together. As we saw in Chapter 1, it has sometimes been defined – misleadingly – as the one type of language interaction where each variety preserves its character. At the same time, data collected in many communities has shown that there is no one-to-one correlation between CS and language change or shift. Thomason (2001)

---

[1] 'ιχ' is also a pun on his name (Eyck).

Box 2 Code-switching in the 'ethnic' press

Publications intended for communities of immigrant origin are often rife with CS. The magazine *Latina*, addressed to young Hispanic women in the USA, started in 1996 and has a circulation of 175,000. Mahootian (2005) claims that in this context, CS is used "as a direct and undeniable assertion of bilingual identity" and that "linguistic necessity is not the driving force" behind it – rather it is evidence of its acceptance and propagation, i.e. of linguistic change.

Gentlemen prefer *gorditas*

Flacas, beware! *Mujeres con curvas* have a lot to offer

orget those *flaca* cover girls! What Latinos love most about Latinas *son las curvas*. Think Iris Chacón, the quintessential Latina showgirl. But with affection come nicknames. Full-figured Latinas are called many things, from *mujerona* to *amazona*. Some men call them pleasantly plump or plus-size, but Latinos usually call them *gorditas*.

Y Ave María, they do call them—on the phone, on the street, at the clubs. *Gorditas* are hot property. Consider this. Of the Latinos who responded to this magazine's 1998 sex survey, a whopping 62 percent said they prefer women with hourglass figures: full breasts, hips, and good legs. Even that runty Taco Bell Chihuahua worships them when he cheers, "*Viva gorditas*" in those cheeky television ads. But despite the adoration, many *gorditas* struggle with emotional conflicts that pit self-image against popular media images.

Vivian Torres (not her real name) hated her full-figured body when she was growing up. "At age 15, I developed large breasts, hips, and legs that attracted unwanted attention from men and boys," recalls the executive director of a social service agency in New Jersey.

Even acclaimed erotic film star Vanessa Del Rio had tough beginnings. "As a teenager I kept getting mixed signals. Men loved my body and wanted to see it, but my parents wanted me to cover it up," says Del Rio, now well over 40 and over her early self-image conflicts.

The psychology of appearance makes heavy demands on *gorditas*, especially teenage girls. "It's a difficult adjustment period because you want to fit in, but your body won't let you," says Sharlene Bird, Psy.D., a licensed clinical psychologist in New York. "It's important for teenage girls to feel

BY ROBERTO SANTIAGO

LATINA MARCH 1999

Translation

Article taken from *Latina* magazine, which is aimed at young Hispanic women in the USA, March 1999 *gorditas*: lit. 'little fat ones', here used as a term of endearment to refer to chunky/chubby women

flaca(s): skinny(ies)

mujeres con curvas: women with curves

mujerona: big woman

amazona: amazon

y Ave María: and hail Mary

viva gorditas: (long) live chubby women

This article is discussed in Mahootian (2005).

has considered this question at length and concludes that CS is not a major mechanism in contact-induced change, as it does not result from "imperfect learning", though it is one of the principal mechanisms of borrowing. She is at pains to point out how varied and heterogeneous the sources of language change are, and that most of the general rules are there to be broken. For example, language change often takes place when a minority group becomes bilingual and adopts features of the L2, as in the case of Greek spoken in Asia Minor adopting features of Turkish. As a general rule, the language of the majority is adopted by the minority rather than vice-versa. However, this tendency is in conflict with another one, i.e. that the language of the *elite* is adopted by the subordinate group, and the elite is, almost by definition, the minority. Thomason points out that native speakers of Turkish may also have played a role in bringing features of Turkish into Asia Minor Greek, as some had learned Greek as a second language, in spite of being the majority (2001:67).

Backus (2005) provides a description of the complexity of the relationship between CS and structural change. He lists numerous problems, both methodological and conceptual, with the hypothesis that structural change is directly brought about by CS. For example, at a methodological level, one would need to have a complete picture of the range of variation of the structure within the monolingual variety in order to establish that it was indeed CS, and only CS, which had brought about the change. At a conceptual level, one would need to understand *how* exactly the fact of code-switching could bring about a change in the structure of a language, and distinguish this from calques (i.e. expressions taken over literally, either word for word or morpheme for morpheme, from one language to another) in the idiolect of the individual code-switcher.

2.2.2   *Studies which show code-switching to be bound up with shift or change*

In most communities where there is CS, there is a correlation between the speakers' *age* and the type of CS which they use. For example Bentahila and Davies (1991; 1998), in analysing the CS of Arabic–French bilinguals in Morocco, found clear differences in the patterns characterizing the younger and the older groups, related to differences in the role played by French in their education and background. In a study of Arvanitika, a dying Albanian dialect spoken in Greece, Trudgill (1977) found that CS into Greek made it very difficult to identify which aspects of Arvanitika were being lost because CS was being used as a compensatory strategy. Lavandera (1978) reports a similar phenomenon in Buenos Aires, where migrants of Italian origin switch between their own dialect of Argentinian Spanish, Cocoliche, and Standard Argentinian Spanish to compensate for reduced stylistic options available to them in either variety. Schmidt (1985) shows how among the older, more fluent speakers of Dyirbal, a dying Aboriginal language of Australia, only individual words are said in English, e.g. **all right, now, finish ('period')**. Moderately proficient speakers use many more imported English words in their Dyirbal, which are often adapted to Djirbal morphology, e.g. ***ring**-iman* 'she phoned him', ***jayil**-gu* 'to jail', *one night, down there*, etc. Finally the younger speakers, who are much less fluent in Dyirbal, code-switch copiously between the two varieties.

Example 1
We tryin' to warn   ban wuigi nomo wurrbay-gu.
We were trying to warn her not to speak [Dyirbal]   (Schmidt, 1985)

Apart from intergenerational comparisons, there is also evidence from historical linguistic work which suggests that CS is an important component of change. This has been notably been studied in the context of Middle English, which relexified[2] under the influence of Norman French and Latin. "Bilingualism and CS must have played a major role in the process of lexical borrowing and mixed-language texts can thus provide interesting information on the process of widespread relexification of English in the ME period. As Rothwell pointed out, "Generations of educated Englishmen passed daily from English into French and back again in the course of their work", a process which must have led to specific lexical transfers both in the field of technical and of general vocabulary" (Schendl, 2002:86). Schendl's paper gives numerous and varied examples of CS between English, French and Latin from a variety of medieval genres (business, religious, legal and scientific texts) to back up this claim.

---

[2] *Relexification* is the process by which a language which retains its basic grammatical identity replaces part or all of its lexical stock with words from another variety.

2.2.3   Counter-examples

It is important to point out that CS takes place in a context where there is shift in progress, rather than *constituting* shift of itself. This was shown in Gumperz's early study of Hindi–Punjabi CS in Delhi (1964), where two related varieties had substantially converged at a grammatical level, through being in close contact for decades, while retaining a different lexical stock. As a number of specific differences between them remained, Gumperz concluded that these differences must be functional, as they would long ago have been wiped out if they were not serving a specific purpose.

In Rindler-Schjerve's (1998) study of Italian–Sardinian CS, she emphasizes that although the switching occurs *in a context* of language shift, it "should not be seen as a mechanism which *accelerates* the shift" (1998:247).[3] In Sardinia, it is the more balanced bilinguals who switch most, and who "contribute to the maintenance of Sardinian in that they change the Sardinian language by adapting it to the majority language thus narrowing the gap between the two closely related codes" (1998:246). In Example 2, the Italian expression *secondo me* 'in my opinion' is inserted in a Sardinian sentence, but adapted to Sardinian phonology to minimize the transition (*segunnu me*). Its function is to highlight or separate the parenthetical expression 'in my opinion'.

Example 2
Non m'an giamadu 'e veterinariu ma segunnu me   **fi calchicosa chi a mangiadu**
They didn't call a vet but   *in my opinion* *it was something*
which it has eaten   (Rindler-Schervje, 1998:243)

2.2.4   A sign of doom or of vitality?

CS can arise in situations of widely varying stability. It can be a feature of stable bilingualism for an extended period, and then, following social changes, it may persist and become implicated in language shift. The shifting and the shifted-to varieties are necessarily in contact, at least in some sections of the community and/or contexts, over a period of time: This is the case of Sauris in the Carnian Alps, described by Denison (1984; 1986). This small community had preserved a local variety of German for some 600 years, Friulian being the regional norm and Italian the national norm, with which speakers, until this century, had relatively little contact. Now the local dialect is declining at the expense of, above all, Italian, but is as yet evident in the frequently code-switched speech of the community. "Functional and substantial linguistic substitution within a total repertoire can (and usually does) proceed selectively, over quite a long period,

---

[3] My italics.

involving many generations, before the stage is reached when what was once an entire linguistic tradition … is … jettisoned" (Denison, 1987:73).

Change can be fast or slow and can affect all aspects of language (Gumperz and Wilson, 1971; Dressler and Wodak-Leodolter, 1977). It can take place over several generations or, effectively, within a single generation. It may be difficult to detect, losses being masked by code-switches (Trudgill, 1977) or internal restructuring (Tsitsipis, 1998), and it can occur either with heavy linguistic symptoms such as morphological loss or without them (Dorian, 1981; Schmidt, 1985). A range of linguistic configurations can arise along the road to extinction. There are descriptions of the characteristics of semi-speakers' competence, such as loss of subordinative mechanisms, word-retrieval problems and phonological distortions or hypercorrections in relation to a number of languages and sociolinguistic settings (Tsitsipis, 1998; Schmidt, 1985). Dorian (1981), however, points out that there are circumstances where, depending on the speed with which a variety is abandoned, languages may die without their morphology having altered at all, and Tsitsipis argues against any "direct correlation of structural intactness with the functional survival of a language" (1998:65).

Auer (1999) describes CS as the first point in a chronological progression along a continuum. At the CS stage, the point in the sentence where there is a switch is a significant aspect of the conversation. The next stage is *language mixing*, where, as in Example 2 above, it is not the individual switch points which carry significance, but the use of the overall switching mode – this stage is also described by Myers-Scotton (1993a) as "switching as an unmarked choice". The third stage is *fused lects*, which are stabilized mixed varieties.

In conversation analysis, the "proof" that speakers are drawing on two separate systems lies in the reactions of their interlocutors to the contrasts and conversational effects which they bring about. Thus Auer's definition of CS is "the juxtaposition of two languages perceived and interpreted as locally meaningful by participants" – here "locally meaningful" applies to the juxtaposition itself. In *language mixing* on the other hand, the combination of varieties does not give rise to local, but to more global, meanings. Individual switches no longer serve a conversational purpose as in Example 2 above, but the distinction between the languages has not collapsed completely. In the third stage, the development of fused lects, there is a loss of variation: the use of elements from one or other variety is no longer a matter of choice, but of grammatical convention. Structures from each variety, which are equivalent in monolingual usage, develop specialised uses.

Auer claims this process is unidirectional. It may never be completed, as bilingual communities may stabilize at any point along the way, but it does not allow for any movement in the opposite direction. Auer goes so far as to say that the movement from fused lects to language mixing to CS is "prohibited".

If you begin with a fused lect – i.e. a fully conventionalised mixed variety, presumably with no more internal variation than any other natural language – it is indeed difficult to see how this could spontaneously "split up" into its historical component parts. The social circumstances which gave rise to the mixing cannot be "put into reverse": English is not likely to split up into Anglo-Saxon, Norman French, etc. On the other hand, if the starting point is two varieties which are somewhere towards the middle of the continuum, say between CS and language mixing, then these could in theory split or become more similar to (one of) the component varieties; this is what happens in decreolization. If we take the example of the Creole–London English mixture described in Sebba (1993), one of the elements, London English, has an independent existence anyway, and it is conceivable that this type of creole could begin to be used independently, if the identity associated with it were to develop further.

We should be careful to distinguish situations where there is a *progression* from one state to another from those where all we know is that different phenomena overlap chronologically. We will see in Chapter 3 that different kinds of CS can co-exist in the same community at the same time. As Crowley pointed out with respect to pidginization in Bislama (1990:385): "Rather than trying to divide the history of Melanesian Pidgin into chronologically distinct developmental phases, we should regard stabilization, destabilization, and creolization as all contributing simultaneously to the gradual evolution of the language from the very beginning."

There are also circumstances where contact-induced change does not proceed smoothly through all three stages. After some convergence has taken place, instead of the old variety being abandoned in favour of the new, the altered (code-switched) variety, brought about through contact, may assume distinct functions of its own. This type of case was discussed by Gumperz (1964) in relation to varieties in contact in Delhi, and may explain the formation of certain creoles.

The stabilization of CS varieties arises when these varieties assume an identity function. They are often characteristic of young second-generation immigrant communities which develop a pride in their mixed identity. Such an intra-community variety is, for example, emerging among the second-generation Portuguese in France. Known as "immigrais" (*immigrese*), by their own description a "bastard" Portuguese, including French words and colloquialisms, this variety is intolerable to purists, but understood by the 900,000 strong immigrant population. In Albatroz, a literary review trilingual in Portuguese, French and immigrais, the proponents of this variety write (Muñoz, 1999:71):

Example 3
Through no will of our own, we're foreigners. But we have a tool: the Portuguese language contaminated by <u>positive pollution</u>. Be that as it may, we write in both languages, copulating frenetically, with the outcome that literary and pictorial objects are

pleasantly produced. It'll be alright. We respect none of the spelling or vocabulary rules of the immigrese language and although we may perturb, we demand that making mistakes be recognized as a technique for exploring the ambiguity of a text or as a gimmick of polysemic amplification. Don't you agree? And while we're at it, let's do away with the cedilla! Irreverence, dear reader, irreverence.[4]

Hewitt (1986) and Sebba (1993) have described types of CS which occur with symbolic and discourse-related functions in London, between Creole and London English speaking young people. Although used sparingly, creole is said by Sebba to have a *we-code* function and CS is described as an "insider activity". Creole is almost certainly preserved by being used in this way, as the majority of young people who were the subject of his study would not be able to use it as a means of expression on its own. Recent novels such as *White Teeth* by Zadie Smith, which portray the lives of young Afro-Caribbeans in London, show this type of CS as an intrinsic – if somewhat inconsistent – aspect of their speech.

Finally, there are an increasing number of popular singers and bands whose lyrics are code-switched, e.g. Ricki Martin, Raggasonic and various Punjabi bands in Britain (Asian Dub Foundation, Bali Sagu, Apache Indian), attesting the vitality which code-switched varieties can have in their own right. Example 4 is taken from the lyrics of Raggasonic Crew Feat,[5] sung by Raggasonic, a Rasta band who sing in English, French and a mixture of both. Along with English–French CS, their lyrics contain morphologically adapted words, borrowed from one language to the other (e.g. *toaster*); elements of creole; and *verlan* (shown in example 4 in capitals), a type of French slang which involves inverting the first and second syllables of multisyllable words and pronouncing single syllable words backwards (from *envers* 'back to front').

Example 4

1	Les femmes sont **nice**	*The women are **nice***
2	et la **dancehall** roule	*and the **dancefloor** is rolling*
3	La basse percute tous les Rastas	*The bass hits all the Rastas*
4	dans la foule	*in the crowd*
5	Le sélécteur joue du **rub-a-dub**	*The selector plays some **rub-a-dub***
6	ou de la **soul**	*or some **soul***
7	Les **bad-boys** sont là	*The **bad-boys** are here*
8	Les **bad-boys** sont là	*The **bad-boys** are here*
9	Eclaire le chemin	*Light the way*
10	Quand Raggasonic SSEPA [=passe]	*When Raggasonic goes by*
11	La **dancehall** est **full**,	*The **dancefloor** is **full***
12	Mory, Big Red sont vraiment là	*Mory, Big Red are really here*
13	Je viens d'Ivry, le Sud	*I come from Ivry, the South*

---

[4] My translation.
[5] The transcription is taken from the lyrics attached to the CD. The translation is my own.

14 est le **best** dans le ragga	*is the **best** at reggae*
15 Si t'es pas d'accord bwoy[6]	*If you don't agree bwoy*
16 viens donc nous CHECLA	*come on and clash us*
[= **clash**er, i.e. 'to clash', adapted to French spelling and morphology]	
17 J'ai pas peur de la compétition	*I'm not afraid of the competition*
18 j'ai pas peur de toi	*I'm not afraid of you*
19 Tu peux **toast**er comme Buju	*You can **toast** like Buju*
20 ou tester comme Shabba	*or test like Shabba*
21 **Toast**er comme Beanie Man	***Toast** like Beanie Man*
22 ou bien comme Bounty Killa	*or else like Bounty Killa*
23 Je n'ai peur d'aucuns **deejays**	*I'm not afraid of no **deejays***
24 des Antilles à RIPA [=Paris]	*from the Antilles to Paris*
25 **People massive** écoute ça	***massive people** listen to that*

Here, prescriptive "rules" such as speaking only one language at a time are deliberately and playfully broken – a function of CS which has been described as *ludic* (Caubet, 2001; McCormick, 2002). The mixing is not a precursor of any of the varieties involved disappearing, at least not among the writers and consumers of such lyrics as these, who are fluent multilinguals – rather it is the purists who should feel threatened! The various functions of CS in rap music are explored in Sarkar and Winer (2006) and in North African-French *rai* music by Bentahila and Davies (2002). Both claim that one of its functions is to reconcile the conflicting trends of localization and globalization.

CS can therefore occur both in situations of decline and as a mechanism of vitality. Aikhenvald (2002:Chapter 8) shows how an Amazonian community, the Tariana, have a strong inhibition against any kind of mixing of their language with that of other local tribes, such as the Tucano, who are gaining dominance over them, and the Makú, whom they despise, comparing them to dogs and accusing their language of containing "inhuman sounds". When such mixing occurs, it evokes ridicule and pity. However, they are increasingly allowing CS with Portuguese and even with English, which symbolizes "everything a capitalist paradise could offer" (2002:211). Gibbons (1987) describes a variety called 'MIX' spoken by students at Hong Kong University, principally among themselves. Unlike a creole (see below), MIX has emerged within a single community and the processes which have occurred have taken place entirely *within* this relatively homogeneous group.

In reviewing research which shows the variety of circumstances where CS may arise, Heller suggests as a priority for CS research to look at "the extent to which different types of CS are related to different types of boundary maintenance/change processes" and "the generalizability of findings concerning

---

[6] In lines 6 and 11, phonological CS serves an artistic purpose: by pronouncing *soul* [su:l] and *full* [fu:l] they rhyme with the French words *roule* (line 2) and *foule* (line 4). In line 15, *bwoy* is creole.

the social conditions under which CS is or is not found" (1988a:268–269). More comparative research is needed (cf. Appendix) for us to realize this aim.

2.3   Code-switching in language interaction

The search for regular correspondences between language interaction and its accompanying social factors has a relatively short history. Traditionally it was thought that change followed universal, language-internal principles such as simplification, and therefore took place *in the absence of* any contact with other varieties (J. Milroy, 1998).

Equally, CS has not always been considered an aspect of language change. Data from the Puerto-Rican community in New York (Poplack, 1980; 1983) was used to argue that. CS was simply the alternation of two varieties, English and Spanish, which preserved their monolingual characteristics. CS was opposed to *borrowing*, which was seen as a form of convergence (see Chapter 5). On the other hand, Mougeon and Beniak (1991:9) suggested that Poplack downplayed the role of CS as an explanation of language change, as a reaction to exaggerated claims that immigrant varieties are hybrid and their speakers inferior. They themselves set out to "rehabilitate" the role of *interference* in language change, refusing to see the term as pejorative. CS is viewed as the most likely *source* of borrowings (see Chapter 1). The exact role of contact in language change is, however, still very much a matter of discussion (Clyne, 2003; Harris and Campbell, 1995).

2.3.1   *Code-switching, interference and borrowing*

Romaine (1989) and Myers-Scotton (1992) reviewed the extensive discussions in the literature concerning the relationship between borrowing and CS, which was mentioned as a significant issue in Chapter 1. One reason why this question has been raised so often is that single-word code-switches/loans are, in many situations, though not always, the commonest kind of CS. Any aspect of a language, however, including its structures, can be borrowed (Boeschoten, 1998).

Within single words, common nouns are the most frequently borrowed items (Poplack, Sankoff and Miller, 1988:62). One explanation of this is provided by Bynon (1977:231), who says this just reflects the size of the grammatical categories concerned. Another is suggested by Aitchison (2000:62), who points out that nouns are freer of syntactic restrictions than other word-classes. Both these explanations involve falling back on "language-internal" factors rather than sociolinguistic ones. Another reason for the prevalence of single-word switches/loans is that these are accessible to bilinguals with any degree of competence, even minimal, in the language from which the borrowing is taken. It was argued in Chapter 1 that there is no reliable way of distinguishing *synchronically* between loans and code-switches; loans must start life as code-switches and then generalize themselves among speakers of the borrowing language (Haust, 1995). When this happens at different historical stages of contact between the same two languages, the loans may go through quite different processes of integration and end up looking quite different in the receiving language. Heath (1989), for example, has shown how some French verbs, borrowed in the early French colonial period, were adopted in Moroccan Arabic without inflectional verb frames. Others, borrowed more recently, have been instantly provided with Moroccan Arabic inflectional frames. Their phonemes have also been imported wholesale, and show signs of stabilizing as such (1989:203).

Sankoff (2001) descibes CS as the "royal road" to borrowing although, somewhat paradoxically, she still supports Poplack's idea that there is an essential distinction between the two. The distinction, it is claimed, is demonstrated by the fact that loan words and "ambiguous lone items" show different statistical patterning in the corpus of Poplack and Meechan (1995). This difference, however, could be a matter of how the two concepts have been defined for research purposes – Sankoff claims that it is preferable to study borrowing processes independently from the "muddy waters" of CS. This preference for studying categorical – and preferably countable – phenomena leads us back to the argument about essentialism (Chapter 1).

2.3.1.1 Grammatical category Nouns may be the most frequently borrowed – and switched – word-class owing to their grammatically self-contained character, but all grammatical categories are potentially transferable. In some data-sets, other types of CS are more frequent. In a comparative study of Punjabi–English bilinguals and Greek Cypriot–English bilinguals, intra-sentential switching was almost three times as frequent as single-word switching among the Punjabis, whereas single-word switching was the commonest among the Greek Cypriots (Cheshire and Gardner-Chloros, 1998). The Punjabi speakers switched massively more than the Greek Cypriots overall, so a possible hypothesis is that the more CS there is overall, the smaller proportion single-word switching represents. Clyne (2003) has rightly pointed out that it would be worth investigating the role of typological factors also in this situation – although at first glance, it should be easier to produce complex switches between Greek and English than between Punjabi and English.

2.3.1.2 Morphophonemic integration with the surrounding language Code-switches as well as loans can be morphophonemically integrated with the borrowing language. Borrowed/code-switched verbs frequently take the morphology of the borrowing variety, e.g. Alsatian *déménagiert* 'moved house' from French *déménager* (Gardner-Chloros, 1991); Maori *changedngia* 'to change' (Eliasson,

1991); Spanish *coughas* 'you cough' (Zimman, 1993); German **gedropped** 'dropped' (Eppler, 1991); etc.

2.3.1.3 Native synonym displacement   There are examples of both loans and code-switches filling lexical gaps in the borrowing language, *and* of their adding themselves as a further option to the native equivalent. The fact that CS is not always the result of an inability to find the right word or expression, is demonstrated by the fact that a common conversational function of CS is repeating (more or less exactly) what one has just said in the other language.

Example 5

RENU: **and she was sleeping all   over the place,   so I had to stay awake**
        digdthi-firdthi   si   **everywhere,   so I had to stay awake**
        *she was falling around **everywhere, so I had to stay awake***
                (Gardner-Chloros, Cheshire and Charles, 2000:1319)

The speaker is clearly fluent enough to have the relevant expression available to them in both varieties. The repetition is functional in terms of its effect within the discourse, breaking up the monotony of repeating the whole expression in English (Gardner-Chloros, Cheshire and Charles, 2000). Similarly, bilingual parents issuing brief orders to their children ("Come!", "Put it on!") often both soften and reinforce the instruction by repeating it in the other language. By contrast, in *mot juste* switching (Poplack, 1980), speakers switch precisely because the other language contains the most accurate term.

Example 6

No me precipitaré en el famoso **name-dropping**
*I will not throw myself headlong into the famous practice of **name-dropping***
                (McClure, 1998:134)

Switching of this type may lead to the word becoming a fully fledged loan, although this never depends on linguistic factors alone, but also on socio-cultural ones.

    This was, for example, the conclusion reached by Treffers-Daller (1994). First of all she found, in her study of French–Dutch contact in Brussels, that the two varieties shared numerous phonemes: many words such as *unique* and *sympathique* could belong to either variety. Second, both French and Dutch have limited morphological marking, so that the criterion of morphological integration could often not be used. Third, both borrowings and code-switches varied as to whether they were syntactically integrated or unintegrated. Treffers-Daller therefore concluded that a unified theory of borrowing and CS was needed.

    Those who disagree would point to the fact that in a given corpus, loans and code-switches may be clearly distinguishable. For example, in Jones (2005), speakers of Jersey French ("Jèrriais") tended to flag code-switched forms (with pauses, self-corrections, etc.), but not borrowings; furthermore those informants with the most positive attitude towards Jèrriais avoided CS entirely (see also Poplack, 1988, discussed in Chapter 3). It is clear that even where a continuum between linguistic varieties exists, speakers are able to use different points along it in a contrastive manner (phonological examples spring to mind). This is different from the question of whether those phenomena are intrinsically, or invariably, distinct.

2.3.2   Code-switching and pidginization/creolization

CS is found alongside pidginization and creolization/decreolization in many parts of the world, and contributes, as they do, to the convergence and divergence of different varieties. Gumperz (1964) and Gumperz and Wilson (1971) identified the close relationship between CS and creolization in the early days of CS research; more recently the trend has been to emphasize the differences. Differences there clearly are, but this should not distract us from the fact that these processes often co-occur, derive from similar social factors and may sometimes lead to similar outcomes.

Crowley (1990), for example, argues that in Melanesian Pidgin, access to the substratum (i.e. indigenous languages) persists at all levels: stabilization, destabilization and creolization should all, he claims, be regarded as contributing simultaneously to the gradual evolution of the language (pp. 384–386). As to CS, its presence or absence seems to be largely a function of the prestige attached to the pidgin. Comparing usage on the radio in Vanuatu and the Solomon Islands, Crowley finds much more CS in the Solomon Islands, where the pidgin's prestige is low, than in Vanuatu, to such an extent that in the case of the Solomon Islands announcers, "It is sometimes difficult to know which language they would claim to be speaking."

In Papua New Guinea, Romaine (1992) shows how CS occurs within the context of a post-creole continuum which had emerged in the preceding twenty years: "In town, Standard English, English spoken as a second language with varying degrees of fluency, highly anglicized Tok Pisin, more rural Tok Pisin of migrants, and the creolized Tok Pisin of the urban-born coexist and loosely reflect the emerging social stratification" (p. 323). Whereas some have been adamant that this situation should be seen in terms of ongoing CS between Tok Pisin and English (Siegel, 1994), Romaine believes that there is no principled way for determining to which language many utterances belong to (1992:322).

Le Page and Tabouret-Keller (1985) give examples of creole speech from sources in the Caribbean, Belize and London. At its most fluid, CS involves shifting at particular linguistic levels rather than a wholesale transition from one variety to another – indeed discrete codes are hard to come by in linguistic contexts as unfocused as those they describe. Sometimes, as in the case of London Jamaican, the switching between the codes is more symbolic than real:

London Jamaican is more a set of norms to be aimed at than an internally coherent and consistent system. Speakers behave as if there were a language called "Jamaican", but often all they do (perhaps all they know how to do) is to make gestures in the direction of certain tokens associated with Jamaican Creole which have a stereotypical value. (1985:180).

Finally, one linguistic phenomenon which shows what a fine line there is between creolization and CS, is bilingual compound verbs (Muysken, 2000; Myers-Scotton, 2002a; Edwards and Gardner-Chloros, 2007). Romaine (1986) showed how in English–Punjabi CS, Punjabi verbal "operators" meaning 'do, make' are commonly combined, in the speech of bilinguals, with a major category (noun, verb, adjective) taken from English, to make new verbal compounds which function as a single syntactic/semantic unit, e.g. *ple kerna*, where *ple* is from English *play* and *kerna* means 'to do/make' in Punjabi. The new compound, which means 'to play', is synonymous with an existing Punjabi verb. Parallel creations have been attested in other, typologically diverse, language combinations, including some, such as Greek Cypriot–English, where, unlike Punjabi, *neither* language provides a native model for the compound verb formation, e.g. *kamno use*, *kamno respect*, *kamno developed*, *kamno spelling*, where the Cypriot form *kamno* 'make/do' is combined with various English words, to make new verbs. These compounds appear superfluous in that the same meaning could in each case be conveyed by a single equivalent in Greek (Gardner-Chloros, 1992). Although generally considered under the heading of CS, these formations show features of creolization, as they involve grammatical convergence and an analytic approach to vocabulary. Heath (1989) gives examples from French borrowings into Arabic and Arabic borrowings into Turkish. These are interesting because, as Heath points out, they occur in intensive contact zones with alternative, productive adaptation routines. Along with the avoidance of inflections reminiscent of pidgins, some of these importations also show unstable word-class, such as *himri* in Moroccan Arabic (from English *hungry*), which fluctuates between noun and adjective (1989:202). This also may be viewed as a product of the fuzziness of the borders, in linguistic terms, between different types of contact languages. But whereas prototypical pidgins and creoles arise as lingua francas in situations involving contact between several languages, other types of mixed languages arise where there is widespread bilingualism and where the new variety serves mainly as a marker of ethnic group identity (Thomason, 2001:197).

2.3.3   Code-switching and mixed languages

"Mixed languages" are generally thought of as a limited and marginal group of languages, spoken in very specific contexts. Their social genesis is crucial to understanding their grammatical make-up. Unlike pidgins, they do not arise in circumstances where there is no common language, but rather as the outcome of particular cases of bilingualism.

They are of interest here because they appear to represent a kind of fossilization of CS (Bakker and Mous, 1994; Bakker, 1997). They characteristically have the grammar of one language and the lexis of another, but in practice this split is "rarely if ever consistent" (Matras, 2000a). Hamers and Blanc (2000) and Thomason (2001) have discussed the differences between CS, mixed languages and pidgins and creoles. Some mixed languages show much more specific and regular patterns than is generally the case with CS. Michif, for example, spoken by the Métis in western Canada and North Dakota and described in Bakker (1997), has a split grammar. The structure of the nominal phrase is essentially French, and that of the verb phrase essentially Cree. A more doubtful candidate for membership of this group is Chiac. A variety of Acadian French–English spoken principally by young people in Moncton, Canada, Chiac is age-graded and highly variable. It can perhaps best be described as a slightly conventionalised type of CS (Perrot, 2001).

As Matras says, most languages are mixed to some extent, and although mixed languages represent a particular type of focusing, the processes underlying them are not fundamentally different from those operating in other forms of contact. The motivation underlying mixed languages, as Bakker points out in relation to Michif, is probably similar to the motivation for CS: the linguistic expression of a dual identity. English could be seen as a mixed language, consisting of an Old English grammatical base with partial relexification from Norman French. "At first those who spoke French were those of Norman origin, but soon through intermarriage and association with the ruling class numerous people of English extraction must have found it to their advantage to learn the new language, and before long the distinction between those who spoke French and those who spoke English was not racial but largely social" (Baugh, 1951:135). In line with Bakker's (1997) account of mixed language formation, there were numerous marriages between Norman men and English women (Baugh, 1951:141), which is consistent with Norman being the lexifier and Old English the principal provider of grammatical structure. Most striking of all is the evidence that the introduction of French words into English is closely correlated with the progressive adoption of English by the upper classes. According to Jespersen (1928:94), slightly over 10,000 French words entered the English language between 1250 and 1400.[7] This corresponds exactly to the period when the upper classes were adopting English (these words represent 40 percent of all the French words in English, of which about 75 percent are still in current use). From the fifteenth century onwards, when English had become

---

[7] The calculation is based on these words' first recorded usage.

the language of the majority within the ruling classes, there was a sharp drop in borrowings from French (Jespersen, 1928:94; Baugh, 1951:214).

2.4   Structural v. social influences

Since the work of Thomason (1986) and Thomason and Kaufman (1988), it has become accepted that many aspects of language change are due to contact – and conversely, that contact often gives rise to change over a longer or a shorter period of time. Chambers and Trudgill (1999) showed that many changes arise from contact between different dialects of the same language, so what appear to be internal developments are often due to processes such as inter-dialect accommodation, imperfect learning and koineization (i.e. the creation of a common variety from existing ones). Trudgill set out "to link a typology of languages and language change to a typology of societies" (1997:3). To do this, he sought out isolated dialects and languages so as to discover which changes arise, and why, in the absence of any contact. Thomason and Kaufman also aimed both to systematize the linguistic factors and to make generalizations about the social influences which affect them (1988:36). The quotation above from Heller set out similar aims specifically relation to CS.

The novelty of Thomason and Kaufman's approach lies in their conviction that social factors determine fundamental aspects of language change. "It is the sociolinguistic history of the speakers, and not the structure of their language, that is the primary determinant of the linguistic outcome of language contact" (1988:35). As in other taxonomies of language interaction, they divide the outcomes of contact into categories: the first is *borrowing*, which can affect both the influenced and the influencing variety, and which, they claim, results first in the adoption of *lexical* elements. Extensive *structural* borrowing, on the other hand, is a one-way process which requires extensive bilingualism among the borrowing-language speakers. Another outcome is *interference through shift*, which does not begin with vocabulary, but with sounds, syntax and morphology, and occurs in the absence of full bilingualism.

Thomason and Kaufman do not specifically discuss CS, but their claims are highly relevant to it owing to their emphasis on the *asymmetric* quality of contact, which links it to the social context within which it occurs. The idea that it is sociolinguistic rather than structural – and potentially universal – factors which determine the outcome of language contact is relevant to the proposed universal grammatical constraints on CS (Chapter 5). In the past, linguists similarly tried to establish universal rules governing the outcome of "interference" generally. For example, Thomason and Kaufman quote various authors who claimed that contact-induced change results in *simplification* of the structures of the contact-receiving language. They then show, by means of counter-examples, that the reverse can also be the case. For instance, contact between the Cushitic language Ma'a and Bantu led to the wholesale adoption by Ma'a of highly marked Bantu inflectional structures. Second, Asia Minor Greek adopted morphological, phonological and syntactic features of Turkish. Their explanation for the latter is that it was the Greeks who were under cultural pressure, and who therefore *became bilingual*. The Turks, for their part, merely borrowed from Greek at a lexical level. As we saw, the minority language is likely to be significantly influenced by the majority one rather than the other way round. Just as there is usually an imbalance in power/status between social groups in contact, so the resulting CS reflects this imbalance and is itself non-symmetrical. Johanson (2002) avoids the terms CS, borrowing and interference and instead discusses "code copying", which is neither a clear switch from a basic code to a foreign code nor a fusion of the two. He proposes that some linguistic features are more "attractive" than others and thus more likely to be borrowed. But the concept of "attractiveness" is not clearly operationalized and Johanson himself agrees with Thomason and Kaufman that "social factors ultimately determine the extent to which attractiveness leads to influence" (2002:3; see also the discussion in Backus, 2004).

Structural factors still have a role to play. Heine and Kuteva (2005) argue that "in situations of intense language contact, speakers tend to develop some mechanism for equating 'similar' concepts and categories across languages". However the speakers' perception of equivalence may not be the same as the linguist's and the course of contact is not always smooth or obvious. For example, Heine and Kuteva claim that it does not always result in simplification, structural parallelism is not always favoured, and, as Tsitsipis (1998) points out, changes may not always be completed, and may be continuous or discontinuous.

An example of the interplay of structural and social factors is provided by Treffers-Daller (1994; 1999), who compared CS between French and Brussels Dutch in Brussels with that between French and the Alsatian dialect in Strasbourg (using data in Gardner-Chloros 1991), reaching slightly different conclusions in the earlier and the later study. The impetus for the comparison was the fact that both in Brussels and in Strasbourg, the local varieties of a Germanic language are in contact with French, from which they have borrowed extensively. However, whereas a mixed identity, relating both to French and Alsatian, is the norm in Strasbourg, in Brussels, where the two linguistic groups are more polarized, all except the oldest members of the population identify *either* with French or Dutch, but not with both. Consequently, as Treffers-Daller points out, Brusselers "no longer consider the mixed code to be an appropriate expression of their identity" and intra-sentential CS is accordingly infrequent.

In the later paper (Treffers-Daller, 1999), the differences between CS in the two situations are downplayed, and it is argued that the typological similarities between the two contact situations are determinant and lead to similar out-comes de*spite* sociolinguistic differences. However, in both these instances of French–Germanic contact, French is the more prestigious language, and this too might help explain certain similar outcomes in terms of structural transfer. Further systematic comparisons will be necessary in order to establish with more certainty the relative role of structural and sociolinguistic factors.

The examples below are first from Brussels and second from Strasbourg. In both, the Germanic sentence structure with the main verb at the end provides the template for the mixed utterance:

Example 7
(a) **Surtout** ze hebben een brief gemaakt.
   Above all they have   a   letter made
   Above all, they have made a letter.   (Treffers-Daller, 1994:192)

(b) Wäje   dem han se **faillite**   gemacht.
   *Because of   that have they **bankruptcy** made*
   Because of that, they went bankrupt.   (Gardner-Chloros, 1991:131)

In both cases, the Germanic variety has imposed its characteristic word order on the code-switched sentence, with the direct object placement before the main verb, which comes at the end. Treffers-Daller does not claim this as a universal feature of French–Germanic contact, and in fact contrasts this situation with that described in Clyne (1987). The latter found evidence of this structure giving way to English word order in Australian Dutch as a result of the impact of English, which exerts a powerful sociolinguistic influence on the minority variety.

Nonetheless, Treffers-Daller's findings require some explanation. One pos-sibility is that, in spite of some differences, the two situations are still *sufficiently* similar at a sociolinguistic, as well as a linguistic, level for the outcome of language contact to be similar, whereas in Australia the situation is much more different than it is between these two. Another possibility is that, although the two linguistic situations differ in many respects, they are nevertheless broadly similar in terms of the overall *balance* of the linguistic vitality of the Germanic and the Romance variety. This could explain a similar linguistic outcome despite some significant differences of detailed sociolinguistic distribution. Bearing in mind that CS is an unstandardized form of speech, a third possibility is that idiolectal factors intervene. There is in fact a difference between example 7a, where the verb–subject order is not inverted as Dutch would require (*ze hebben*), whereas in the Alsatian case it is (*han se*). Internal variation and/or inconsis-tency undoubtedly arises in both communities. In Alsace, structures based on an Alsatian "template" can be found in French as in example 7, but the opposite can also be found, e.g.:

Example 8
Es saat mir nix
It tells me nothing
[*It doesn't appeal to me*, calqued from the French expression *Ça ne me dit rien*].
(Gardner-Chloros, 1991:177).

In general terms, the Alsatian situation supports Thomason and Kaufman's proposals: Alsatian borrows extensively from French at a lexical level; some Alsatian words are also borrowed into French, but less than four times as often (Gardner-Chloros, 1991:164). This assymetry is in accordance with their predictions (Thomason and Kaufman, 1988) as to the likely outcome of shift from a low-vitality to a high-vitality language. "Contact-induced shift", the other outcome predicted in the model, whereby imperfect learning of the target language results in alterations to that language (here French) of a mainly structural nature, can also be found, e.g.:

Example 9
Toujours il était bon
Always   it was good
It was always good.   (Gardner-Chloros, 1991:177).

The Alsatian word order, with the adverb placed at the beginning of the sentence, is used (instead of French: *il était toujours bon*) although there is no inversion of the verb and subject as required in Alsatian (see example 7b above). The outcome of "incomplete" Alsatian influence on French is therefore a hybrid construction.

In some cases, sociolinguistic factors can be seen to override the structural closeness/distance between the languages. We saw above that CS patterns in two broadly comparable immigrant communities, the Greek Cypriot community in London and the Punjabi community in Birmingham, diverged widely: "On every count which we were able to compare, the Punjabis switched massively more than the Cypriots and more *intra-sententially* than through any other form of switch … Whereas there were under five intra-sential switches per ten utterances for the Cypriots, there were over sixty for the Punjabis" (Cheshire and Gardner-Chloros, 1997:270). This is the *reverse* of what one would expect on the basis of structural closeness/distance between the two varieties, Greek and English being typologically closer than Punjabi and English.

2.5   Conclusion

CS is one of the possible outcomes of contact between two (or more) varieties, often co-existing and overlapping with other outcomes. Owing to the huge range of linguistic guises which it adopts, it has sometimes been ignored altogether in studies of language contact, and sometimes defined as being more neat and tidy

Box 3 Medieval Code-Switching

Many code-switched texts, both official and non-official, survive from medieval times (see Trotter, 2002). These cover a variety of genres, including sermons, medical texts and business documents. In Britain, English was code-switched with Latin but also with Norman French. Schendl (2002:81) quotes the following letter, from the Dean of Windsor, Richard Kingston, to King Henry IV (1403). He points out that the use of inter- and intrasentential CS in a letter to the king indicates the social acceptability of code-switching at the time.

Letter from R. Kingston to King Henry IV (1403)

Please a vostre tresgraciouse Seignourie entendre que a-jourduy apres noone…qu'ils furent venuz deinz nostre *countie* pluis de .cccc. des les rebelz de Owyne, Glyn, Talgard, et pluseours autres rebelz des voz marches de Galys … *Warfore, for goddesake, thinketh on your beste frende, god, and thanke hym as he hath deserved to yowe! And leueth nought that ye ne come for no man that may counsaille yowe the contrarie* … Tresexcellent, trespuissant, et tresredouté Seignour, autrement say a present nieez. Jeo prie a la benoit trinité que vous ottroic bone vie ovc tresentier sauntee a treslonge durré, *and sende yowe sone to ows in help and prosperitee; for in god fey, I hope to almighty god that, yef ye come youre owne persone, ye schulle have the victorie of alle youre enemyes* … Escript a Hereford, en tresgraunte haste, a trios de la *clocke* apres *noone*. le tierce jour de Septembre.

Translation

May your most gracious Lordship be pleased to hear that today, in the afternoon … more than 400 of Owen, Glyn and Talyard's rebels, and several other rebels from your Welsh borders, entered our *county. Wherefore, for God's sake, set your mind on God as your best friend, and thank him for the favours he has bestowed upon you. And do not for any reason fail to come, whatever advice to the contrary you may receive from anyone* … Most excellent, most powerful and most redoubtable Lord, let me be denied / refused in some other way! I pray the blessed Trinity that you be granted good life with perfect health for a long time to come, *and may [the Trinity] send you to us soon in help and prosperity; for I faithfully pray to almighty God that, if you yourself come in person, you will be victorious over all your enemies* … Written [by R. Kingston to King Henry IV] at Hereford in the utmost haste at three o'clock in the afternoon on the third day of September [1403].

NB: In the original edition, the words *please*, *noone* and *clocke* were italicised as if they were English, but they are in fact French words of French origin (just like *deserued, counsaille, prosperitee*, etc.), so they are not italicized here in the original or in the translation.

than it actually is. There are examples of relatively stable bilingual situations where two varieties appear to alternate without affecting one another's essential character, but in other cases CS is rule-breaking behaviour, which should be seen not in relation to static norms but in terms of language change and convergence. A fuller exploration of the mechanisms by which the latter occurs is called for (see the papers in *Bilingualism, Language and Cognition*, 7(2), August 1974). Toribio, for example, explores the different factors involved in convergence, and argues that the "semantics–pragmatics interface" is crucial (2004:167). She agrees with Otheguy (1995) that bilinguals select "the most parsimonious grammar that serves both languages". Bullock and Toribio (2004) distinguish it clearly from interference and transfer; rather than implying the imposition of a structural property from one language on another, they see it as an "enhancement of inherent structural similarities found between two linguistic systems" (p. 91). It is to be hoped that the relation of CS to these processes will continue to be investigated.

It increasingly appears that sociolinguistic factors are the key to under-standing why CS takes the form it does in each individual case. Such factors affect different sub-groups in different ways, so there are often different types of CS within the same community. At a social level, CS may be seen as the product of a power struggle between two varieties (Pujolar, 2001) (see Chapter 3). At an individual level, it reflects varying bilingual competences and serves as a discourse-structuring device. Its functionality is discussed in Chapter 4, which reinforces the view that CS is not a passive victim of linguistic forces.

3   Social factors in code-switching

3.1   Introduction

In Chapter 2, we saw that CS is often manifest within the process of language change, which can lead to the creation of new varieties such as pidgins or mixed languages. In other cases, it may be a temporary phenomenon, leading only to some limited borrowing. The outcome of language contact situations is determined by social and economic variables: the relative prestige of one variety as opposed to another, or its association with a more powerful or up-and-coming group. In this chapter, we will look at social factors in CS – factors which, as we saw in Chapter 2, are as important as, if not more important than, the linguistic characteristics of the varieties in determining the linguistic outcome. Whether used in a deliberate way, as above, or not, CS provides a variety of clues as to the social identity of the speaker – the groups which, to paraphrase Le Page, she or he wishes to resemble. In Chapter 4, we will see that bilingual speakers often use CS as "conversational scaffolding" while *at the same time* using it to convey aspects of their identity. The motivation to code-switch relies on factors independent of the varieties as such, including the speakers' relative competence and that of their interlocutors, the identities they can express through each language, the acceptability of CS in their network and in particular contexts, and a variety of further factors.

3.2   Types of factor

As Thomason and Kaufmann pointed out (see Chapter 2), there are a range of factors which determine whether or not CS occurs at all in a given language contact situation. From a sociolinguistic point of view, three types of factor contribute to the form taken by CS in a particular instance:

(1) factors independent of particular speakers and particular circumstances in which the varieties are used, which affect all the speakers of the relevant varieties in a particular community, e.g. economic "market" forces such as those described by Bourdieu (1997), prestige and covert prestige (Labov, 1972; Trudgill, 1974), power relations, and the associations of each variety with a particular context or way of life (Gal, 1979).

(2) factors attaching to the speakers, both as individuals and as members of a variety of sub-groups: their competence in each variety, their social networks and relationships, their attitudes and ideologies, their self-perception and perception of others (Milroy and Gordon, 2003).

(3) factors *within the conversations* where CS takes place: CS is a major conversational resource for speakers, providing further tools to structure their discourse beyond those available to monolinguals (see Chapter 4).

There are many overlaps and inter-relations between the three sets of factors, and some understanding of all three is necessary in order to apprehend why particular CS patterns arise. The classification provides a semblance of order within the huge range of factors which attach *neither* to the varieties themselves as linguistic entities, *nor* to cognitive/psycholinguistic factors which affect the individual. For example, the individual's *competence* in the relevant varieties is a product of their (reasonably permanent) psycholinguistic make-up; at the same time, it has sociolinguistic implications, as it is closely connected with factors such as age, network and identity. Thus, whether or not a second- or third-generation member of the Chinese community on Tyneside can converse fluently in Chinese determines the extent to which they can take part in conversations with the oldest members of the community, who may be to all intents and purposes monolingual Chinese speakers. At the same time, their social networking with people their own age is also partly determined by their linguistic abilities, and their association with English or Chinese speakers is likely to reinforce their preferences and abilities in those languages (Milroy and Li Wei, 1995; Li Wei, 1998a).

3.3   Code-switching in two communities: Strasbourg and London Cypriots

Two examples based on field-work in Alsace (Gardner-Chloros, 1991; 1997) and among Greek Cypriots in London (Gardner-Chloros, 1992; 1995; Gardner-Chloros, McEntee-Atalianis and Finnis, 2005) are presented below, in order to illustrate how these various factors interact in real-life situations. The two cases contrast in that one is a native plurilingual and the other an immigrant setting. The main similarities are that both settings are European, and the varieties involved all Indo-European.

In order to assess the contribution of the linguistic and sociolinguistic factors properly, one would need to systematically compare a variety of situations where CS occurs. For example, one would need to contrast situations where there is switching between closely related varieties with other situations where the varieties involved are typologically far apart from one another. Similarly, one could try to assess the importance of sociolinguistic factors by contrasting cases where the social situation is similar with others where it is quite different. Some attempts to evaluate the relative weight of these aspects have been made (see below). The purpose of the LIPPS/LIDES enterprise is partly to permit such comparisons, by setting up a database of CS texts (see Appendix).

3.3.1   Strasbourg

3.3.1.1   Background   Strasbourg is the capital of Alsace, the easternmost region of France, and a historic town of some quarter of a million inhabitants. Originally part of the Germanic Holy Roman Empire, this disputed region changed hands between France and Germany five times between 1648 and 1945. Since the last return to France after the Liberation, a clear French identity has prevailed. French is the language of the state, of education and the media and, increasingly, the mother tongue of the younger generation.

Surveys have revealed that the Alemannic dialect known as *Alsatian*, which is on a dialectal continuum with dialects spoken in the adjoining areas of Germany, is still widely spoken by various sectors of the population (Gardner-Chloros, 1991; Schuffenecker, 1981; Tabouret-Keller and Luckel, 1981a and 1981b). The existence of this dialect has always been an important element of the area's identity, particularly during the times when it formed part of France rather than Germany. It is used more in rural than in urban contexts, and varies with the age and gender of the speaker, being spoken most by the sociolinguistic groups where one would expect a traditional dialect to be used, i.e among older, rural males. In Strasbourg, it also functions as an in-group marker of Alsatian identity, as opposed to the overarching French identity (French people from other parts are known as "les Français de l'Intérieur" in Alsace). The dialect also distinguishes locals from the international community associated with European institutions based in Strasbourg, whose staff may speak French, but very rarely Alsatian. Alsatian was rigorously avoided after the Second World War for its Germanic associations, but has recently enjoyed a revival among younger generations, including young parents when speaking to their offspring. It is used in adolescent groups as well as by local comedians, playwrights and poets, for humorous, emotional and vernacular purposes of all kinds. There is even a version of Microsoft Office currently being translated into Alsatian by a team of dialectologists.

In spite of this, the surveys document a slow but inexorable falling off in its use as one goes down the age groups. Bister-Broosen's more recent research (2002) identifies positive attitudes towards the dialect among the young generation, but points out that such positive attitudes are common in the final stages of language loss and that they should therefore in fact be interpreted as a warning of the dialect's impending disappearance. In Strasbourg, Alsatian is more often than not mixed with French, i.e. it is heard more in the context of code-switching than in its "pure" form.

3.3.1.2 Types of code-switching   The following example is typical of CS as heard in Strasbourg. It represents the full text of a telephone conversation between a woman in her thirties working in an insurance office, Mrs F, with a technician who had already tried (unsuccessfully) to repair the air-conditioning system.

Example 1

1 MRS F: Do isch d'Madame F. De **bureau de Saint-Paul. Bonjour.** Wissen'r
2   warum ich schunn widder anruef? Unseri mache schunn widder uf siewene
3   zwanzig Grad … Jo, **c'est impossible,** hein. **Madame Jund, quand elle**
4   **est arrivée ce matin, il y en avait 29** … Do het se Tüer e bissel ufgemacht.
5   Mir kann awwer ken … ich weiss nitt. **Ce gars était là l'autre jour** un
6   dann het er ebbs gemacht, het g'saat … **et puis tout d'un coup ça a fait**
7   **clic et effectivement ça a remarché; vendredi il faisait bon,** angenehm
8   **et tout. Et aujourd'hui ça va être pas tenable parce que's** gibt ken Luft,
9   **hein** … Siewene zwanzig Grad, isch e bissel viel … Ja, **j'compte sur**
10   **vous, hein. Merci Monsier Raab, au revoir.**

It's Mrs F here. **The** *Saint-Paul office.* *Hello.* *Do you know why I'm ringing up yet again? Our (thermometers) have gone up again to twenty seven degrees … Yes, it's impossible, eh.* **Mrs Jund, when she arrived this morning, it was 29** *… So she opened the door a bit. But we can't … I don't know.* **This guy was here the other day** *and then he did something, he said … and then all of a sudden it went click and it did work again; Friday it was fine, pleasant and everything. And today it's going to be unbearable because* *there's no air, eh … Twenty seven degrees, it's a bit much … Yes,* **I'm counting on you, eh. Thanks, Mr Raab, bye bye.**

(Gardner-Chloros, 1991:98–99)

When the speaker was asked, after the recording, why she had switched so much – she was entirely capable of speaking monolingually in either French or Alsatian – the only answer she was able to provide was that her interlocutor had been switching as well. Interruptions (marked with …) mark the points where the other speaker was replying, but the whole extract was delivered at high speed and the fifteen or so switches in no way interrupt the flow (note for example the switch in L8 between the complementizer *parce que* and the (abridged) pronoun *es* which follows). Since Mrs F's switches do not noticeably coincide with the other speaker's contributions, there is no reason to think that the actual points at which she switches are determined by her interlocutor – though the overall decision to code-switch was allegedly connected with her knowledge that he was a fellow code-switcher.

Mrs F is a typical Strasbourg code-switcher, but as one would expect in a town of that size, there are many variations on the theme. CS varies from a limited alternation which can be described in terms of "French plus Alsatian" (or vice-versa) to a mixed code with some "third system" phenomena present. Example 2, though within a private conversation, is typical of the switching which occurs as a result of French dominance in official and administrative matters:

Example 2

MRS B: E **promesse de vente** isch unterschriwwe, nitt, awwer de **contrat de vente** nitt,
         denn … der het's kauft vor zehn Johr, am achzehnte **janvier; s'il le revend
         avant**, hett'r e **plus-value**.
         *The **exchange of contracts** has been signed, you see, but the **sales contract**
         hasn't, because … he bought it ten years ago, on the eighteenth of **January**;
         if he sells before (ten years are up), he'll have to pay **gains tax**.*

The use of French for the technical terms (*promesse de vente, contrat de vente,
plus-value*) and for the name of the month, 'January' – along with greetings,
numbers, time of day/days of the week/years, are typical features of Alsatian
switching. Here, they spill over, or "trigger", in Clyne's (1967) term, the phrase
s'il le revend avant. So even within such a short utterance, at least three types of
CS can be identified: switching for technical terms, for months/dates and owing
to triggering. A further motivation – accentuating the contrast between the *if*
clause and the rest of the sentence, i.e. a discourse-related reason, may well
account for the switch back to Alsatian in the last line.[1] Although it is tempting
to say here that the "base" language, which provides most of the grammatical
"glue" is Alsatian, in many cases it can rapidly become impossible to say which
is the dominant language of the conversation, as below in Example 3.

The use of CS is not much constrained by topic in Strasbourg, but is associated
with informal contexts and a "chatty" register. In a comparison between family
and workplace settings, it was found to be more frequent, and more intensive, in
workplaces, between colleagues or peers than between family members, though it
is more frequent in families than between people who do not know each other. For
example, in an anonymous study carried out in three department stores, modelled
on Labov's study of "r" in New York, salespeople code-switched far more among
themselves than when talking to customers (Gardner-Chloros, 1997). In families,
CS reflects inter-generational competence differences, i.e. the switches take place
more *between* speakers and less *within* their utterances. An example of this will be
found in Chapter 4.

Particularly intriguing are cases of CS with no apparent motivation. Such CS
is found in situations where both varieties are intrinsic to people's identity –
what Myers-Scotton called "switching as an unmarked choice" (1983; 1988). In
such cases, in the words of Boeschoten (1998:21), CS begins to acquire
"language-like" properties. Speakers who never speak otherwise than in a
code-switching mode have been observed in many contexts (Swigart, 1991;
Meeuwis and Blommaert, 1998; McCormick, 2002).

---

[1] According to Myers-Scotton's theory (1993b), we are dealing here with Alsatian as a *Matrix
Language* and the conditional clause *s'il le revend avant* is an *Embedded Language Island*.
According to Muysken (2000), this represents *Insertional* CS. Grammatical interpretations of CS
are discussed in Chapter 5.

Example 3 is a case of such unmarked CS, in which the individual language changes are not "indexed" with any particular significance. Three men in their twenties, all fluent bilinguals, are chatting at work about their leisure occupations. One of them, Gérard, starts excitedly describing a motorbike video game. The immediacy of his action-packed description is reflected in his use of the present tense, his short, staccato, sentences and his unconstrained CS.

Example 3

GÉRARD: Wenn d'mit drüewwer witt, **alors il cogne, alors la moto se renverse, puis il faut la remettre sur pied. Moi, je suis arrivé à 80**. S'isch e **truc**, wenn's e paarmol gemacht hesch, hesch's hüsse, **après il y a des difficultés**, kannsch e **programme deux** mache, noh muesch, pour pouvoir traverser, isch dann d'**distance entre le début et la fin de l'obstacle**, un vorhär hesch e so grosser Platz g'hett, **disons**.

If you want to get across with it, **then he knocks, and then the motorbike turns over and you have to right it again. I got up to 80.** *'Thing is, when you've done it a couple of times*, **then there are difficulties**, *then you can put on* **programme 2**, *then you must*, **in order to cross**, *there's the* **distance between the beginning and the end of the obstacle**, *and before that you've had, say, this much space*, **let's say**.

(Gardner-Chloros, 1991:153)

Although the speaker starts in Alsatian, in the first part of the utterance, French appears to be dominant, but Alsatian seems to take over more in the latter part. This "turnover" in the dominant language is quite common, and it would be difficult to assign a "base" or "Matrix" Language to the utterance as a whole (Myers-Scotton, 1993a). Such examples challenge the usefulness of the Matrix Language as a descriptive tool – an issue which is considered further in Chapter 5.

Signs of convergence or melding of the two varieties, going beyond the phonological level and the borrowing of individual words or expressions, can also be found in the Strasbourg context. They include the following:

(1) Expressions calqued from French into Alsatian and vice-versa:

e.g. *es saat mir nix* 'it doesn't appeal to me' – modelled on the French expression *ça ne me dit rien*, lit. 'it doesn't say anything to me'; *achtung mache* 'to pay attention'; French: *faire attention*, Alsatian: *ufpasse*, German: *aufpassen*. Although the French expression has provided the model, Alsatian word order (verb last) is used. This is an example of "covert" borrowing, since the expression remains ostensibly in Alsatian.

(2) Composite word order, as in the utterance:

Toujours il était bon

French: *il était toujours bon* 'it was always good' v.

Alsatian: *immer war er guet* 'always was it good'

The adverb placement at the beginning of the sentence is modelled on Alsatian, but the subject–verb order is French.

(3) Bilingual verbs: like Standard German has done at various times in its history, Alsatians freely borrow French verbs and integrate them thanks to the ending *-iere* (or *-iert* for the past participle), e.g. *camoufliere* 'to camouflage', *engagiert* 'taken on, employed', *arrangiert* 'arranged', *confirmiere* 'to confirm', *forciert* 'forced'. Some of these have entered Alsatian *via* German, but the process remains productive in the dialect, with examples such as *demenagiere* 'to move house', *enregistriere* 'to record' and *choisire* 'to choose' being good examples of spontaneous CS creations which can instantly acquire loan status owing to their being based on an existing well-attested borrowing paradigm.

Alsace provides a useful example of historically rooted CS in a European regional context. It illustrates how several trends and motivations can simultaneously spark off CS, leading to co-existing forms of it within the same community. Despite its diversity, and despite the fact that *in some cases* it signals the loss of the dialect, CS as a whole functions as a marker of being Alsatian in the twenty-first century.

3.3.2   Greek Cypriots in London

3.3.2.1 Background   The Greek Cypriot community in London consists of around 200,000 people (Christodoulou-Pipis, 1991), and is therefore comparably sized with the population of Strasbourg, though obviously more dispersed. In other respects there are significant differences: the Cypriots represent an immigrant community within multi-ethnic London, as opposed to an indigenous one surrounded by rural areas where related varieties are spoken.

Full-length studies of language contact in immigrant communities include Auer (1984), Backus (1996), Clyne (1967; 1991b); Halmari (1997), Li Wei (1994), Nortier (1990), Sebba (1993) and Zentella (1997). The range of linguistic phenomena in such contexts is as varied as in indigenous ones, though Dabène and Moore (1995) point to a few characteristics commonly found in migrant settings which are likely to affect the linguistic picture. First, the circumstances of the migration have an immediate impact on the restructuring of the different groups' social networks; second, there may be a split between the behaviour of those members of the community who develop close links with the host society and those whose lives revolve around the home (for example, housewives or the elderly), who may acquire only minimal skills in the host language and/or take on a role as guardians of the home language. On the other hand, adolescents are often strongly motivated to adopt the language habits of the host community and this may lead to non-reciprocal language use within the home. Finally, the mutual teaching of languages developed within families is conducive to linguistic creativity and each family cell may become a "privileged setting for specific linguistic behaviour and interactional patterns" (p. 30).

Differences between the generations in the London Greek Cypriot community are heightened by the fact that different waves of immigration occurred in different circumstances. Immigration started in the 1930s, for economic reasons. Most migrants of that period were peasants with little schooling, who moved to England because they did not have enough land to live off at home. Some who are still alive now can be found in north London community centres and lunch clubs, sitting round in communal rooms in single sex groups as if in a village square in Cyprus, the women all in black and wearing black headscarves, the men playing backgammon or watching TV and drinking coffee.

Many of them never learned English fluently, but they borrowed from English a large number of words which they adapted to the Cypriot dialect, and which are now considered the archetypal marks of London Greek Cypriot Dialect or GCD (see below). They worked in the catering or hotel trade, clothing or shoe manufacturing or hairdressing and grocery shops. Often wives and families joined the breadwinner after he had been established for a few years (Anthias, 1992). Many women remained in the home, taking in "part-work", which they did at a sewing machine in the kitchen. Most settled in the Borough of Haringey, around Green Lanes, where there are still a succession of Cypriot shops and offices (doctors, lawyers, travel agencies, etc.). Children were sent to Saturday schools, of which there are around fifty. There they were taught Greek by teachers sent over by the Greek government, who made no concession to the fact that their pupils spoke a dialect at home which differs in significant respects from Standard Greek.

The largest migratory wave, in the 1950s and 1960s, was again dictated by economic factors. Finally, after the Turkish invasion of Cyprus in 1974, a number of refugees from all walks of life came over to Britain to make a fresh start. The children of this latter group, having often started school in Cyprus, stand out for their proficiency in Greek; many take GCSE Greek. Each of these waves now comprises several generations, and the youngest in the community are on the whole heavily anglicized. Nevertheless, the rate of intermarriage with the local non-Cypriot population has been relatively low. Many younger people, when interviewed, said they would prefer to marry another member of the community rather than either an English person *or* a Cypriot from Cyprus (Gardner-Chloros, McEntee-Atalianis and Finnis, 2005).

3.3.2.2 Types of code-switching   English words, principally nouns, were adopted and morphologically/phonologically adapted into the London GCD at an early stage in the migration history, and have become part of the community repertoire – known as BBC ('British-born Cypriot') Grenglish. Some, like *marketa* 'market' have displaced native equivalents, others, like the expression for 'fish and chip shop', have been coined to cover concepts which would not have been relevant in Cyprus.

Example 4

BBC Grenglish	English	Greek
marketa	*market*	*aγora*
χoteli	*hotel*	*ksenoδoχio*
taspin	*dustbin*	*skupiδia*
kuka	*cooker*	*furnos*
fishiatiko	*fish and chip shop*	[no equivalent]
kitSi	*kitchen*	*kuzina*
ketlos	*kettle*	[no equivalent]
χaspas/-aδes	*husband/s*	*andras*

Such items are loan words in that they are used community-wide in preference to the "native" equivalent, as well as being morphologically and phonologically adapted to GCD. The younger and more balanced bilinguals use them alongside unadapted code-switches, i.e. English nouns or compounds in a GCD framework (e.g. *situation, GP, flat, second cousins, Mediterranean, privacy, factory, nine-to-five jobs, dinner dance, receptionist, very tight community*, etc.). As was the case with French–Alsatian switching, there are also switched adjectives, adverbs, conjunctions and, less commonly, other parts of speech. Appel and Muysken (1987:170–171) refer to a "switchability hierarchy", in which nouns tend to be the most frequently switched elements owing to the referential weight which they carry.

Although nouns may be switched more frequently, a frequent type of CS involves the formation of new verbs. A common way of doing this in Alsatian, as we saw, was by using the productive verb-ending *-iere*. In GCD–English, the Greek verb ending *-aro* is added to various English verbs (e.g. *kanselaro* 'to cancel', *tʃekaro* 'to check', *muvaro* 'to move', *fixaro* 'to fix'). A further technique involves formations using a verb meaning 'do/make' (in this case the Greek Cypriot *kamno*) in combination with a verb, noun or adjective from the other language, to make a new compound verb. This construction has been found to be prevalent in several diasporic Greek–English contexts: Montreal (Maniakas, 1991), Chicago (Seaman, 1972) and in Victoria, Australia (Tamis, 1986). It is of particular interest in CS as it constitutes a widespread "intermediate" or innovatory process found not only in Greek–English but in a huge number of CS contexts (see 2.3.2).

Example 5
[Mixed compound verb formations in London Cypriot Dialect]
kamno *use*   *to use*
kamno *respect*   *to respect*

kamno *developed*   *to develop*
kamno *spelling*   *to spell*
kamno *improve*   *to improve*

[Occasionally the verb *eχo* 'to have' is also used in such formations, as in:]
Ksero oti eχis very busy *I know you are* [lit. 'have'] *very busy*

The fact that the speaker uses 'to have' rather than 'to be', which would be closer to the relevant expression in either language, suggests that we are dealing with a new verbal formation rather than straightforward CS. Perhaps there is underlying interference from the expression 'to have a lot of work', which is the same in Greek. Perhaps also the speaker cannot recall, or does not know, the Greek for 'busy', *aposχolimenos*, which is long and erudite compared with *busy*. The following examples present similar questions:

Example 6
ekamna **upset**
*I was **upset***
Here the past tense of *kamno* is used instead of the past tense of 'to be' (lit. '**I made** upset')

Example 7
I agli   en   kanun   except   **tus ksenus**
the English** NEG do*   *except **(the) foreigners
the English do not make exceptions for foreigners

Here **kamno** + *except* departs from both English and Greek models. The English would be *make an exception for* and the Greek would require either a monomorphemic verb, or, more colloquially, an expression exactly equivalent to the English one.

3.3.2.2.1 Grammatically deviant examples   Such examples show that there is a grey area where borrowing, code-switching, convergence and innovation cannot easily be distinguished. The tidiness of the switchability hierarchy breaks down as soon as the switched element is a complex, rather than a simple, noun phrase, e.g.:

Example 8
to mono pu mu aresi δamesa ine oti ise **very tight community**
*the only thing which I like here is that you are **very tight community***

The compulsory article required in English before the switched phrase *very tight community* is missing, which violates the equivalence constraint (see Chapter 5).

Example 9
bori na δiavazi ke na γrafi ala oχi ke **a hundred percent**
she can read and write but not actually [lit. *and*] ***a hundred percent***

This is another violation, as the Greek for 'a hundred percent' (**ekato tis ekato**) does *not* take an article. Morphosyntactically deviant structures also arise when the obligatory subject is omitted, in utterances such as 'is' for 'it is' below:

Example 10
ama thelis na χrisimopiisis ta trapezomandila tus, ta pramata tus, **is not inclusive**
if you want to use their tablecloths, their things, ***is not inclusive***

or:

Example 11
kseri ime kipreos tshe nomizo oti **suspect you** an men tu miliso ellinika
he knows I am a Cypriot and I think (he) ***suspect(s) you*** *if I (actually) speak Greek to him*

The verb *suspect* is a "bare form" with no ending. It also lacks a pronoun subject from the point of view of English and the VO order is incorrect from the point of view of Greek.

Switches are also found at locations where adjective placement rules conflict, as in this unpublished example:

Example 12
irthe δaskala **private**
came teacher ***private***
a private teacher came

This example is of interest from the point of view of *constraints* and is commented on in section 5.3.1.

3.3.2.3 Symbolic duality   Below, as in the case of Alsatian, a longer extract from a typical conversation has been selected. The interviewer was a Greek Cypriot from Cyprus, and the respondent is a second-generation member of the London community. The passage is revealing in terms of content as well as CS. Maro is linguistically typical of teenagers and young people, who are not generally fluent bilinguals, and many of the switches appear to be due to a lack of fluency in the GCD.

Example 13

[Conversion with Maro, age 20, social worker]
1   o: **Se pio meros menete tora?**
          where do you live now?
2   M: Palmers Green
3   o: **Thelis na pas piso stin kipro i thelis na minis eδo mesa?**
          Do you want to go back [sic] *to Cyprus or do you want to stay here?*
4   M: δen thelo na mino eδo ala pros to paron –
          I don't want to stay here but for the time being –

5   um, I don't want to go back to Cyprus but I might go to another country but it
         won't be Cyprus
6   O: **iati?**
         why?
7   M: because **persi to kalokeri**.. um …**ðen mu aresane ta … ta provlimata**
         last summer   *I didn't like the … the problems*
         you know I didn't like- I didn't like the way – I don't want to sound like an
         outright feminist but I don't – I don't like the way they treat the women …
         like my cousins right – [*to another interlocutor who says something
         inaudible in the background*] – YOU INTIMIDATED ME – they'll be
         sitting there and their husbands will come in and go: **kori sofia, piene
         ferta ruχa mu ia na kano banio**
         Sophia my girl, go and fetch my clothes so that I can have a swim
8   and I mean things like that, know what I mean. I can't … **ðen boro na sinithiso** …
                                                                  I can't get used to …
9   O: **niothis kseni otan pas kato?**
         do you feel foreign when you go down? [*i.e. to Cyprus*]
10 M: **ne niotho-**
         yes I feel-
11   one of the things I like when I go to Cyprus is that the language is not alien to
         you, people are speaking the same language that you were brought up with
         so that's – you know you get a sort of warm feeling from that, but still I do
         feel like a foreigner over there
12 O: uh..**ðilaði vriskis provlima na milisis kato kipriaka?**
         you mean you find it difficult to speak Cypriot when you're there?
13 M: **oχi ðen..ðen vrisko provlima-ine oti**
         no I don't..I don't find it difficult-it's that
14   you know **ine orea otan pas kapu ke milun ti γlosa pu katalavis**[2] you know
         *it's nice when you go somewhere and they speak the language which you
         understand*

In L5, 7 and 10, Maro breaks off speaking GCD to explain what she means, or to
play for time (*you know*) in English. She is ill at ease because of her halting –
though by no means elementary – Greek – but perhaps also because she is being
questioned about her identity and life plans by an interviewer from Cyprus, i.e.
effectively a foreigner, in front of giggling friends who, at one point (L7), put
her off her stride by saying something in the background to which she reacts
strongly. She is also being questioned about speaking GCD *in* GCD, in which
she is not fully fluent, in the context of a rather tricky conversation about
feelings and allegiances. In L12 there is an indication that the interviewer
herself has not properly understood Maro's comments, and that is why Maro
tries to rephrase them in GCD in L14.

---

[2] Incorrect ending. The correct form would be *katalavenis*. Maro makes various "mistakes" in her
    Greek.

Maro claims that she does not have a problem with speaking GCD (L14) and that it gives her a *warm feeling* to hear the language spoken in Cyprus. She is at her most fluent and confident when she imitates her cousins' macho remarks in Cyprus, showing that she identifies with the values of British youth – equality for women. In this she identifies with the values of her country of residence, the UK. Older members of the immigrant community would tend to be more conservative than the society where they live, hankering after an outdated image of their country of origin. Other girls of a similar age and background said that they would neither want to marry a Cypriot from Cyprus, nor an English person, but only a Cypriot from Britain.

The conversation is revealing at various levels, not least the psychological. Maro's attitude to GCD is like that of an adolescent towards their family – torn between feelings of belonging and the desire at the same time to distance herself, to express a separate identity. The "dual voicing" which CS allows symbolizes this split (see Chapter 4). In conversations with peer-group members, Greek Cypriots of Maro's generation make use of CS for a variety of expressive and identity-creating/reinforcing purposes (Gardner-Chloros and Finnis, 2004).

These two case-studies, the Alsatian and the Cypriot, show how the study of CS in any given community brings in factors at many different levels and, of necessity, involves some ethnographic knowledge and engagement. In both these cases, for example, there are significant differences between the generations in terms of their motives for CS; these difference stem from the speakers' personal and collective history. Considerable caution should be exercised in relation to analyses, be they grammatical or psycholinguistic, which rely on de-contextualized data.

3.4   Macro-linguistic approaches

Sociolinguistics covers a wide range of issues, from language policy and the description of "linguistic markets", via the different linguistic behaviour of women v. men, middle class v. working class, and other social groups, right down to conversations between individuals. Similarly, CS can be studied at the level of whole societies where multilingualism is prevalent (e.g. India), but is also telling at inter-individual and idiolectal level, being closely bound up with the ways in which conversation is structured.

Gumperz and Hernandez wrote that "CS occurs whenever minority language groups come into close contact with majority language groups under conditions of rapid social change" (1969). However, the majority of studies have placed the emphasis on explaining CS from a microlinguistic perspective rather than on showing how it relates to broader aspects of the societies where it occurs. In the next section a few of the broader-based studies are described.

Heller's (1988a) volume *Codeswitching: anthropological and sociolinguistic perspectives* contains various papers in which CS is described in terms of its connection with characteristics of the communities where it occurs: Heller's own paper (1988b) shows how CS can be used to manage and avoid conflict when different varieties are associated with different roles in a society. She gives examples from a Montreal company and a school in Toronto to show how CS allows people to gain access to different roles or "voices" by switching from French to English or vice-versa, and thereby exploit various ambiguities inherent in the situation. Woolard (1988) describes a comedian, Eugenio's, use of Catalan–Castilian CS in Barcelona, not as a test of in-group membership but rather as a way of addressing two audiences at once and thereby *levelling*, rather than maintaining, the boundary between them. McConvell (1988) describes switching between dialects of an aboriginal language, Gurindji, and English in terms of the inter-related social "arenas" where these are used, as Denison had done earlier (1972) for Sauris, a German-dialect speaking enclave in the Friulian Alps.

Gal (1988) points out that CS often involves one state-supported and one stigmatized minority language. Vernacular linguistic forms continue to be used because they represent a form of resistance to domination, so such patterns of use do not simply *reflect* the socio-political situation, they help to shape it. The latter point is an important one: several others have also pointed out that traditional sociolinguistics tends to present the stratification which it portrays in society (e.g. class or gender based) as if it were the result of a consensus, and thereby to gloss over the fact that the observable differences may in fact embody conflict or dissatisfaction (Williams, 1992; Cameron, 1992; Pujolar, 2001). As Cameron puts it, "The language reflects society account implies that social structures somehow exist before language, which simply 'reflects' or 'expresses' the more fundamental categories of the social" (1997:57).

3.4.1   *Diglossia, marked choices and networks*

Ferguson's description of certain linguistic situations as "diglossic" (1959; reprinted in Li Wei, 2000), continues to form a useful basis for discussing bilingual situations. This is not because the diglossic communities described by Ferguson are unchanged – the description was not totally accurate even when first written – but because these proposals focused attention on the *functional* differences between different varieties of the same language and provided a set of structural parameters which allowed one situation to be compared with another. Language use in bidialectal situations – the model was subsequently extended by others to bilingual ones – is described in terms of complementary *domains*[3] of usage, of the

---

[3] Fishman defines domains in terms of "institutional contexts and their congruent behavioral co-occurrences", e.g. family, employment (1972:441).

varieties' relative *prestige*, their role in official life, religion, education and literature. The schema was the subject of significant amendments by Fishman (1965; 1967; also reprinted in Li Wei, 2000). Breitborde (1982) subsequently pointed to some difficulties with connecting the abstract notion of domain with its impact in actual interactions: the features which make up a domain are rarely a perfect fit, so in each case some aspects are likely to be more significant than others. The concept of diglossia was discussed in relation to CS by Myers-Scotton (1986), via the notion of *marked* and *unmarked* choices, mentioned above and further described in Chapter 4. Markedness Theory was developed in the context of explaining the socio-psychological motivations for CS, using data collected in various settings in Africa, Kenya in particular (Myers-Scotton, 1993a).

Li Wei, Milroy and Pong Sin Ching (2000) proposed social networks as an alternative means of relating CS and the language choices of individuals to the broader social, economic and political context. They claim that a *social* – as opposed to sociolinguistic – theory which associates network patterns with the sub-groups which emerge from political, social and economic processes, remains to be developed. Højrup's (1983) division of the population into sub-groups described in terms of different "life-modes" provides one possibility. Li Wei *et al.* found that these life-modes corresponded well with the linguistic behaviour of members of different types of network in their study of the Tyneside Chinese.

3.5   The Gumperz tradition

John Gumperz, whose early work on CS put it on the sociolinguistic map, investigated it in contexts ranging from Delhi to Norway, from the point of view of its historical genesis, its linguistic consequences, its significance for speakers and its conversational functions. Some of this work has already been discussed in Chapter 2. Here, the discussion concentrates on two aspects of his analysis which continue to be influential: the notions of *we-code* v. *they-code*, and the distinction between *situational* and *conversational CS*. Much of Gumperz's earlier work on CS, originally published in less accessible sources, was recapitulated in *Discourse Strategies* (1982), so for the sake of convenience most of the references here are to that volume.

3.5.1   We-*codes and* they-*codes*

As a direct consequence of diglossia, Gumperz (1982) suggested that the ethnically specific, minority language comes to be regarded as a *"we-code"* and to be associated with in-group and informal activities, whereas the majority language serves as the *"they-code"*, and is associated with more formal, out-group relations. However, he emphasized that the relationship between the occurrence of a particular set of linguistic forms and the non-linguistic context is indirect, and that there are only very few situations where one code exclusively is appropriate. "Elsewhere a variety of options occur, and as with conversations in general, interpretation of messages is in large part a matter of discourse context, social presuppositions and speakers' background knowledge" (p. 66). In CS, the *we-code* and the *they-code* are often used within the same conversation, as in Example 14. A Punjabi–English bilingual, Umi, talks to a friend about the likely loss of Punjabi culture in Britain

Example 14
UMI: **culture** tha   aapna …..rena tha   hayni
         culture [tha = stress marker] our …… stay [stress marker] is-not

         we know it, we know it, we know it's coming
         *Our **culture** is not going to last, **we know it, we know it, we know it's coming***
                                          (Gardner-Chloros, Charles and Cheshire, 2000: 1322)

The threat to Punjabi culture is poignantly embodied in the switch from the *we-code* to the *they-code* half way through the sentence, and by the use of the English word for 'culture'.

From an early stage, variations on the classic *we-code/they-code* dichotomy have been reported. Singh (1983) wrote that, although the minority language is usually the *we-code*, this is not always the case. In India, for example, speakers with social aspirations may use English as their *we-code* and Hindi with ironic intent, to show themselves to be a different kind of minority, whose apartness is based on privilege. Sebba and Wootton (1998) also state that even where there are two or three distinct codes available, a multiplicity of social identities may be evoked and manipulated through them, and the relationship between code and identity is far from being one-to-one. They illustrate the point by showing unexpected configurations of *we-* and *they-codes* in various contexts: Cantonese is the *we-code* in Hong Kong classrooms, where English is learned as an L2, but cannot be equated to an insider code as Cantonese is the majority language. For British-born Caribbeans, London English and London Jamaican are both *we-codes*, since it is the ability to use *both* which characterizes the "Black British" speaker.

The *we/they-code* distinction breaks down in situations such as that described in Meeuwis and Blommaert (1998). In the Zairian community in Belgium, CS can be a variety in its own right, with the same functions and effects as those usually attributed to "languages". In communities where this is the case, speakers vary in the extent to which they are able to speak the two varieties monolingually. All the national languages of Zaire are spoken as CS varieties peppered with French (French being the official language in Zaire). Lingala–French and Swahili–French code-switched varieties (Lingala and

Swahili being the two most widespread national languages), have their own range of social, stylistic and register-related variation. A similar situation is reported in Swigart (1991) with respect to the CS variety known as Urban Wolof in Dakar. Such cases point to the dangers of viewing CS from a monolingual reference point in which meaning is seen as being negotiated through the interplay of two differentially marked "languages". Beyond this, there are cases where the *we-code/they-code* distinction completely fails to account for the variation and CS which are observed. Instead, the contrast between the two varieties is used to bring about "local" meanings in a variety of ways, only some of which make use of the associations of the two languages (see Chapter 4).

Indeed the adoption of CS may in itself be an "act of identity", a fact which we see clearly in the case of "crossing" (Rampton, 1995). Rampton describes adolescents in Britain using features of Punjabi and Creole in order to create a trans-racial "common ground". By contrast with other types of CS, crossing "focuses on code-alternation by people who are not accepted members of the group associated with the second language they employ. It is concerned with switching into languages that are not generally thought to belong to you" (p. 280; see also Hewitt, 1986; Jørgensen, 2005). Franceschini (1998) gives a bilingual example:

Example 15
In a fashion house in Zurich, I am served by a ca. eighteen-year-old shop assistant in Swiss-German. After about ten minutes, a group of young men, obviously friends of the shop assistant, enter the shop. All of them use the common Swiss-German/Italian CS style, which is certainly not surprising. There is nothing unusual about the scene. The group seems to me to be one of many second-generation immigrant peer-groups. In order to exchange my purchase, I go to the same fashion house the following day. I am now served by the owner of the shop, a ca. forty-year-old Italian. In the course of our conversation, I am told that the shop assistant I overheard the previous day is not a second-generation Italian immigrant at all but a Swiss-German. She grew up in a linguistically strongly mixed area of the town and has had Italian friends since her school years. (Franceschini, 1998:56–57)

The young shop assistant code-switches, not out of linguistic necessity, but in order to identify herself with a particular peer-group. However, CS due to necessity and CS as the product of choice, are not always easy to separate. Many instances of CS are combinations of the two, or somewhere on the border *between* the two. Auer (2005) shows that it is not always easy in practice to disentangle *discourse*-related CS (see Chapter 4) from such displays of identity.

3.5.2   *Situational and conversational code-switching*

Equally influential with the *we-code/they-code* distinction was Gumperz's sub-division of CS into *situational* and *conversational* types. Situational CS occurs when distinct varieties are associated with changes in interlocutor, context or topic, and is therefore a direct consequence of a diglossic distribution of the varieties. Conversational CS occurs when there are changes in variety without any such "external" prompting. Such switching is further termed *metaphorical* when the purpose of introducing a particular variety into the conversation is to evoke the connotations, the metaphorical "world" of that variety. Blom and Gumperz (1972) gave the example of two villagers in a social security office in the Norwegian village of Hemnesberget, switching from Standard Norwegian to discuss business, to the local dialect to discuss family and village matters.

Although this type of switch, and the compelling motivation for it, are familiar to anyone who has observed CS in this type of minority situation, it was asserted by Maehlum (1990) that the dialect and standard varieties taken as a prototype by Gumperz were in fact "idealized entities" which in practice are subject to interference at different linguistic levels: "Most probably, the switching strategies which Blom and Gumperz recorded in Hemnes actually represent some form of *variant switching* whereby, in certain contexts, single words, (idiomatic) expressions and grammatical forms from the standard are introduced into otherwise dialectal utterances" (1990:758). Maehlum claims that the misapprehension is due to the researchers' insufficient knowledge of the ins and outs of the dialectal situation in that area. Gumperz himself remarked that recordings of informal conversations in the same town, which *speakers* claimed were conducted entirely in the local dialect, "revealed frequent conversational switching into standard Norwegian" (1982:62). Along with classic diglossia, situational CS appears to be a somewhat idealised notion, rarely found in practice.

3.6   Comparisons between and within communities

As we saw in Chapter 1, one of the challenges posed by CS is to explain the variation within it, or, viewed another way, to decide how broadly it should be defined. It has been defined here as inclusively as possible, because, in the present state of knowledge, it has not been demonstrated that the differences between CS and other language contact phenomena are categorical differences as opposed to differences of degree. CS merges with lexical borrowing at one end of the scale, one of the most "minimal" manifestations of contact, and with convergence/interference/code-mixing at the other end, which can be seen as the last step before total fusion. If the process of language contact always started and ended in the same way and always proceeded along a similar path, it would be easier to divide it into distinct phases. Instead, our task is a messier one – to try and apprehend the variations involved and to tie them in with the factors which may help explain this variety. Variation in CS can, however, be divided for practical purposes into variation *between* communities and variation *within* communities. Variation *within* communities can be considered from several points of view, including age, gender and network, some of which are discussed elsewhere (see above and Chapter 4). Some of the studies of variation *between* communities are discussed below.

3.6.1   Variation between communities

Making systematic comparisons between CS in different language combinations and different contexts is the best way to elucidate the contribution of typological factors on the one hand, and sociolinguistic ones on the other, to the patterns of CS in different communities. So far, only a few such comparisons are available. On the whole, researchers base their discussions of CS on their own data, collected in a single community, and do not have access to comparable data-sets from other communities. The LIPPS Project, mentioned in Chapter 1, has as its purpose to set up a database of CS texts coded according to a common protocol and thus facilitating such comparisons (LIPPS Group, 2000) (see Appendix). Meanwhile, some existing comparisons between communities or sub-groups are discussed below. Treffers-Daller (1994;1999), discussed in Chapter 2, Cheshire and Gardner-Chloros (1998), discussed in Chapter 4 and Muysken (2000), discussed in Chapter 5, also employ a comparative approach.

3.6.2   Comparisons between communities

3.6.2.1 McClure and McClure (1988)   McClure and McClure (1988) set out to take a broader perspective than in much CS research by describing a multi-lingual Saxon community in Romania in terms of the macrolinguistic relation-ships between the groups. The Saxon and Romanian communities are quite separate, but unlike other minority groups, the Saxons do not occupy a sub-ordinate position vis à vis the majority. Consequently, their CS is more limited in type than that described elsewhere. Situational switching, mainly dictated by changes in participant, is dominant over the conversational variety. Where the latter does occur, its main function is to highlight quotations.

McClure (1998:141) compares written CS between English and the national language in Mexico, Spain and Bulgaria. The characteristic type of CS encoun-tered in each of these countries reflects the functions of, and attitudes towards, English. In Mexico and Spain, English is widely known, and is used in the press in various expressions denoting concepts expressed more economically in English or using "English" concepts (e.g. *Latin lover)*. But in Mexico, which shares a frontier with an English-speaking country and resents the latter's economic and cultural hegemony, CS is functionally richer than in the other two settings. It is used in ironic contexts to reflect a certain rejection of the US culture, as for example in the use of *by the way* in this quotation from the Mexican press:

Example 16
La hipocresia norteamericana no estriba tanto en los lamentos exagerados por la muerte de un agente de la DEA, y en la indiferencia o incluso el desprecio ante la muerte de decenas de agentes mexicanos (o, **by the way**, de miles de civiles panameños).

*The North-American hypocrisy does not rest so much on the exaggerated laments over the death of an agent of the DEA, and on the indifference or even the scorn with respect to the death of tens of Mexican agents (or, **by the way**, thousands of Panamanian civilians).* (*Proceso*, 15 January 1990).

By contrast, in Bulgaria, English has increasingly been used, since the fall of the Communist regime, as a symbol of the West, a cultural and economic world to which many Bulgarians aspire. English is not yet sufficiently well known for more subtle uses of CS, but is widely present in advertizing and in other documents such as the Yellow Pages for Sofia.

3.6.2.2 Poplack (1988) Poplack (1988) made a three-way comparison between data collected in the Puerto-Rican community in New York (Poplack, 1980) and a later data-set from five neighbourhoods within the Ottawa–Hull community in Canada, which is divided by a river which constitutes both a geographic and a linguistic border (not in the dialectician's sense of "isogloss", but in a sociolinguistic sense). On the Quebec side (Hull), French is the official (and majority) language, and on the Ontario side (Ottawa), it is a minority language. The comparison is of particular interest as any differences between the communities must presumably be attributed to the different status of French in the two communities. The method of data collection and the definition of what constituted CS was the same in both cases. For the purposes of this study, Poplack considered as CS the use of English material in the context of French conversations (i.e. in practice she operated with the notion of French being the *base language*). In keeping with her view as to the demarcation line between CS and borrowing (Poplack and Sankoff, 1984), she did not count single English words which were morphologically or phonologically integrated with French as CS.

The most striking finding was that in the Ottawa communities, where French is a minority language, CS was "three to four times as frequent" as in Hull, i.e. the stronger influence of English in the environment was directly reflected in the amount of CS (1988:226). The same switch-types were found in both communities, but the distribution of the four main types was radically different.

Tabel 3.1 shows that in both communities the commonest switches were *mot juste* switches, switches for metalinguistic comments, switches where the English intervention is "flagged", as in:

Example 17
Excuse mon anglais, mais les **odds** sont là
*Excuse my English, but the **odds** are there*

Table 3.1. *Functions of code-switching in five Ottawa–Hull neighbourhoods*

	OTTAWA (ONTARIO)			HULL (QUEBEC)	
	VANIER	BASSE-VILLE	WEST-END	VIEUX-HULL	MONT-BLEU
# OF SPEAKERS:	23[a]	23[a]	22[a]	24	24
FUNCTION OF CODE-SWITCH:					
EXPRESSION/"MOT JUSTE"	19	18	22	20	13
META-LINGUISTIC COMMENTARY	9	18	9	24	36
ENGLISH BRACKETING	10	17**[b]	8	15	12
REPETITION TRANSLATION, EXPLANATION	8	8	7	10	7
REPORTED SPEECH	10**	13**	14*	16*	18*
PROPER NAME	4	3	4	5	7
CHANGED INTERLOCUTOR	18*	4	17	2	7
FALSE START	5	7*	4	0.7	0.7
AT TURN BOUNDARY	2	0.7	0.7	0	0
SENTENTIAL	13*	6	12*	2	4
INTRA-SENTENTIAL	3	5	2	6	1
TOTAL[c]	552	423	514	148	136

(a) Four sample members whose use of English greatly exceeded that of the other informants and whose status as French L_1 speakers is not clear, were excluded from this study.
(b) Asterisks indicate that the effect is essentially due to that number of individuals.
(c) Percentages may not add up to 100 due to rounding.

and switches in the context of explaining/translating. This points to a fairly self-conscious use of English in both cases, with switches in Quebec being largely restricted to metalinguistic commentary, which, as Poplack points out, show the speaker's full awareness of using English, e.g.:

Example 18
Je m'adresse en français, pis s'il dit "**I'm sorry**", ben là je recommence en anglais
*I begin in French and if he says, "**I'm sorry**", well then I start over in English.*

Poplack comments that this reflects the fact that in Hull, people believe that good French must of necessity exclude Anglicisms.

3.6.2.3 Reasons underlying the differences   The comparison with Puerto Ricans in New York is less direct. There is a wide range of differences between the two situations, such as the fact that the Puerto Ricans are of immigrant origin, which could account for the differences in the prevalent types of CS. We are also dealing with another language combination, but as Poplack points out, the linguistic distance between English and Spanish is not much more remarkable than that between English and French. It is probably more significant that different data collection techniques were used, the Puerto Ricans being studied through participant observation, whereas the Canadian studies were conducted by means of interviews with out-group interviewers. The latter technique might mask the extent of CS and give rise to heightened purism on the speakers' behalf. Regardless of this, Poplack describes switching found in New York as fluent and varied, with many unflagged switches, as opposed to the limited, and more stilted, CS found in the two Canadian contexts. She ascribes this mainly to the fact that for the Puerto Ricans both languages are an intrinsic part of their identity and of their communicative practices. The cohabitation of the two varieties within CS is a natural consequence of this integrated duality.

CS therefore arises, in different forms, in a wide variety of sociolinguistic circumstances. There are also, more unusually, communities which appear to shun it, as in the case described by Sella-Mazi (1997). This is the Moslem, Turkish-speaking community in Thrace (Greece), who were afforded a special status and protection of their linguistic rights under the Treaty of Lausanne (1923). Although the younger members of this community are perfectly fluent in Greek, they are described as avoiding CS, owing to a high level of awareness of the need to protect their language and culture from Greek influence. A second reason given is that the two languages are of widely differing importance in terms of speaker attitudes.

3.7   Conclusion

Broadly "sociolinguistic" approaches to CS are extremely varied and cover multiple levels of engagement with plurilingual data, from the societal to the intra-individual. Dividing these approaches up is a partly arbitrary exercise, since the societal level and the individual are in constant dynamic interaction. The issue of gender, for example, could have been treated here with other major sociolinguistic variables; instead, it is discussed in Chapter 4, as it appears to be bound up with more detailed conversational factors rather than being a broad differentiator within CS behaviour.

CS should be seen as a technique which has clear analogies in the monolingual sphere. Theories linking the social phenomenon of register and style variation to individual performance are highly relevant to CS (see for example the papers in Eckert and Rickford, 2001). Barrett (1998), for example, has illustrated style alternation, largely in phonological terms, amongst African American drag queens, identifying three basic styles (AAVE,[4] gay male style,

---

[4] African American Vernacular English.

and a style based on stereotypes of white women's speech) and showing how the subjects' performances are "tuned" to highlight the audience's assumptions about sex, class and ethnicity (see also De Bose, 1992; Mishoe, 1998).

The concept of "audience design" developed by Bell (1984; 2001) and Coupland (1985), can help explain many cases of CS, such as Example 1 above. Mrs F herself explained her abundant CS on the telephone in terms of reciprocation of her interlocutor's style, and furthermore, during the course of a working day, she switched between several different styles of CS – and mono-lingual speech – depending principally on her interlocutor (Gardner-Chloros, 1991:92–94). The effect of audience design/accommodation on CS is well illustrated in Wei Zhang (2005), where callers to a radio phone-in programme in a bidialectal area of China are addressed in Cantonese by the host unless they themselves reply in Putonghua, in which case the host switches to match. It is to be hoped that in future, there will be more studies systematically comparing CS and dialect – as well as style/register-shifting.

More recently, the linguistic *styles* adopted by individuals have become an important focus of interest in sociolinguistics (Bell, 2001; Coupland, 2001; 2007; Eckert and Rickford, 2001). Broad, quantitative approaches which obscure the differences between individuals are being put into perspective by approaches such as that of Eckert (2000) based on the notion of "community of practice". This notion too could prove extremely useful in relation to CS, which is, after all, no more than the bilingual manifestation of universal discourse practices.

4 Code-switching in conversation

4.1 Introduction

In Chapter 3, CS was considered as a sociolinguistic phenomenon – a linguistic product of language contact, determined in various ways by the social circumstances in which it occurs. One of the principal challenges in CS research is to determine to what extent the social circumstances affect the form which CS takes in any given case. As we will see in Chapter 5, there is also a great deal of research which emphasizes the linguistic and typological factors which shape CS, and it is often considered that the CS patterns found in any given context represent a choice among grammatical options, which are themselves defined by the contributing languages (Halmari, 1997; Muysken, 2000).

Although there is evidence that typological factors influence the type of CS which is found at a grammatical level (Muysken, 2000), there is *no* hard and fast evidence that CS is constrained in any absolute way by the characteristics of the languages involved. First, proving that it was would involve proving a negative – that some kinds of CS *could never* occur. Second, this would imply that speakers *cannot* break, or rewrite "rules". But we should consider carefully what we mean by "rules" when talking about language. As Le Page (1997) has observed, "A language is best thought of as a game in which all the speakers can covertly propose and try out rules, and all the listeners are umpires" (p. 32). Since we know that certain kinds of CS are often found within certain language combinations, and that certain kinds can be expected in certain social circumstances, the challenge is to find the limits of these influences – no more, no less. This can best be achieved by carrying out systematic comparisons between CS involving the same language-pairs in different sociolinguistic contexts, and between different language-pairs in similar ones.

In this chapter we consider three further sociolinguistic determinants of CS: conversational/pragmatic motivations; social psychological influences, including Attitudes and Communication Accommodation Theory (CAT); and gender (with some reference to Politeness Theory). The first of these has been written about extensively in relation to CS; the other two have lagged behind, although they are the subject of massive research efforts in their own right. It goes without saying that each instance of CS, being a highly complex form of speech behaviour, requires a multilevel explanation, so all these aspects, and more, may be relevant simultaneously. The separate presentation of these factors here therefore inevitably involves some oversimplification.

4.2   Conversational/Pragmatic motivations

Myers-Scotton (1993a:49) drew a distinction between the "allocational" paradigm, in which social structure determines language behaviour, and the "interactional" one, in which individuals make "rational choices" to achieve their goals (p. 49). Milroy and Gordon (2003: Chapter 8) similarly contrast pragmatic uses of CS which exploit the symbolism or connotations of each of the codes, and those which purely exploit the *contrast* which the two varieties provide, regardless of their connotations. They emphasize the need to pay attention to both aspects in order to achieve a full understanding of CS.

4.2.1   Using the external symbolism of the two codes

Gumperz (1982) provided examples of both uses of CS. Using the distinction, outlined in Chapter 3, between the *we-code* and the *they-code*, he described the conversational functions of CS with examples from Slovenian–German, Hindi–English and Spanish–English CS in the USA. He conceded that the range of interpretations that results is much greater than one would expect from describing the language usage in terms of the simple "we" and "they" dichotomy. In the conversation below, Gumperz describes the speaker as alternating between *talking about* her problem in English and *acting out* her problem through Spanish: the code contrast "symbolize(s) varying degrees of speaker involvement in the message":

Example 1
[A Chicano professional talks about her attempt to cut down on smoking]
    They tell me "How did you quit Mary?" I don't quit. I … I just stopped. I mean it wasn't an effort that I made **que voy a dejar de fumar por que me hace daño o** (*that I'm going to stop smoking because it's harmful to me or*) this or that uh-uh. It's just that I used to pull butts out of the waste paper basket yeah. I just used to go look in the … **se me acababan los cigarros en la noche** (*if my cigarettes would run out on me at night*). I'd get desperate **y ahí voy al basarero a buscar, a sacar** (*and then I go to the wastebasket to look for some, to get some*) you know. (Gumperz, 1982:81)

Another example shows German–Slovenian bilingual Austrian farmers discussing the origin of a certain type of wheat, and switching from Slovenian to German in order to give countering statements more authority. This is typical in that the majority language is often linked to objectivization or depersonalization of the statement.

The symbolic associations of the two codes are also often exploited in advertisements, as we have seen in the case of McDonald's of (Box 1, p. 6). All over the world, adverts make use of English words, phrases and slogans to convey images of modernity, Westernization, etc. (Bhatia, 1992; Martin, 2002; Takashi, 1990; Cheshire and Moser, 1994). Often the contrast between the local script and the Roman characters used for the English insertions provides an iconic equivalent to the different accents or voices which characterize oral CS – as in the case of the Coca-Cola logo, embedded the world over in hundreds of languages on thousands of hoardings. The fact that code-switching sells products is attested by the fact that some of the biggest multinational companies use it. In Example 2, the 'foreign' flavour is introduced by the use of a different script.

4.2.2 Code-switching as a discourse-structuring device

Goffmann's concept of footing, developed with reference to monolingual speech, is highly relevant in CS: "A change in footing implies a change in the alignment we take up to ourselves and others present as expressed in the way we manage the production or reception of an utterance" (1979:5). Gumperz referred to CS as a "contextualization cue", that is a "verbal or nonverbal cue that provides an interpretive framework for the referential content of a message" (1982:131). His list of conversational functions coinciding with switches also

Example 2

Box 4 Code-switching and script-switching

This example of a Japanese make-up ad illustrates a type of script-switching which is inherent in the Japanese writing system, and shows that certain kinds of CS can be subsumed within what might otherwise be considered a monolingual system. Japanese uses a combination of three scripts: Chinese-derived characters called *kanji*, and two phonetic *kana* scripts called *hiragana* and *katakana*. *Kanji* are pictographic–ideographic characters used to write nouns, adjectives and verbs. *Hiragana* are used to communicate the grammatical functions of a statement, for example, verb conjugation/tense, particles and adverbs. *Katakana* by contrast is used in contemporary Japanese mainly to transcribe foreign words phonetically.

The three scripts may be switched so that words written in *kanji*, for example, can be phonetically transcribed in either of the *kana* scripts. Although convention and context require that a combination of scripts should be used in standard texts, the three scripts offer great possibility for experimenting with language, and depending on how the scripts individually and in combination are manipulated, one can play with meaning, the relationship between sounds and characters, the relationship between words and gender, class, age, ethnicity and so on.

As an example of how the scripts work in a standard setting, consider line 1 from this ad:

キュート	な	小箱	に、	パーリイ	な	グロス	と	口紅。
Kyuuto	na	**kobako**	ni,	*paarii*	na	*gurosu*	to	**kuchibeni**.
Cute	*	**little box**	in,	*pearly*	*	*gloss*	and	**lipstick**.

Pearly gloss and **lipstick** in a *cute* **little box**.

* *na* – adjective particle

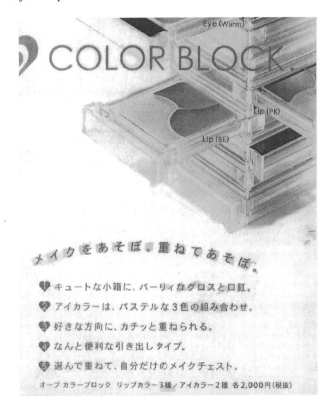

'Cute' and 'pearly gloss'; are approximated phonetically into Japanese pronunciation using *katakana* (in *italics*). In contrast to the more formal *kanji* (in **bold**) and functional *hiragana* (normal font), *katakana* in this context lends a light-hearted sense of fun, trendy youthful fashion and cute feminine style. (For more information on the Japanese writing system, see Florence, 2003.)

includes quotation, addressee specification, interjection, reiteration, message qualification and personalization v. objectification (see similar lists in Saville-Troike (1982), Valdès-Fallis (1977) and Zentella (1997)).

4.2.2.1 Markedness Theory and the Rational Choice Model

Myers-Scotton's 'Markedness Model' (1983; 1993a) represented an attempt to integrate these functions into a more comprehensive model. She argued that in any given social circumstances, a particular variety is the expected or "unmarked" – i.e. the unremarkable – one. So, for example, switching to the local vernacular to talk about home/family is "unmarked", whereas switching to the local vernacular in a public speech is a "marked" choice. Myers-Scotton coins a new "conversational maxim" (Grice, 1989) which corresponds with marked choices: "Negotiate a change in the expected social distance holding between participants" (1993a:132).

Myers-Scotton set out to answer the question "What do bilingual speakers gain by conducting a conversation in two languages (i.e. through CS) rather than simply using one language throughout?" (1993b:3). She drew on numerous theories linking behavioural choices to social constraints, including that on Power and Solidarity (Brown and Gilman, 1960), Politeness Theory (Brown and Levinson, 1987), Speech Accommodation Theory (Giles and Smith, 1979; Giles and Coupland, 1991) and Conversational Principles (Grice, 1989).

In a development of this theory, she presented bilingual speakers as "rational actors" (Myers-Scotton, 1999; Myers-Scotton and Bolonyai, 2001), who are constrained by social norms and conventions. In any given situation, they are in a position to make linguistic choices, which may either conform with the prevailing social norms and pass as "unmarked", or, alternatively, redefine the current set of "rights and obligations". CS itself is the unmarked choice in situations where two sets of identities are normally indexed simultaneously in the community (this would not be possible under strict diglossia). CS can also be an "exploratory" choice, when speakers are feeling their way to the most advantageous way to conduct the conversation. This is the case in Example 3, where a young man is trying to get a dance out of a young woman in a Nairobi hotel. He starts off with the "neutral" choice, Swahili, but it is his switch to English, *following her lead*, which seems decisive in persuading her to dance with him.

Example 3

HE: **Nisaidie na** dance, **tafadhali.**
*Please give me a **dance.***
SHE: **Nimechoka. Pengine nyimbo ifuatayo.**
I'm tired. Maybe the following song.
HE: **Hii ndio nyimbo niyayopenda.**

This is the song which I like.
SHE: **Nimechoka!**
I'm tired!
HE: **Tafadhali –**
Please –
SHE: (***interrupting***)
Ah, stop bugging me.
HE: I'm sorry. I didn't mean to bug you, but I can't help it if I like this song.
SHE: OK, then, in that case we can dance.

(Myers-Scotton, 1993b:146)

Li Wei (1998a) describes the application of Markedness Theory to CS as arguably the most influential model since Gumperz made the distinction between situational and metaphorical CS (see below). However, it places the emphasis on the analyst's interpretation of participants' intentions rather than on the – crucial – creation of meaning by participants within conversations. As we will see below, the notion that speakers make choices between codes and code-switch in accordance with indexical values external to the conversations and the speakers themselves has increasingly been regarded as insufficient.

4.2.2.2   Code-switching as "verbal action": Auer and Li Wei   In a critique of the "Rational Choice" Model (2005), Li Wei demonstrates by means of four extracts from conversations involving a young Chinese girl in England that many of the turn-by-turn switches have a specific meaning which can be interpreted *within* the conversation, not by reference to an external set of norms. Gafaranga (2005) makes similar points in relation to a quite different linguistic situation, that of Kinyarwanda-speaking Zairians in Belgium, for whom the mixing of French and Kinyarwanda in itself already constitutes the *medium* of most conversation. Therefore CS has to be identified on a case-by-case basis, when speakers depart from the normal pattern of mixing in some fashion.

As Meeuwis and Blommaert (1994) have pointed out, in real conversational interactions, it is not always possible to define the situation unambiguously in terms of language choices, and speakers may pay attention to the participants' conversational moves without referring to external precedents. Meeuwis and Blommaert (1998) show that, within a community where CS is commonplace, differences between "languages" may be much less salient than differences between dialects, sociolects, speech styles, etc. In such circumstances, contrasting the two languages for a particular effect is just one way of using CS, and one needs to look at the actual linguistic practices in any given community in order to understand how the various (mixed) varieties are deployed.

A similar caution is expressed by Giles and Coupland (1991): "Speech is far more likely to be dependent upon how speakers cognitively represent their characteristics and subjectively define the scene than upon any objective classification imposed from without" (1991:15). Burt (2002) remarks that in a given bilingual situation, the various maxims and sub-maxims within Myers-Scotton's model can lead to opposite choices. For example, the "Deference" Maxim dictates that one speaks the mother tongue of one's guests to them, but the "Virtuosity" Maxim dictates that one speaks the language which is understood by all the speakers present (p. 995). So if one is in the presence of guests, along with others who do not share the latters' mother tongue, the maxims are in conflict and an ad hoc decision to prioritize one over the other has to be taken. Sachdev and Bourhis (2001:415) point out that CS also occurs in the absence of, or in spite of, a normative framework. At a methodological level, they observe that the "maxims" are often defined by using examples of code-choices which are then in turn re-cited as empirical evidence of those maxims, introducing a certain circularity.

Auer (1998a; 2005), like Li Wei, considers CS to be part of "verbal action", and that its meaning can best be found at a level of conversational structure which is neither grammatical nor dependent on larger societal structures, although both of these are considered to have some relevance. In keeping with the CA tradition, he looks for meaning in units going beyond the sentence, and believes that the only way the analyst can prove that a given set of co-occurring linguistic features is perceived by participants as a distinct code is "by showing that switching between this set and another is employed in a meaningful way in bilingual conversation" (1998a:13).

He takes an example of a conversation from Myers-Scotton. The farmer speaks Lwidakho and some Swahili (italics), and is asking for some money. Myers-Scotton interprets the divergent language choices as follows: the worker shows his rejection of the farmer's appeal for solidarity by using varieties which are marked ("out-group") in this context, English and Swahili:

Example 4

1 FARMER: Khu inzi khuli menyi hanu inzala-
            As I live here, I have hunger-
2 WORKER: [interrupting] **Njaa gani?**
            What kind of hunger?
3 FARMER: Yenya khunzirila hanu-
            It wants to kill me here-
4 WORKER: [interrupting again, with more force) **Njaa gani?**
            What kind of hunger?
5 FARMER: Vana veru-
            Our children-[said as an appeal to others as brothers]
6 WORKER: **Nakuuliza, nja gani?**
            I ask you, what kind of hunger?
7 FARMER: Inzala ya mapesa, kambuli.

> *Hunger for money.; I don't have any*
> 8 WORKER: **You have got a land.**
> 9   **Una shamba**.
>   *You have land [farm]*
> 10   Uli nu mulimi.
>   *You have land [farm]*
> 11 FARMER: ... mwana meru-
>   *... my brother-*
> 12 WORKER: ... mbula tsisendi.
>   *I don't have money*
> 13   **Can't you see how I am heavily loaded?**
>
> (Myers-Scotton, 1993a:82; Auer, 1998a:9–10)

Auer points out that the conversational "moves" made by the participants are at least as significant as the conversation-external factors invoked by Myers-Scotton in explaining the language choices. While not denying the relevance of the wider, "macroscopic" factors, he shows how an analysis of CS which simultaneously pays attention to the sequential structures in conversation – initial request, clarification request, elaboration, indirect decline, second attempt at request, etc., can uncover patterns of convergence or divergence between the speakers which would otherwise not have been apparent (1998a:9–13). For example, in L8–10, the worker does in fact move from English to Swahili to Lwidakho, thus achieving both emphatic repetition and gradual convergence to the farmer's variety. It is only in the third and last request/decline sequence that the worker decisively diverges from the common language and refutes the request.

Li Wei (1998a) makes a similar point and also contrasts Myers-Scotton's analysis with the CA approach, which focuses on speakers' procedures for arriving at *local* meanings. He shows how CS can be used to draw attention to a new conversational move, regardless of the direction of the switch, and analyses the productions of Chinese–English bilinguals in terms of Preference Organization. In a rich database gathered in the Chinese community on Tyneside in the UK, in which inter-generational talk is the prime site for CS, he argues that it is not the structural contrast between Chinese and English which provides an explanation for the switching patterns. A shift to English is taking place over three generations, from Chinese monolingualism to English-dominant bilingualism, and CS varies according to generation, network patterns and the particular group studied (Li Wei, 1998b).

Example 5 shows how Li Wei's subjects' language choices simultaneously reflect their linguistic preferences and authority structures in the family. Speaker A addresses her mother in English, asking her to help with making a folder out of cardboard. The failure of A to switch to her mother's preferred language, Cantonese, in spite of the latter's repeated attempts to encourage her, are indicative of a lack of cooperation which ends, as Li Wei points out, practically in a communicative breakdown.

Example 5
[A is an eight-year-old girl, and C is A's fifteen-year-old brother. B is their mother who is in her forties.]

A: Cut it out for me (.) please
B: (2.5)
A: Cut it out for me (.) mum.
C: [Give us a look
B: [**Mut-ye?**
     What?
A: Cut this out.
B: **Mut-ye?**
     What?
C: Give us a look.
     (2.0)
B: **Nay m ying wa lei?**
     You don't answer me?
A: [To C] Get me a pen.

(Li Wei, 1998a:171–2)

The dual use of CS and pausing shows how CS complements or reinforces discourse structuring devices which are available to monolinguals. This *reinforcement* function of CS parallels the use of such devices in combination with one another in monolingual speech: for example the use of a discourse marker like *well* in English is frequently accompanied by a pause – both before and after – as well as a change in voice quality.

Another example of CS used to signify *non*-compliance occurs partly as a result of the mismatch between the linguistic preferences of the younger and the older generation: Li Wei found switching between turns in such cases to be characteristic of "dispreferred" responses, as in the following example:

Example 6
[B, a twelve year-old boy, is playing on the computer in the living room. A is his mother]

A: **Finished homework?**
B: [2 second pause]
A: **Steven**, yiu mo wan?
     want to review your lessons?
B: [1.5 sec. pause] **I've finished**.

The boy's long pauses and his use of English are both indicative of his lack of enthusiasm for telling his mother anything about his homework (Li Wei, 1998b:163).

4.2.3   Code-switching compared with monolingual conversational moves

In Gardner-Chloros, Charles and Cheshire (2000), a direct comparison is made between the functions which CS has been shown to fulfil in bilingual conversations, and the equivalent expression of these functions in a monolingual context. Two assumptions were made. The first is that bilingual code-switchers and monolinguals accomplish basically the same conversational functions with the different means at their disposal. Bell writes, for example: "having two discrete languages available rather than a continuum of styles simply throws into sharper focus the factors which operate on monolingual style-shifting. The social processes are continuous across all kinds of language situations" (1984:176). The second assumption is that, except in the case of "unmarked" CS, it is more likely that switches are functional than non-functional. Whether such switches are an instance of "rational choices" in Myers-Scotton's terms, or simply capitalize on contrasts within the conversation, we expected most genuine switches be motivated.

In order to get round the problem of obtaining matched samples of monolingual and bilingual speech, code-switched and monolingual passages *within the same conversations* were compared. This allowed a direct comparison to be made of the way in which particular conversational effects are realized monolingually and through CS. The conversations analysed were between members of a close Punjabi family/friendship network in London. Its members were bilinguals, of varying degrees of dominance in English and Punjabi, and habitual code-switchers. The use of discourse features in bilingual and monolingual conversations was compared, concentrating on four common types of transition, which one would expect to be flagged both in monolingual and code-switched conversational contexts. These were: (1) asides; (2) quotations; (3) reiterations; and (4) "but" clauses. The occurrence of each of the four features was noted and then classified as either monolingual or code-switched, according to whether the feature in question coincided with a change in language or not. Examples 7 (a) and (b) illustrate the use of asides used monolingually and bilingually in the same conversation.

In monolingual conversation, speakers often mark off "parenthetical" parts of their utterance by a change in voice quality – in English often to a lower pitch. This may be accompanied by other paralinguistic features such as a gesture, facial expression or change in the direction of their gaze.

Example 7(a)
[Context: talking about one of the participants' future son-in-law]

RENU: What does he do? – to ask the usual question

The aside (underlined) is marked by lower pitch. The speaker is highlighting a metaphorical change in addressee, as the aside is a metalinguistic comment addressed to herself as much as to her interlocutor. The way in which such a device may be used to mark the change from speaking to an interlocutor to thinking aloud (and thus addressing oneself) can equally be seen in the following bilingual example:

Example 7(b)
[Context: talking about the speaker's son's friend)

1	UMI:	saada na, **Charanpreet's friend and er**
		*our now **Charanpreet's friend and er***
2		orna dtha munda siga
		their of boy was
3		**how old is Davan now**?
4		**eleven? So he's about twelve**
		now our Charanpreet's friend, they had a son, how old is Davan now? eleven? So he's about twelve

The speaker uses English and Punjabi in lines 1 and 2, and then switches to English to pose the parenthetical question (underlined) in line 3. This is marked by a change in voice just as in the previous, monolingual example. Here the aside also serves a "fact-checking" function, in which confirmation is implicitly sought from the interlocutor (Gardner-Chloros, Charles and Cheshire, 2000:1317).

Dual marking of a discourse function through CS and voice tone was also seen in relation to reiteration. Typically, repetition and reiteration achieve a number of discourse functions simultaneously (Tannen, 1989; Coates, 1996). In our corpus, the functions included emphasizing or clarifying certain stretches of an utterance, and acting as a floor-holder. These functions have been identified for reiteration in monolingual discourse. When reiteration coincides with CS, however, the functions are marked twice over. Furthermore, switching languages for repetition allowed speakers to hold the floor and to create coherence between different parts of their utterance without the marked connotations of monolingual exact repetition, which can appear rude or condescending.

When CS occurred in quotation sequences, the additional dimension it can bring to discourse was often very clear. It is a well-known function of CS to frame a quotation – here the quote was sometimes framed twice over, once with its quotative verb and then with the change in language. The use of CS not only marked the boundary between the quotative verb and the quote itself. It also gave speakers another "voice" in which they could encode expressive meanings. In monolingual discourse, such effects can be achieved by using a higher proportion of a specific phonetic variant (Eckert, 1996; Eisikovits, 1991;

Holmes, 1995). A subtle change in the use of a single phonological or morpho-logical variant, although in essence comparable to the use of CS as a "we-code", is presumably less salient to interlocutors than a change of language.

Finally, switches coinciding with *but* and its Punjabi equivalent *par* are quintessential examples of the way that the speakers in this study marked textual connections within and across their utterances twice over – once with the contrastive conjunction itself and, simultaneously, with a contrast in language.[1] When CS occurred with these conjunctions, additional effects of CS could be observed: a precise mapping of form and content, implying a habitual action in contrast to a single event, or as an aid to turn-taking. *But* can also have these roles in monolingual discourse. The point is that the function is doubly marked when CS occurs and, presumably, doubly salient to interlocutors as a result.

Example 8
[Context: Renu regretting that pictures of family in India were not evident in a home video made by some of her British Asian relatives who recently visited India]

1 RENU: me kya ki   saria   nu fir   dthek sugdthi
          I   said that everyone to then see   can
2   kutho **I haven't been to India for a long time**
          because
3 UMI: **oh yeah so they didn't take the <family>**
4 RENU: <par>   kisi   dthi **family** dthi ni eye   vich
          *but   anyone of **family** of   not come in*
5   I said [to myself] that I'd be able to see everyone because **I haven't been to**
          India for a long time
6 UMI: **oh yeah, so they didn't take** [ie. take pictures of] **the family**
7 RENU: but nobody from the family was in it [ie. in the video]

Renu begins in Punjabi and then, in line 2, switches to English. Umi then takes the floor in English. Then in line 3, Renu overlaps with Umi's last word (*family*) and switches back to Punjabi, signalling her reclaiming of the floor with the Punjabi *par* 'but'. At the same time, the use of 'but' in this position links her utterance to her preceding turn, continuing the story about how, because she had not seen the relatives in India herself for a while, she was disappointed that they are not included in the home video. The language switch is therefore at the same time both contrastive and cohesive (Gardner-Chloros, Charles and Cheshire, 2000:1333–1334). In a study of Mandinka – Wolof – English CS in the Gambia, Haust similarly found that a high proportion (63.4 percent) of the insertions of grammatical morphemes were formed by the two English words *so* and *because* (1995:369).

---

[1] Oesch-Serra (1998) shows how the French and Italian words for 'but' have become complemen-tary in terms of referential meaning in the bilingual speech of Italian migrants in Switzerland. Therefore, which one is used at a particular juncture depends on the intended meaning and not on the base language which is in use in that sentence or utterance.

Although the discourse functions achieved by CS can be performed monolingually, they are more salient when they are marked by CS, because they are
marked twice over. The discourse functions of CS have long been recognized,
but thanks to this direct comparison, we can see more clearly how these
functions relate to the features that occur in monolingual speech.

4.2.4   A Western view of "intentionality"?

A different view on ascribing motivations to CS is provided by Stroud (1992;
1998). Stroud studied CS in a non-Western context, between Tok Pisin (one of the
three national languages of Papua New Guinea) and Taiap, a language spoken in the
village of Gapun by a mere eighty-nine people. He pointed out the inapplicability,
in this context, of Gumperz's "in-group/out-group" view of bilingualism, as he
claims that no domain, speech genre or topic is conducted exclusively in one
language. More fundamentally, he criticizes the whole notion of "intentionality",
which he claims is based on an inappropriate, Western view of "personhood".
Drawing on work by Duranti (1988), and Hill and Hill (1986), itself influenced by
the Bakhtinian notion of "voices" (or points of view on the world), he claims that
CS in Gapun should be seen as a series of rhetorical moves which highlight
contrasts, and/or perceptual shifts providing different points of view on a situation.
"The words of others carry with them their own expression, their own evaluative
tone, which we assimilate, re-work and re-accentuate" (Bakhtin, 1986:89). There is
little doubt that CS can provide different "voices" to the same speaker. This finding
ties in with research on reported speech in monolingual contexts: Tannen (1989),
for example, points out that most reported speech is "constructed dialogue", i.e. has
never in fact been spoken.

Although Stroud is much closer to a CA interpretation than to one based on the
social connotations of the two languages like that of Gumperz or Myers-Scotton, he
is critical of CA as well, arguing that it is unclear what conversation analysts mean
by "language as social action", and what the latter's relationship is to other kinds of
(non-linguistic) action (1998:340–341). This is to some extent a general critique of
sociolinguistics for not making clear exactly how the structures described are
related to their social uses. He implies that only a deeply ethnographic approach
can get anywhere near understanding the "meaning" of CS from an emic perspective. In Gapun, meaning is not something the individual brings to the conversation
and tries to put across to others, it is a "negotiated product" which emerges from the
conversation. In such a case, the problem, he claims, of assigning meaning to code-
switches is first of all that of deciding: "Whose meaning is it?" (1992:151). Stroud's
approach is illustrative of the diversity of approaches which CS has attracted, and
while his critique may be correct, he gives little indication as to how one should best
proceed in the light of it. It seems likely that all these levels of insight about CS have
their place and that the main challenge is to decide how they can be fitted together.

4.3   Accommodation, attitudes and audience design

Compared with other areas, there is a relative lack of work on the social psychological aspects of CS, although the concepts used by social psychologists are extremely relevant to an understanding of it and such results which exist should be seen as complementary to research on other aspects (Sachdev and Bourhis, 2001).

4.3.1   Accommodation and audience design

CS is one of the possible ways of accommodating to the interlocutor's linguistic preferences (Coupland, 1985; Sachdev and Bourhis, 1990; Scotton, 1976; Wei Zhang, 2005). It can serve as a compromise between two varieties, where these carry different connotations or social meanings for speakers and interlocutors (see above). It may also, of course, be the only possibility open to a speaker where there is a mismatch between their level of competence in the relevant languages and that of their interlocutor.

This compromise function – particularly where it allows the speaker to address an audience made up of people with disparate linguistic competences – is not limited to spontaneous speech. It is also exploited by politicians in their speeches and comedians in their jokes (Woolard, 1988). Generally, it is used in the media which are aimed at multilingual audiences for multiple functions.

For example, Hindi–English CS is extensively used in programmes on the Asian cable television channel Zee TV. This channel aims to appeal to the widest possible audience, including young second-generation Asians whose main language is English, as well as to their parents' and grandparents' generation, whose main language may be one of a variety of Indian languages (e.g. Punjabi, Gujerati), but who have Hindi as a language of literacy. This extract is taken from a drama serial or soap shown on Zee[2] (Gardner-Chloros and Charles, 2007). The scene opens with the male speaker pacing around impatiently, when a well-dressed, older woman rushes in, obviously late for their appointment. By reading the original and ignoring the translation, the non-Hindi-speaking reader can experience the role of the CS as a prop to comprehension.

Example 9
MALE: **Oh, hi**
FEMALE: Ajay, **I'm sorry, tyre flat** horgya tha ….. [HINDI] ….
                  *Ajay, **I'm sorry**, I got **a flat tyre**…. [Hindi]* ….

---

[2] Some monolingual Hindi stretches have been glossed over with the word HINDI, in order to highlight the parts containing CS, where it can be seen how the few English words used provide a useful prop, along with the visual action, to following the story.

MALE: Vese **you can afford a driver**, khud kyor **drive** kurthi he?
Mera mutlaab he **it's not safe**   **these days**.... [HINDI] .....
Actually, **you can afford a driver**, *why do you* **drive** *yourself?*
I mean, **it's not safe these days**.... *[Hindi]* .....
[HINDI] .... aap ko barri **problem** hothi howgi .... [HINDI] ....
..*[Hindi]* ....*it must give you* **a problem**....*[Hindi]* ....
Aap jesi **progressive** xxxx esi barth kurri he?
a **progressive** *xxxx check? like you, saying things like that?*
FEMALE: [HINDI] ...
MALE: *[several seconds' pause]* **Oh** *[another long pause]* **I see**

The last switch to English by the male speaker is punctuated by portentous pauses, implying that the previous speaker's utterance in Hindi was a significant revelation which explained her late arrival in a more thorough-going fashion than the flat tyre could do. Thus the CS here is both a compromise to suit an audience with various levels of competence in English and Hindi – many themselves code-switchers – and simultaneously functional within the conversation itself.

Local radio stations aimed at immigrant communities are also often rich seams for CS. This is the case for London Greek Radio, aimed at the London Cypriots, and also of Beur FM, a French community station aimed at the North African population. Aitsiselmi (2003) has identified pretty well every known category of CS on this station, including inter-sentential, intra-sentential, flagged, identity-related, unmarked and humorous or ludic. As an example of "unmarked" CS with no apparent function, he reports the following:

Example 10
Ils sont revenues **laHqu**   juste **m3a**   la grève des huit jours
They came back **they arrived** *just* **with**   *the one week strike*
tal3u fi   Air France **a sidi, ki diKularte** l'avion avait des problèmes. **Umba3ed**,
so they took Air France **When the plane took off** *the plane had problems.*
l'équipage **kifash y-anunsiw** la nouvelle   *L*   les passagers?
How was **the crew** *to announce* the news   *to*   the passengers?

                                              (Aitsiselmi, 2003:4)

Another major function of CS is what Gumperz called "addressee specification". Using the appropriate language to address different interlocutors allows the participants to continue the conversation smoothly, without undue flagging of who they mean to address ("flagged" switches involve inserting a conversational marker or comment at the point where the switch occurs). This is common in Alsace, where balanced bilingual speakers of the middle generation often use CS in this way. For example in the Beck family, the following conversation took place over a meal between the parents, Mr and Mrs Beck. They are balanced bilinguals but generally speak to one another in Alsatian. The grandfather is markedly more at ease in Alsatian, and the Becks' two teenage daughters are basically French speakers. CS allows Mrs Beck to minimize the confusion which could be caused by her holding two conversations at once, one with her aged father about the weather, and the other with her husband and daughters about serving the meal.

Example 11

MR BECK:	Awwer hit morje isch kalt gsinn, oh kalt!
	But this morning it was cold, oh so cold!
MRS BECK:	's isch kalt, 's isch Winter!
	It's cold, it's winter!
MR BECK:	**A table, les enfants!**
	Lunch is ready, children!
MRS BECK:	De Putzlumpe isch gefrore sinn. **Allez vite maintenant, allons!**
	The mop was frozen. ***Come on now, quickly!***
GRANDFATHER:	Hit morje haw ich gelööjt, sinn's vier Grad g'sinn.
	I had a look this morning, it was four degrees.
MRS BECK:	Ja, s'isch unter nul gsinn. S'isch g'frore g'sinn. **Des pommes de terre, qui veut des pommes de terre?**
	Yes, it was below zero. ***Potatoes, who wants potatoes?***

(Gardner-Chloros, 1991:114)

Addressee specification of this type overlaps with accommodation. As we have seen, however, the concept of "audience design" as such has mainly been applied to monolingual style-shifting. Specific attempts to investigate accommodation in the context of CS have been made by Lawson-Sako and Sachdev (1996; 2000). The definition of CS used in these studies should be noted, in that the object of their study is in fact *language choices*. In a series of anonymous roadside surveys in Tunisia, researchers of different ethnicities posed as passers-by asking the way to the station. They used Tunisian Arabic, French or a combination of the two. Results indicated that subjects converged most readily to the linguistic stereotype of in-group usage when the questioner looked as if they belonged to the in-group (i.e. when they were Arab as opposed to European), whether or not the questioner addressed them in the in-group language. The "unmarked in-group code which most accurately represents the bilingualism of the country" turned out to be CS between Tunisian Arabic and French (2000:1358).

If the desire to accommodate sometimes manifests itself through CS, as the above study seems to show, then we should bear in mind that accommodation is itself a more complex phenomenon than might appear at first sight, and that like CS, it is not found equally across all members of a population. Woolard (1997) found, in a survey of Catalan adolescents, that girls reported a greater tendency towards linguistic accommodation to their interlocutor than boys did. Catalan-dominant female speakers maintain Catalan with Castilian speakers, but converge by using Castilian *if* they consider the Castilian speakers as their friends. As Woolard observes, for girls, "social distance allows one to carry on a bilingual conversation, while closeness and friendship demand a shared language ... For the girl, solidarity demanded accommodation and social distance allowed linguistic mismatch. For the boy, social distance demanded accommodation, and solidarity entitled individuals to use their own languages" (p. 549). A monolingual parallel to this can be found in Brown (1994), who found that women show more positive politeness (PP) than men towards friends, and more negative politeness (NP) in public.

4.3.2 Attitudes

Attitude studies of CS are still relatively few and far between, and most of our information on this is gleaned from a variety of studies where responses are elicited about attitudes along with other aspects. An early exception to this was Chana and Romaine (1984), who reported negative attitudes towards CS among Punjabi–English bilinguals in Birmingham, in spite of their almost exclusively using a CS mode. Bentahila (1983) carried out a matched guise experiment among 109 Arabic–French bilinguals in Morocco, and found a large majority expressing disapproval of the CS guise, with attitudes ranging from pity to disgust. Gibbons (1987) found similar reactions among Cantonese–English code-switching students in Hong Kong, although he also identified an element of covert prestige associated with it. Gumperz's subjects attributed CS to characteristics such as lack of education, bad manners or language inability (1991), and Zentella's to language deficiency, rather than language skill or discourse needs (1997).

Lawson-Sako and Sachdev (2000) report on a matched guise among 169 Tunisians in which they found CS to be rated lowest of all the guises which were used, regardless of the speaker's gender, although gender did affect reactions to the other varieties. Nevertheless, in a follow-up language diary study, the use of CS was widely reported in a range of circumstances (2000:1353–1354). McCormick (2002) found a variety of attitudes towards CS within the same South African community.

A study of London Greek Cypriots revealed reasonably positive attitudes towards CS in this community, with some variation depending on education, occupational group and age (Gardner-Chloros, McEntee-Atalianis and Finnis, 2005). Subjects from lower occupational groups had the most favourable attitudes towards CS; in fact, the more educated the respondents, the less favourable their attitude towards CS. The younger respondents disapproved less of CS, and saw it as more advantageous, than the older ones. Several significant differences were found between attitudes – and in reported CS practices – among Cypriots in London and in Cyprus itself, although the language combination is the same and several significant cultural values are shared. This was ascribed to the languages having a different "market value" in

Cyprus and in London (Bourdieu, 1997). Overall, it seems that CS is gradually gaining acceptability in many contexts, as cultural, racial, musical, culinary and other types of hybridity or "fusion" are better tolerated and indeed become fashionable.

Much work remains to be done, however, for a full understanding of attitudes to CS. Results such as those of Aikhenvald (see Chapter 2) and Bentahila (see above), where extremely negative attitudes are expressed – often at odds with people's behaviour – suggest that attitudes to CS are learned rather than spontaneous. In order to get a picture of people's spontaneous reactions, one should look at contexts where speakers are in no way insecure about their language use, where they do not feel their language to be threatened and, at the same time, where they are not taught or indoctrinated to believe in "purity" as a linguistic ideal. Unfortunately, the world can be roughly divided into the less developed areas, where the first condition applies, and the more developed world where the second one does (Le Page and Tabouret-Keller, 1985:181–182).

4.4   Gender

Gender is considered one of the most important sociolinguistic categories. Studies of the interaction of gender with linguistic performance have become increasingly subtle, avoiding the facile generalizations of the 1970s studies. Gender has assumed more prominence within the discipline rather than less, as the ways in which it is studied have become more diversified.

The research surveyed below shows that CS cannot be correlated in any direct way with gender, but intersects with a large number of intervening variables which are themselves connected with gender issues. Following this, a piece of research is presented in greater detail (Gardner-Chloros and Finnis, 2004) which shows how CS is woven in with female discourse strategies and discourse needs, via the notion of politeness (Brown and Levinson, 1987).

4.4.1   Code-switching and gender in various communities

The long-established finding that women use more standard forms than men (Labov, 1972; Trudgill, 1972; Chambers, 2003) derives from monolingual settings. In its simplest form, it can usefully be tested in bilingual contexts. First, we need to know whether, in a given case, the choice of one or the other variety corresponds with a choice between the vernacular and the prestige code. In some cases, it is the CS mode itself, as we have seen, which carries the "in-group" connotations and may be considered the "local" type of speech (Swigart, 1991).

Given the generally negative judgements of CS outlined above, a study was carried out to find out whether the widespread finding that women use more standard, and less non-standard, language than men was reflected by a clear gender difference in the amount of CS they used. The finding would gain support if women were found to code-switch substantially less than men (Cheshire and Gardner-Chloros, 1998). Transcribed recordings from two immigrant communities in the UK, the Greek Cypriots and the Punjabis, was used to test the hypothesis. The results were negative – there were no significant differences between men and women in either community regarding the use of any kind of CS, though there were substantial differences *between* the two communities, both as regards quantity and type of CS.

Some other studies, on the other hand, *have* found differences in either the amount or the type of CS used by women and men within the same community (Poplack, 1980; Treffers-Daller, 1992). In a study in the Gambia, Haust (1995) found that men used CS twice as much as women, especially using discourse marker insertions, whereas women tended to change varieties outside the turn unit.

Such differing findings in different communities should come as no surprise, given the shift which has taken place within language and gender studies from essentialist to constructionist views (Winter and Pauwels, 2000). As Swigart (1991) argued, women, even *within* a given society, do not all behave as a monolithic group. Gender is not a fixed, stable and universal category whose meaning is shared within or across cultures. It cannot be separated from other aspects of social identity and its meaning varies in different domains: "A nonessentialist view sees gender as a dynamic construct, which is historically, culturally, situationally and interactionally constituted and negotiated" (Winter and Pauwels, 2000:509). Conversely though, the variety within these findings should lead us to relativize the usual pattern of sex differentiation, which Chambers (2003) referred to as a "sociolinguistic verity". This can come about if we look not only at statistical information about how many instances of variant X are produced by women or men, but at the discourse context and the reasons why particular choices are made (see Stroud above).

Furthermore, use of particular linguistic forms does not always signal the same underlying motivations. Traditionally polite or indirect forms do not necessarily indicate underlying compliance. Brown (1994) found that in Tenejapan society, even when women are not being polite in essence, characteristic female strategies of indirectness and politeness are nevertheless manifested in their speech. Brown suggests that this might help us make sense of the finding that women appear more cooperative than men in interaction. While cooperative strategies are being used, what is being achieved may be opposition and disagreement. The way in which this is done in particular instances, the strategies which are typical of women or of men in specific communities, and the particular types of discourse where CS is brought to bear, are often associated with different sexes in a given community.

4.4.2   Code-switching, gender and politeness

In Gardner-Chloros and Finnis (2004), the link between language and gender was explored by considering whether *certain specific functions* of CS are more common among women or men in the Greek Cypriot community. Various findings were taken up from Cheshire and Gardner-Chloros (1998), mentioned above. The earlier study did not eliminate the possibility that, although the overall switching rate between the sexes did not differ significantly, women and men were code-switching for very different purposes.

Two sets of data were used, thirty interviews carried out in the London Greek Cypriot community (Gardner-Chloros, 1992) and transcriptions of recordings carried out at meetings of a Greek Cypriot youth organization. These meetings were informal, and took place at a range of venues, including a community centre, a coffee shop and the home of one of the participants. The participants were five males and five females between the ages of twenty-three and twenty-nine who had all completed higher education.

Sifianou's (1992) comparative study of politeness in England and Greece proved particularly useful. It was pointed out there that different cultures place emphasis on different values, which values are moreover interpreted differently. Basing her work on Brown and Levinson's (1987) theory of Positive and Negative Politeness, Sifianou argued that "Politeness is conceptualised differently and thus, manifested differently in the two societies; more specifically that Greeks tend to use more positive politeness devices than the English, who prefer more negative politeness devices" (1992:2). It is not the case that some cultures or societies are *more* polite than others. The difference is the quality, rather than the quantity of politeness strategies, in that speakers are polite in different, culturally specific, ways.

For example, Greek speakers are more direct when it comes to making requests, when giving advice or making suggestions. The cultural norm in England requires a more distant code of behaviour, and requests, among other speech acts, are expressed more elaborately and indirectly. Sifianou argues that, in England, requests are perceived to a greater extent as impositions, and as such need to be accompanied by more elaborate politeness strategies. Therefore a variety of options are available to the interlocutor when making a request, allowing the imposition created by the request to be minimized, e.g. *You don't have a pen, do you?* (p. 140).

In contrast, Greeks define politeness in very broad terms. Sifianou found that their definition included attributes which might be better described in English in terms of "altruism, generosity, morality, and self-abnegation" (p. 88). Greeks reported that "a warm look, a friendly smile, and in general a good-humoured disposition and pleasant facial expression are integral parts of polite behaviour" (p. 91). Her overall message is that English culture values distance, and Greek culture values intimacy.

This is supported by several examples in Gardner-Chloros and Finnis (2004), which indicate that, when being direct, Greek Cypriot speakers prefer to switch to Greek, as directness is more acceptable in Greek culture. This seems especially to be the case for women, of whom, as in many Western societies, there is an expectation that they will be more polite and consequently more indirect than men. At the same time, because Greek is a more positively polite language, when being intimate, speakers may also prefer to use Greek. Similarly, Zentella (1997) notes that in the Puerto Rican community in New York, commands are often repeated in Spanish, after being delivered in English, in order to soften their impact/harshness.

Three of the functions which are noticeably associated with CS, which were labelled *humour*, *bonding* and *dampening directness*, are illustrated below. There are significant overlaps between the three, which reinforces the idea that there is a general politeness function associated with CS. For different reasons, which are discussed in each case, it was considered that these uses of CS were particularly typical of women in the community, though by no means exclusive to them.

4.4.2.1   Code-switching used for humour

Example 12
1   M I :[3]   ...??? happen to know anyone that has like a colour laser jet..
2   F I :   I know a place where they do???
3   M I :   yeah
4   F I :   ???
5   M I :   what make are they?
6   F I :   **En iksero, en leptomeries**
            I don't know, these are details
            [general laughter].

(Gardner-Chloros and Finnis, 2004:524)

Speaker F1 is relying on her interlocutors' familiarity with Greek culture, in that she adopts the "voice" of a particular Greek stereotype, that of a laid-back type who won't bother with too much detail (line 6). The fact that she is "playing a part" is indicated by a change in voice quality for the remark in Greek. In this way, she justifies her ignorance of the technical details of the photocopier by bringing in a persona who represents this particular Greek attitude.

4.4.2.2   Code-switching used for bonding   CS was often used to indicate identification or intimacy. In the following example, the speakers are talking about a conference they are organizing. Speaker F1 suggests the topic of arranged

---

[3] In this study M1 indicates the first male speaker, M2 the second male speaker, F1 the first female speaker, etc. '???' indicates inaudible speech.

marriages, a traditional aspect of Greek Cypriot culture. She refers to her own mother's concern about her finding a husband and getting married:

Example 13

1 FI: Am I the only person that gets??? by their parents already?
2 MI: What, about getting married?
3 FI: Yeah, she started today.
4 F2:   ???**mana sou?**
       your mother?

(Gardner-Chloros and Finnis, 2004:525)

In line 4, Speaker F2's intervention in Greek can be viewed as an act of positive politeness, or identification with F1, as another female Greek Cypriot. She uses the language of the culture in which such traditional maternal attitudes towards the marital status of daughters prevail. Gender therefore plays an important role in this switch. Whilst the topic of marriage within the community is relevant to all its members, it has much greater consequences for women, and, as such, requires more positive politeness strategies in order to indicate solidarity.

4.4.2.3   Code-switching used for dampening directness   In example 14, speaker F1, after asking the same question in English twice and failing to get a response from speaker M1, switches to Greek to elicit a response. Having succeeded in doing so, she then switches back to English.

Example 14

MI: All right
FI: Stop, how many days is the conference?
MI: Guys, I wanna finish at seven o'clock
FI: I'm asking ! How many days is the conference?
MI: ??? It's half past six.
FI: **Kirie Meniko, poses imeres ine?**
     Mr Meniko, how many days is it?
MI: It will be around four days, I imagine
FI: Ok, four days, good … and what time?

(Gardner-Chloros and Finnis, 2004: 527)

The potentially face-threatening act – an escalation of repeated questions which had been phrased pretty directly from the beginning – is carried off thanks to the switch to Greek, which not only allows greater directness but is also the *we-code* and the language of humour. CS is shown to offer a powerful toolkit for women in the community, who can get away with jokes, strong repartee, etc. without appearing aggressive or unfeminine.

Among the London Greek Cypriots, women seemed to make use of these strategies to get round some of the traditional constraints on female discourse, such as the expectation that it will be less forceful, pressing or direct than that of men, or that making jokes is unfeminine. Women also use CS for solidarity in certain contexts which are directly relevant to them, e.g. in talking about mothers and their attitudes towards their daughter's marital status. It would not be surprising if, being more directly concerned, women talked about these issues more than men, and so had occasion to use these PP strategies to a greater extent, though this is obviously an empirical question.

To the extent that one can show that gender differences are contingent upon culturally determined norms, the role of gender as such is relativized. It is shown to be mediated by other factors, such as the power relationship between the speakers and the conventions governing behaviour – which of course include gendered behaviour – in the community. "We must criticize explanations of difference that treat gender as something obvious, static and monolithic, ignoring the forces that shape it and the varied forms they take in different times and places ... Feminism begins when we approach sex differences as constructs, show how they are constructed and in whose interests" (Cameron, 1992:40).

4.5   Conclusion

In Chapter 3 and in this chapter, we have considered CS from a sociolinguistic perspective. In Chapter 3, we saw how CS could reflect social realities, from the dominance relations between language groups to differences within groups, for example between generations. The importance of making comparisons between different CS situations was stressed, and illustrated by instances where such comparisons were made. In this chapter, we have seen how the uses of CS are woven in a complex fashion with various social motivations, from the desire to accommodate to one's interlocutor to the expression of gender identification. There is rarely a simple, one-to-one correspondence between such factors and the use of CS, even if – naively – one treats CS itself as a simple, on-or-off, phenomenon. As Nilep has put it, CS is "the practice of individuals in particular discourse settings. Therefore, it cannot specify broad functions of language alternation, nor define the exact nature of any code prior to interaction. Codes emerge from interaction, and become relevant when parties to discourse treat them as such" (2006:63). Cashman (2005) also describes how social structures, social identities and linguistic identities are all "talked into being", and are alternately constructed, accepted and rejected within the same conversation. The participants' role-taking is much more subtle than their simple social identities (in this case, as Chicano/Latinos and Anglos) would suggest. Authors including Auer, Li Wei and Gafaranga have all shown how the indexing of varieties with particular values is subordinate, or at least complementary, to the particular uses which bilinguals extract from CS in their conversations.

The ways in which those varieties are manipulated by bilinguals are so varied, and the linguistic configurations are so diverse, that it is tempting to think that there are no limits at all to how languages can be combined, or to what end. In some senses this is true. As we saw, borrowing, for example, arises at all linguistic levels, not only the lexical level with which it is often associated. Nevertheless, synchronically speaking, individuals are limited by their knowledge and perceptions and the ways in which they find it possible – or acceptable – to combine them. The pragmatic approach to CS is marked by the struggle between attempts to demystify and systematize – such as Myers-Scotton's model – and the realization that, having once constructed such systems, speakers can then turn round and deliberately ignore them or subvert them, in their online productions, for their communicative ends.

In the next two chapters, we will look at two different aspects of the *combining* which takes place in CS, first from the point of view of grammar, and then from the point of view of how linguistic elements, which may or may not belong to separate "systems", interact in the brain. Both these factors can in theory set the outer limits on the possibilities of code-switching. But both grammatical and psycholinguistic limitations rest first and foremost on our understanding of what constitutes a separate variety or language in the first place, a question raised in Chapter 1, and which impacts on every aspect of the study of CS.

Box 5 Code-switching in antiquity

CS was common all over the ancient world where Latin and Greek were in contact with local language. This has been discussed in two recent volumes (Swain, 2002; Adams, 2003).

The Roman orator Cicero, who styled himself as a philhellene, wrote a series of letters in the first century AD to his friend Atticus (Cicero, 1999), code-switching copiously from Latin to Greek (Adams *et al.*, 2002). The notable feature of these letters is that they are gossipy in style and were not intended for publication. It is therefore reasonable to assume that the friends code-switched into Greek when speaking, as Cicero does regularly in the letters, as shown in three extracts below (with Shackleton Bailey's translations).

325 (XIII.18)
Scr. In Arpinati IV Kal. Quint. An. 45
<CICERO ATTICO SAL>

Vides propinquitas quid habet, nos vero conf<ic>iamus hortos. colloqui videbamur in Tusculano cum essem; tanta erat crebitas litterarum. sed id quidem iam erit. ego in-terea admonitu tuo perfeci sane argutolos libros ad Varonem, sed tamen exspecto quid ad ea quae scripsi ad te primum qui intellexeris eum desiderare a me, cum ipsehomo **πολυγρώτατος** numquam me lacessisset; deinde quem ζηλοτυπεῖν <intellexeris. quod si non Brutum. multo Hortensium minus aut eos qui de re publica loquuntur. plane hoc mihi explices velim in primis, maneasne in sententia ut mittam ad eum quae scrips an nihil necesseputes. sed haec coram.

325 (XIII.18)
Aprinum, 28 June 45
<CICERO TO ATTICUS>

*You see the virtue of propinquity. Well, let us secure a property in the suburbs. When I was at Tusculum it was as though we talked to one another, letters passed to and fro so rapidly. But it will soon be so again. Meanwhile I have taken your hint and finished off some neat little volumes addressed to Varro. None the less I am awaiting your answer to my questions: (a) how you gathered that he coveted a dedication from me, when he himself, extremely **prolific author** as he is, has never taken the initiative, and (b) whom you gathered him **to be jealous** of: if it's not Brutus, much less can it be Hortensius or the speakers on the Republic. The point above all which I should really be glad if you would make clear to me is whether you hold to your opinion that I should address my work to him or whether you see no need. But we shall discuss this together.*

391 (XV.16)
Scr. Asturae (?) III Id. Iun. an. 44 (?)
<CICERO ATTICO SAL>.

Tandem a Cicerone tabellarius; sed mehercule litterae πεπινωμένως scriptae, id quod ipsum **προκοπὴν** aliquam significaret, itemque ceteri praeclara scribunt. Leonides tamen retinet suumillud 'adhuc'; summis vero laudibus Herodes. quid quaeries? vel verba mihi dari facile patior in hoc meque libenter praebeo creduum. tu velim, si quid tibi est a tuis scriptum quod pertineat ad me, certiorem me facias.

391 (XV.16)
Astura (?) 11 June 44 (?)
<CICERO TO ATTICUS>

*At last a courier from Marcus! But upon my word the letter is well written, which in itself would argue some **progress**, and others too send excellent reports. Leonides however sticks to his 'so far'; but Herodes is enthusiastic. Truth to tell I am not unwilling to be deceived in this case and gladly swallow all I'm told. If there is anything in letters from your people which concerns me, please let me know.*

392 (XV.16a)
Scr. Asturae (?) prid. Id. Iun. an. 44 (?)
<CICERO ATTICO SAL>.

Narro tibi, haec loca venusta sunt, abdita certe et, si quid scribere veils, ab arbitris libera. sed nescio quo modo οἶκος φίλος. itaque me referent pedes in Tusculanum. Et tamen haec ῥωπογραφία repulae videtur habitura celerem satietatem. Equidem etiampluvias metuo, si Prognostica nostra vera snunt; ranae enim ῥητορεύουσιν tu, quaeso, fac sciam ubi Brutum nostrum et quo die videre possim.

391 (XV.16)
Astura (?) 12 June 44 (?)
<CICERO TO ATTICUS>

*The district, let me tell you, is charming; at any rate it's secluded and free from observers if one wants to do some writing. And yet, somehow or other, '**home's best**'; so my feet are carrying me back to Tusculum. After all I think one would soon get tired of the **picture scenery** of this scrap of wooded coast. What is more, I am afraid of rain, if my Prognostics are to be trusted, for the frogs **are speechifying**. Would you please let me know where and what day I can see Brutus?*

5   Grammatical aspects of code-switching

5.1   Introduction

Grammatical approaches have been one of the most prolific sub-fields in the study of CS, and there a number of useful summaries of work in this area (e.g. Bhatia and Ritchie, 1996; Muysken, 2000). The volume of work on CS from this perspective derives from the light which it can cast on grammatical theories: "When sentences are built up with items drawn from two lexicons, we can see to what extent the sentence patterns derive from the interaction between these two lexicons" (Muysken, 1995:178). The purpose of this chapter will not be to give a full picture of the theories, since these have been described thoroughly elsewhere (Myers-Scotton, 1997; Muysken, 2000). Instead there will be a brief overview, the emphasis being put on the role which grammar can play in our understanding of CS – i.e. a reversal of the normal formula. It will be argued that the grammatical work done on CS so far has failed to take the *variations* in code-switching behaviour sufficiently seriously. Rather than being peripheral issues, which can be treated under the heading of exceptions or instances of some other phenomenon such as borrowing, the variations in CS grammars should be taken as the central issue to investigate. Grammatical explanations of CS will be more satisfactory to the extent that they can take on board the variations related to differences in competence between speakers, differences related to typological factors and differences due to sociolinguistic parameters – all of which have often so far been regarded essentially as an inconvenience.

This is a product of the fact that we have so far lacked a general debate as to how and why the notion of grammar can apply to CS in the first place (Gardner-Chloros and Edwards, 2004[1]). The different senses of "grammar", like those of "language" (Le Page, 1989), do not all lend themselves to characterizing performance data. There are at least three potential problem areas:

(1) A grammar is essentially a linguist's description of properly formed *sentences*, and hence represents an abstraction over a set of data. In most types of grammar, the sentence (or clause) represents the upper limit. But

---

[1] The discussion here derives largely from that paper.

the sentence – and its component parts of speech, nouns, verbs, etc. – are not necessarily appropriate units for the analysis of spontaneous speech. Second, grammatical approaches which only seek to explain CS *within* the sentence can only account at best for *some* of the data, as much CS occurs between sentences and between conversational moves (Auer, 1998a:3).

(2) There are doubts about a key concept used systematically in much of the literature on CS grammars, namely that of the "Base" or "Matrix" Language (actually a base *grammar*). The assumptions underlying this notion are discussed below, (and more fully in Gardner-Chloros and Edwards, 2004). It is argued that a misplaced faith in the role of the Matrix Language underlies the failure of many grammatical proposals to account fully for CS data.

(3) Much grammatical work on CS is based on an assumption that bilinguals alternate in some meaningful way between two clearly distinguishable sets of rules. But this question is not one which can be decided by grammatical analysis alone, or the procedure is circular. As Alvarez-Cáccamo wrote

> In order to argue convincingly **for** or **against** the existence of "code-switching constraints" and "code-switching grammars" based on the two monolingual ones (…), research should first convincingly prove that (a) speakers who code-switch possess two (or more) identifiable linguistic systems or languages, each with its identifiable grammatical rules and lexicon; and (b) "code-switched" speech results from the predictable interaction between lexical elements and grammatical rules from these languages. None of these assumptions, I believe, is proven yet. (Alvarez-Cáccamo, 1998:36)

Before looking at how grammatical theories have actually been applied to CS, we will look briefly at some of the different senses in which the term "grammar" is used in this research.

5.2   Types of "grammar"

5.2.1   Prescriptive/Pedagogical grammar

Linguists working on the grammar of CS are certainly not consciously putting forward a prescriptive model of bilingual speech; they are attempting to uncover universal regularities which underlie it. Nevertheless, a prescriptive element can creep in: the outcome of specifying a "grammar" of CS is that there appears to be a right and a wrong way to code-switch, or at least a "possible" and an "impossible" way: it is said that certain combinations of words from different varieties are not CS (see the notion of *nonce loans* discussed below in 5.3.1, but also Myers-Scotton's notion of "classic" CS). Some types of CS are seen as "more equal than others", and many grammatical approaches avoid engaging with the variations between what is prevalent in different sub-groups, e.g.

different generations, or the same speakers in different contexts. There is a parallel here with dialect/creole-speaking settings, where speakers often say of their speech-mode that "it has no grammar" – a recognition that in non-focused contexts, speech is not regulated by the rules which apply to standard, especially written, varieties, and may therefore vary considerably both inter- and intra-individually.

5.2.2   Chomskyan/Universalist grammar

Chomskyan Universal Grammar (UG) is not actually a grammar as such, but rather a "metagrammar": it determines the forms that rules of individual grammars can take. It is therefore at several removes from the form of CS utterances. The nature of the principles and constraints formulated within UG theory are generally highly abstract, and liable to change in the light of developments within the theory, the current version being Minimalism (MacSwan, 1999; 2005; Bhatia and Ritchie, 1996).

Chomsky (1986) made a distinction between *E-language*, meaning the totality of utterances that can be made in a speech community, and *I-language*, defined as "some element of the mind of the person who knows the language". He considered CS to be impure, as it does not represent a single set of choices among the options allowed by Universal Grammar. Muysken (2000) offered various possible explanations as to how there may not be a one-to-one correspondence between the E- and the I-language: bilinguals combine modules from different languages, and several E-languages may correspond to a relatively coherent I-language. George (1990) further distinguished between what speakers *know/ believe* about their grammar, and how these beliefs are actually internally represented ("psychogrammar").

In fact, the majority of grammatical studies of CS, including those of Poplack and Myers-Scotton, attempt to explain surface-level regularities. Nortier (1990:169–170) notes this important contradiction in their formulation: on the one hand it is stated that in CS, syntactic rules of either "language" must not be violated, which implies that underlying structures are the focus of attention; on the other hand, the examples given are all to do with points at which the surface structures are the same or different in the two languages. She shows how, in Spanish–English, this contradiction does not raise serious problems, whereas in her Dutch–Moroccan Arabic data, it does. Similarly, Clyne (1987) and Romaine (1986) had suggested that the Government model failed to explain the sites of CS because these are surface-structure properties. As Chomsky wrote, "there is no reason to expect uniformity of surface structures ... Insofar as attention is restricted to surface structures, the most that can be expected is the discovery of statistical tendencies, such as those presented by Greenberg (1963)" (1965:118).

5.2.3   Formal grammars

These are generative grammars, typically expressed in a rigorous phrase-structure formalism, which provide highly explicit grammatical descriptions of particular languages. Cowie (1999) argues that even within generative discourse, the term "grammar" is used to refer to (at least) three distinct objects:

- the system of rules determining well-formed strings in a given language;
- "competence" grammar, suppposedly consisting of a set of rules and principles claimed to exist in the speaker's mind; and
- the linguist's model of the grammar.

The linguist's model of grammar and the content of the mental grammar are only indirectly related. Moreover, CS poses additional problems, in that it often displays grammatical forms which are "hybrids" of the two monolingual grammars (for example, double morphology). Such phenomena, also attested in second language acquisition, do not necessarily undermine the search for UG-type principles of syntactic organisation, but they do suggest that bilinguals may be operating processes which cannot be explained by generative models.

5.2.4   Cognitive/Functional/Word grammars

The common feature of this cluster of frameworks is that they do not recognize strict divisions between grammar/syntax, meaning and discourse functions. For example, Myers-Scotton's "Production approach" (1993b) attempts to tie in the psycholinguistic notion of "activation" with the grammatical form of CS productions, and in order to do this relies on the notion of "Matrix Language" (see below).

Grammatical studies of CS have on the whole been based on the second and third types of grammars. Studies based on Sense 2 (e.g. Di Sciullo, Muysken and Singh, 1986), which seek to demonstrate universal patterns in CS, have so far not succeeded in doing so. Many other studies have been based, implicitly or explicitly, on grammar in the spirit if not the letter of the third type – statements about the structure of particular languages, and how the differences between them are reconciled in CS. In this case, the productions of bilingual speakers are interpreted through the template of a set of regularities derived from a quite different set of data, which is monolingual – and often introspective – and has provided what is considered to be "the grammar" of Language X and that of Language Y.

5.3   The application of grammatical models to code-switching

Broadly speaking, one can distinguish three major trends in the grammatical study of CS:

(1) Variationist approaches: In the 1970s and 1980s, various attempts were made to formulate grammars based on universal *constraints* on where CS could occur in the sentence (Timm, 1975; Pfaff, 1979; Poplack, 1980; Sankoff and Poplack, 1981).

(2) Generativist approaches, which took off in the 1980s (Di Sciullo, Muysken and Singh, 1986; Joshi, 1985, Mahootian, 1993; Belazi, Rubin and Toribio, 1994; MacSwan, 1999; 2000; 2005).

(3) Production approaches (de Bot and Schreuder, 1993; Azuma, 1996; Myers-Scotton, 1993b). Since these concern psycholinguistic aspects of CS, they are mainly dealt with in Chapter 6. Myers-Scotton's Matrix Language Frame, however, is presented as a direct alternative to variationist and generative approches and is therefore considered below. It has been the subject of repeated amendment by Myers-Scotton and her colleagues (see Myers-Scotton and Jake, 2009).

5.3.1   *The variationist approach*

When CS was first studied systematically at a grammatical level, it was quickly observed that switches did not occur at random points in the sentence. Certain kinds of switching, for example lexical switching, were very common, at least in the Spanish-speaking communities in the USA which were originally studied, whereas others, such as switching between a pronoun subject and a verb, were very rare. This led researchers, for example Timm (1975), Pfaff (1979), Joshi (1985) and notably Poplack (1980/2000) and Sankoff and Poplack (1981) to propose that there must be constraints of a universal nature on where switching could occur. Only brief examples of these constraints are given here.

5.3.1.1 The clitic constraint   The clitic constraint states that clitic subject or object pronouns must be realized in the same language as the verb (Timm, 1975:478; Pfaff, 1979: 303). Thus, examples such as such as the following – recorded in Strasbourg – would be marked with an asterisk as violations:

Example 1: French–Alsatian
il koch güet[2]
he cooks well   (Gardner-Chloros, 1991:168)

5.3.1.2 The free morpheme constraint   Poplack's (1980) analysis of a corpus collected in the New York Puerto-Rican community led her to propose that two constraints were operating, the *free morpheme constraint* and the *equivalence constraint*. These appeared simple enough to be universally applicable and have

---

[2] *il* is a clitic pronoun in French according to Jones (1996).

been widely discussed (Clyne, 1987; Myers-Scotton, 1993b; Jacobson, 1998b). The free morpheme constraint stated that a switch is prohibited from occurring between a bound morpheme and lexical form unless the latter has been phonologically integrated into the language of the former (so a form like *catch-eando*, with an English root and a Spanish ending is not a "permissible" code-switch).

As Bhatia and Ritchie among others point out, such coinages do in fact occur, in both agglutinative and non-agglutinative languages. In some communities this is one of the commonest forms of switching (cf. Eliasson, 1989, on Maori–English). Here four different Swahili bound morphemes are affixed to the verb 'spoil':

Example 2
vile   vitu   zake zi-me-spoil-iw-a
*those things her they-perf-**spoil**-pass*
Those things of hers were spoiled
                                        (Myers-Scotton, 1983, quoted by Bhatia and Ritchie, 1996:640)

5.3.1.3   The equivalence constraint   Lipski (1978), Pfaff (1979) and Poplack (1980) all formulated constraints stating that CS cannot occur at points in the sentence where the surface structures of the two languages differ. Again, this is undermined by examples such as:

Example 3: Greek Cypriot Dialect–English
Irthe dhaskala **private**
*Came teacher **private***
a private teacher came   (Aaho, 1999:43)

English adjective–noun order is violated here. Note that English word order would *also* be acceptable in Greek, yet the speaker chooses the *alternative* order which is *not* common to both languages.

The notion of equivalence is itself problematic. Romaine (1989:118) remarked that the equivalence constraint assumes that the two languages in contact share the same categories and does not make predictions for language combinations where this is not the case. Muysken (1995) also discusses the problem as one of equivalence of structures in the two languages. Sebba (1998) goes further and claims that equivalence is *constructed* by speakers rather than inherent in the languages themselves.

None of the constraints proposed stood up when new language combinations or new communities were studied (Agnihotri, 1987; Bentahila and Davies, 1991; Clyne, 1987; Eliasson, 1989; Gardner-Chloros, 1991; Muysken, 1995; Nortier, 1990; Romaine, 1989, etc.). Instances of CS have been found in every grammatical position, not only by looking across corpora but even within a single corpus (Nortier, 1990). The constraints have therefore come to be seen as having a relative rather than a universal value (Romaine, 1995; Jacobson, 1998b; Muysken, 2000).

Poplack's response to such counter-examples was to claim that apparent violations were due to the fact that we were not dealing with CS, but with a different process, "borrowing". In Chapter 2, it was suggested that borrowing affects all aspects of language, and can only ultimately be distinguished from CS in diachronic terms. Poplack, however, claimed that borrowing could be a once-off process ("nonce loan") (see Poplack and Sankoff, 1984). The circularity of this argument dealt the model what many considered to be a fatal blow: "Poplack's defence of the structural integrity of linguistic systems is motivated less by the evidence than by the desire to justify the validity of a particular theoretical model of code-switching" (Romaine, 1989:286). Poplack (2000) describes some relatively minor changes to the original proposals emerging from later work: the fact that phonological adaptation is now recognized as an unreliable indicator that a word is borrowed, and the formalization of the equivalence constraint on the basis that it is a consequence of speakers' production of "hierarchically and linearly coherent sentences" (Sankoff and Mainville, 1986; Sankoff, 1998). But the basic circularity of the argument is unaltered.

Finally, little attention has been paid to the *interaction* of the proposed constraints, and the possibility that they may not always be compatible with one another, or may lead to different outcomes. Maters (1979) pointed out that violating the free morpheme constraint by adapting CS words morphologically *repairs* the ungrammaticality caused by violating the equivalence constraint:

Example 4
Tu peux me pick-up-*er?*
You can me pick up-INF suffix
Can you pick me up?   (Gardner-Chloros, unpublished example).

The speaker here "gets away with" violating the equivalence constraint – switching from French to English at a point where the pronoun object placement differs between the two languages – by giving the verb 'to pick up' a French infinitival ending, -*er*. This sounds more "grammatical" in French than if she had used the bare form. Such tactics should be of particular interest because, rather like "flagging", they indicate speakers' *awareness* of grammatical difficulties such as equivalence – and, simultaneously, their determination to override them.

5.3.2   Generativist approaches

5.3.2.1   Government   Attempts to explain constraints on CS in terms of Government typically contended that there can be no switching between a governor and the governed element (Di Sciullo *et al.*, 1986). This fails, however, to account for many common switches, such as those between verb and adverb (***Uno no podía comer carne*** *every day,* 'We couldn't eat meat every day'), or subject NP and main verb (***Les canadiens*** *scrivono* c, 'The Canadians write c') (examples quoted in Muysken, 1995).

The proposals were modified in Muysken (1990) and restricted to lexical government by non-function words. Even this prediction was too strong. Muysken refers in particular to the numerous counter-examples in Nortier (1990) from Dutch–Moroccan Arabic CS. These include switches between elements canonically related by "Government" such as verbs and direct objects (***anakandir*** *intercultureel werk*, 'I I-am doing intercultural work') or between direct and indirect objects (***ib li-ya*** *een glas water of so*, 'Get for-me a glass of water or so').

The theoretical constructs involved here are, in many cases, highly abstract, and subject to frequent redefinition. In the case of "Government" for example, several successive formulations of the relationship and the domain in which it applies appear in the literature, and the class of governing categories has been the subject of controversy within GB theory. The notion of "Government" has now been abandoned in the Minimalist Program, partly as result of these definitional difficulties (see Epstein, Groat, Kawashima and Kitahara, 1998: Chapter 1).

5.3.2.2 "Null" theories   MacSwan (1999; 2000) is one of the main proponents of applying the Minimalist Program, as a formal model of grammar, to the analysis of CS. The Minimalist model (Chomsky, 1995) is intended to be a model of grammatical competence, and hence does not address aspects of CS grammar which are likely to involve surface factors, or "performance" factors such as processing and production (see section 5.2.2. above).

MacSwan (2000) assumes that the notion of "a language" should play no role in the formal system employed to account for the data under analysis. The focus, then, is on formal systems. Under the assumptions of the Minimalist Program, the mixing of grammars is effectively the mixing (or "union") of two lexicons, as the significant features of grammars, including the parameters of variation between grammars, are assumed to be located in the lexicon. Regarding CS, MacSwan's position is that "nothing constrains codeswitching apart from the requirements of the mixed grammars" and that the grammar of CS will generate all of the well-formed expressions which invoke elements contributed by more than one language, and none of the ungrammatical ones (2005:2). In order to identify ungrammatical expressions in CS, he uses some experimental data (invented examples tested against informants' intuitive judgements), as well as naturally occurring data. However, this raises the problem of which "native speaker's competence" to appeal to, since this is an even more complex and unreliable concept in the case of bilinguals than in the case of monolinguals. Colina and MacSwan (2005) claim, like Poplack did, that phonological integration can help us distinguish between code-switches and (nonce) loans, and thus that in Spanish–English code-switched speech *tipear* ('to type') is a code-switch and *typear* [taipear] a (nonce) loan.

"Null" theories of CS grammar had been proposed by others before, e.g. by Woolford (1983), Pandit (1990) and Belazi, Rubin and Toribio (1994). All specify that CS can be described in terms of the grammatical principles relevant to monolingual grammars, without postulating additional CS-specific devices or constraints. Along with MacSwan, Mahootian (1993) and Chan (1999) have continued this tradition. Mahootian's proposals are couched in the formalism of Tree Adjoining Grammar (Joshi, 1985), while Chan, like MacSwan, assumes a Minimalist version of Principles and Parameters theory. Mahootian's proposal is mainly concerned with the content of *lexical* constituents, as determined by language-specific rules for those constituents. Her proposal – which is essentially concerned with "surface" word order differences between languages – is however called into question by counter-examples such as that below.

Example 5: German–English
Jemand hat gesagt dass er ist **the father of her child**
*Somebody has said that he is **the father of her child***   (Eppler, 1999:287)

As Eppler observes, word-order constraints formulated in terms of the ordering of constituents dominated by a specific node would not admit switches such as this, in which the complement ***the father of her child*** follows *ist*, rather than preceding it as the relevant phrase structure rule for German would require.

By contrast, Chan (1999) argues that certain patterns of switching can be explained by reference to the *types* of phrase that "functional" categories (Tense, Determiners and Complementisers, among others) select as their complements in different languages. He cites the example below from Bentahila and Davis (1983):

Example 6: French–Moroccan Arabic
je peux le dire **had** le truc **hada bas** je commence à apprendre
*I can it say **this** the thing **this that** I begin to learn*
I can say this in order that I begin to learn   (Bentahila and Davies, 1983:323)

What is important here is that the Moroccan Arabic complementiser *bas* must be followed by a finite clause in Arabic. Chan points out that although the complement clause is in another language – in this case French – the syntactic requirement that the subordinate clause be finite holds. Chan proposes that certain instances of CS are constrained by the "Functional Head Constraint", a condition to the effect that a switch can take place between a functional head in one language, and its complement in the other language, provided that the complement matches the type of complement which would be required in the first language. He claims that this constraint is empirically superior to similar proposals by Belazi, Rubin and Toribio (1994), and Myers-Scotton (1993b), in predicting a wide range of data without the need for special filters and let-out mechanisms.

However Chan's analysis leaves several questions open. Firstly, Chan's constraint relates only to a particular set of categories. These categories (the functional categories), as formulated in Chan's theoretical framework, are, as with Government, abstract categories, whose properties are not fully understood, and which do not constitute a homogeneous class. It is not clear, for example, *why* functional categories should impose constraints on CS. An alternative explanation of the example from Bentahila and Davis cited above, for example, might be that verbs such as *say* (or its French equivalent *dire*) require finite complements in most languages. Second, data from a range of sources suggest that some "functional categories" such as agreement may be affected in CS (witness the common phenomenon of the use of "bare" verb forms in CS). It is by no means certain that the specific grammatical properties of these categories are the same across languages. Nor is it clear that such categories would consistently impose "constraints" on the form of switched utterances. Chan's Cantonese data, for example, contain aspectual markers and these are argued to determine the absence of inflectional morphology on English verbs which have been embedded in Cantonese sentences. In addition to the problem of possible non-equivalence between the relevant Cantonese and English functional categories (Cantonese appears to have no functional categories marking tense, for example), it is interesting to speculate how the situation would work in reverse, say when an English verb appears fully inflected inside a Cantonese sentence. Indeed, Chan offers examples of inflected English nouns in Cantonese sentences. To sum up, while Chan's analysis points to a potentially interesting locus of research, it leaves certain questions unanswered. As with other proposed syntactic "constraints", the jury must therefore remain out on these proposals.

5.3.3   *The Matrix Language Frame (MLF) model*

Klavans (1985) and Joshi (1985) among others, posited that CS involved a "frame" or "matrix" into which elements of another language could be embedded. In a series of publications, Myers-Scotton and her colleagues have formulated an elaborate grammatical model based around this concept (1993b.). The *MLF* (Matrix Language Frame) differs from earlier constraints-based explanations in providing a hierarchical framework and in tying in the proposed constraints with:
(1) the role of different types of morpheme in CS. The basic proposal is that in all CS there is a dominant language, the "base" or Matrix Language (ML). This supplies the system morphemes (closed-class items) in the sentence, whereas the embedded language (EL) supplies a proportion of the content morphemes (open-class items);
(2) the psycholinguistic notion of *activation* (see Chapter 6).

"Grammar" as used here does not correspond clearly with any of the types of grammar mentioned above. Language processing is said to involve the construction of a frame, generally dictated by one of the two languages (the ML), into which elements of the other language (the "embedded language" or EL) are slotted. The model is *insertional*, as opposed to the *alternational* approach embodied by constraints (Muysken, 2000). The ML, we are told, is to be thought of not as a language in itself, but as the "abstract grammatical frame of a bilingual CP".[3] In certain cases, the ML may be "composite", i.e. made up of an "abstract frame composed of grammatical projections from more than one variety" (Myers-Scotton, 2002a:22).

In her earlier work, Myers-Scotton had referred to the existence of "switching as an unmarked choice" (1983) – similar to Gafaranga and Torras's "mixed medium" (2001). But what is posited is a composite framework at the *grammatical* level. She claims that this occurs in situations of language attrition or shift, when speakers do not have "full access to the morphosyntactic frame of the ML", or when "the notion of a target Matrix Language is not clear to the speakers themselves". This is a puzzling statement: it appears to imply that the use of a Matrix Language is connected to the individual's education or competence rather than being a necessary aspect of production, as is claimed elsewhere.

5.3.3.1 The Matrix Language   Leaving to one side the – possibly self-contradictory – notion of a composite Matrix Language, which is said to arise in very specific circumstances, various problems surround the definition of the ML (and consequently the EL).

5.3.3.1.1 The quantitative criterion   Originally, the ML was determined by a quantitative criterion. It was said to contribute the greater number of morphemes in a discourse sample consisting of more than one sentence (Myers-Scotton, 1993b; 2002a). By Myers-Scotton's admission, the size of the necessary sample was uncertain: "How large is 'large enough' is an unresolved issue" (1993b:68). Many bilingual conversations, according to this criterion, could be seen as changing ML several times. As Bentahila and Davies (1998:31) asked: "Should an interaction containing four sentences dominated by one language that are followed by two more sentences dominated by the other be analyzed as having a single Matrix Language, calculated on overall morpheme frequencies, or should one recognize a change of Matrix Language within the interaction?" Examples such as the following illustrate the problem: the languages are pretty well equally represented, and some morphemes cannot

---

[3] The CP is defined as a clause with a complementizer, though both the complementizer and other elements in the CP may be null (Myers-Scotton, 1997:220).

easily be assigned to a particular language; *in, de, en* and *is* are all unclear or borderline between English and Dutch.

Example 7: Dutch–English
Ja, *in de, in de* **big place** *is* het **a lot**, nou ja, je kan't, t' *is de same* als *hier.* Je habt **Melbourne** en *de* **other places** met *de* **high flats and so**. Dat heb je in Holland ook. Maar'n, maar **a lot of places** *nou* **(now)**, de **same before we go**. D'r is, **we go to my sister in Apeldoorn**, en zi hef de **same place** noog.   (Clyne, 1987:754)

Second, what is the relevant unit within which to count morphemes? Auer (1998b) illustrates in some detail the problems attendant on segmenting utterances into clauses (or CPs), and the corresponding outcomes in terms of determining the base language. The quantitative criterion was therefore eventually abandoned in favour of other criteria.

5.3.3.1.2 The morpheme-type criterion   The ML was said to provide the function words, except within EL "islands". The class of EL islands is open-ended, so the question is how such islands are to be identified without circularity. According to Myers-Scotton, islands are triggered by the use of a *lemma*[4] which does not exist in the ML (1993b). As such islands are basically inserted chunks, more complex types of CS had to be accounted for separately (thus giving rise to the notion of a composite ML).

The division between function and content words is itself problematic. Muysken (2000) points out that there are at least four different criteria relevant to this kind of classification in different languages; also, the distinction does not operate in the same way across languages. In a later paper, Myers-Scotton's collaborator Jake concedes that "there is variation across languages in the assignment of particular lexical 'concepts' to content or system morpheme status" (1998:354).

The MLF model has been repeatedly amended, partly in response to such criticisms. In Myers-Scotton and Jake (2000), a new "submodel for classifying morphemes into four categories", known as the 4-M model, was presented. This relies on a sub-division of system morphemes into sub-categories which are said to be directly related to, and differentially activated during, the process of language production. Accordingly, it is predicted that these different types of system morphemes will be differently treated in CS, and indeed in other types of language contact and change. But in fact the only evidence that these morphemes are the product of different mental processes consists in pointing to instances where they are treated differently in different instances of CS.

---

[4] Myers-Scotton takes over Levelt's definition of a lemma as the "nonphonological part of an item's lexical information including semantic, syntactic, and sometimes aspects of morphological information" (Myers-Scotton, 1993b:49, quoting Levelt, 1989:6).

No independent criterion for ascertaining their different status is proposed. As Winford (2003:164–165) points out, the classification of system morphemes into four categories is not placed in the context of the earlier criteria. Most recently, a discussion has developed between the MLF proponents and proponents of Minimalism as to whether aspects of both theories could be combined to deal with the grammar of CS (Jake, Myers-Scotton and Gross, 2002; MacSwan, 2005). The Matrix Language proponents argue that the ML concept is the bilingual realization of a "Uniform Structure Principle", which requires that each constituent be uniform. This principle applies to monolingual production as well but is, as it were, "invisible" within it (Jake *et al.*, 2002:72).

5.3.3.1.3 Other characteristics of the Matrix Language   The Matrix Language is also said to be identifiable in other ways:

- *Psycholinguistic*: the ML is said to be more "activated" in the brain. However it is again unclear how this can be independently demonstrated. Also, the connection between the language which is more activated in the brain and the grammatical frame of a sentence is not made explicit.
- *Social*: the ML is said to represent the "unmarked choice" for conversations of that type in the community. Auer (1998a) remarks that this criterion presupposes a very uniform community where linguistic choices are highly constrained. In many cases where there is no social pressure to use either of the two varieties, the alternation is related to discourse factors, as seen in Chapter 4 (e.g. Alfonzetti, 1998 on Italian and Sicilian).

5.3.3.1.4 Further possible grammatical criteria   Others have suggested that the ML is determined by the language of the main verb (Klavans, 1985; Treffers-Daller, 1990). But as Muysken (1995) points out, many languages have strategies to incorporate alien verbs (e.g. through prefixes in Swahili), and taking the borrowed verb as determining the base language can be misleading. Further possibilities include Doron's (1983) and Joshi's (1985) claim that the ML is determined by the language of the first major constituent in the sentence, and Nishimura's (1997) suggestion that word order is the relevant criterion.

5.3.3.1.5 Use of the Matrix Language by other researchers   A different approach to the base language is adopted by Nortier (1990:158), who distinguishes between the *base* language of a whole conversation, and the *Matrix* Language of individual sentences. Moyer (1998) contrasts the *base* language, meaning the language which determines the grammar of the sentence, and the *main* language, which "sets the frame for the entire exchange". The latter "can only be determined by taking into account the wider linguistic context of the conversation or speech event" (p. 223). As Moyer suggests, we are not dealing with a unitary phenomenon: our view of which language dominates will depend on the level of planning – and the size of the corpus – which we have to examine.

The MLF in its various incarnations has continued to be used as a convenient means of describing large data-sets, sometimes despite evidence that it fails to explain aspects of the data. For example, Rindler-Schjerve (1998) illustrated what is described as a change of ML among the younger generation in Sardinia, which is symptomatic of language shift. Most of what is said can clearly be identified as Sardinian, and in over 93 percent of switches the speakers return to Sardinian after a segment in Italian, though with considerable variations based on age and network. At a grammatical level, however, instances of CS which contradict the MLF model are found:

Example 8: Sardinian–Italian
No, deo, dae sos polcheddos suoso non happo tentu mancu ... ca sa veridade, happo accontentadu su cliente
No, I didn't even make any profits from the pigs ... the truth is, I satisfied the customer (1998:243).

If there is a Matrix here, it is clearly Sardinian. But the obligatory prepositional accusative of Sardinian, which does not exist in Italian, is not realized in the final part of the sentence (Italian: ***accontentato** il cliente*; Sardinian: ***accontentadu a su cliente***). The EL has imposed its grammar on the ML – which the model predicts as impossible.

Deuchar (2006), along with many others (Myers-Scotton and Jake, 2000) found her corpus (Welsh–English) to be "overwhelmingly compatible" with the various principles underlying the MLF. The framework deals best with cases of very asymmetric bilingualism such as that which formed the basis of this study. But, as Belazi, Rubin and Toribio (1994) had cautioned, different types and levels of bilingual competence lead to divergent code-switching behaviour: "The distinction between *matrix* and *embedded* language that is crucial to much code-switching work may be indicative of a lack of balance in the two languages in the bilinguals whose speech is at issue" (p. 222). Muysken's *Bilingual Speech* (2000) offers an integrated framework showing that not only the MLF but each of the grammatical frameworks we have considered offers only a partial description of the grammatical possibilities in CS speech.

5.3.4   Muysken's "bilingual speech"

Muysken prefers the term *code-mixing* (CM) to the commoner CS, reserving the latter as a synonym for *alternation*, and distinguishes the following types:

5.3.4.1 Alternation   Alternation occurs when there is compatibility of the two grammars, or at least equivalence at the point where the switch occurs. Models such as Poplack's, in which grammatical equivalence is a precondition for switching, are seen as resulting from the fact that her Spanish–English data are mainly of the alternational variety. Alternation is illustrated in data-sets which vary considerably as to the patterns exhibited, but which share the feature that the elements following and preceding the switched string are not structurally related.

5.3.4.2 Insertion The second type is *insertion*, a process akin to borrowing but where elements longer than a single word may be inserted. Muysken suggests that the MLF model is directly related to the primacy of insertional material in Myers-Scotton's African corpus. Although no single criterion is generally valid for establishing which language is the Matrix, in insertional CM one language remains more activated and tends to provide the language of the main verb and most of the functional elements. Models based on Government represent a particular interpretation of insertion.

5.3.4.3 Congruent lexicalization The third process is *congruent lexicalization*, in which the languages share a grammatical structure but the vocabulary comes from two or more languages. Counter-examples to the constraints and the MLF models, from data such as Clyne's (1987) Dutch–English in Australia, are considered instances of congruent lexicalization. The latter results from grammatical convergence *or* from similarities between languages. Understanding this type of CM involves carefully determining the nature of the monolingual varieties which are mixed. Arguably this should be as much of a priority for the other processes as well.

5.3.4.4 Sociolinguistic factors determining type of code-switching Each of the three types of CM is associated with different linguistic, sociolinguistic and psycholinguistic factors. Alternation is likely to occur in stable bilingual communities with a tradition of language separation, each language being successively activated in the bilingual's brain. Insertion is likely to be found in situations where bilingual proficiency is asymmetric (e.g. colonial or recent migrant settings). This is illustrated for example by Backus's work on Turkish speakers in the Netherlands (1999). Inter-generational language shift may be reflected in a change in the direction of the insertion. Congruent lexicalization is likely to occur between closely related languages, where their relative prestige is roughly equal, or where there is no tradition of overt language separation (e.g. second-generation migrant groups, post-creole continua); here the languages are assumed to partly share their processing systems.

Muysken schematizes the three main types of CM which he identifies in a triangle (see Figure 5.1) and shows how corpora collected in different settings by Myers-Scotton (Swahili), Pfaff (Mexican American in Texas), Poplack (New York and Ottawa) and Gardner-Chloros (Strasbourg) can be localized within this space.

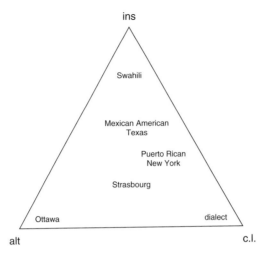

Figure 5.1 Localization of a number of contact settings in the triangle alternation, insertion, congruent lexicalization.

The importance of Muysken's proposed correlations between types of CS and sociolinguistic circumstances is that they provide us with a set of potentially testable hypotheses. Although it is legitimate to describe CM in terms of the grammatical regularities which characterize it *in a given context*, overall we are faced with a degree of variation which no single set of grammatical rules can account for. Muysken argues convincingly that both "constraints" and the Matrix Language are relevant to certain types of CS only. This brings us back to the argument that grammar can only provide one part of the explanation as to why code-switching takes the form it does.

5.4   Is grammar the right framework?

Muysken (2000) remarks that code-switchers break various kinds of "rules" in CS if those rules get in the way of their combining what they want to combine: "If you cannot have equivalence, adopt another form, by bending the rules of the systems a bit" (p. 32). This reinforces the idea that we need to look outside language as a closed system, which has been the focus of research in the structuralist tradition since Saussure and Chomsky, just as pragmaticians and discourse analysts have done so successfully in the last few decades (Nehrlich and Clarke, 1994).

5.4.1   Code-switching outside the grammatical confines

For example, grammatical explanations have little to offer in respect of the CS variously described as *ragged* (Hasselmo, 1972), *paratactic* (Muysken, 1995) and *disjointed* (Gardner-Chloros, 1991), which is found in many contexts. This involves speakers using pauses, interruptions, "left-right-dislocation" and other devices to neutralize any awkwardness associated with CS.

Example 9: French–Brussels Dutch
Les étrangers, ze hebben geen geld, hè?
The foreigners, *they have no money, huh?*   (Treffers-Daller, 1994:207)

A better understanding of this may be found in "the grammar of speech" which provides an alternative way to understand phenomena which formal linguists would explain as a disparity between competence and – often imperfect – performance. Biber, Johansson, Leech, Conrad and Finegan (1999) list various characteristics of spoken English, based on a 40-million-word corpus covering four different registers. They point out that over a third of all the units identified are "non-clausal" and have an average length of two words. Production is "on-line", showing the effects of limited planning time and being characterized by "dysfluency, error, hesitations, repairs, grammatically incomplete utterances and syntactic blends" (p. 1038). Such occurrences can "legitimize" combinations of typologically different languages, for example as regards word order. Aitchison (2000) has pointed out that devices such as left-dislocation (see also Geluykens, 1992), can find their way to being fully grammaticalized parts of the language over a period of time.

"Flagged" switches fulfil a similar function. Such strategies reinforce the notion that grammatical rules are present in the mind of code-switchers – albeit sometimes in the negative sense of being something to be skirted round. A suggestion for future research is to work backwards from examples where code-switchers make use of paratactic strategies to try and see which grammatical difficulties drive them to use such techniques.

5.4.2   Code-switching's "language-like" properties

Boeschoten wrote that: "CS as verbal behaviour has language-like properties, i.e., it is really not assumed to consist just of the combination of two completely independent systems" (1998:21). This is an important remark, as specific examples of innovation noted in the literature show.

5.4.2.1 Bilingual compound verbs   The creation of bilingual compound verbs, as exemplified in 3.3.2, is so widely attested that it may constitute a universal of CS (Muysken, 2000). In Edwards and Gardner–Chloros (2007), these verbs are discussed as an example of bilingual creativity, which highlights the inadequacy of describing CS as the sum of two pre-existing grammars.

5.4.2.2 Compromise forms   Where the languages are related, similar or identical sounding words, or "homophonous diamorphs" (Muysken, 2000), may serve as a "bridge" facilitating the transition to the other language. As we saw in example 7, function words such as *de/the* and *dat/that*, or *in* operate in this way (Clyne, 1972). In a substantial corpus of Dutch–English and German–English CS in Australia (Clyne, 1987), CS often coincided with the use of compromise forms, making it difficult to establish with certainty where exactly the language switch had occurred. Clyne also noted that Vietnamese– and Chinese–English bilinguals sometimes switched unintentionally into English following the use of a word corresponding to an English *pitch* (Clyne, 2003).

5.4.2.3 Further "bridge" phenomena   The use of *compromise forms* serves to reduce the distance between two varieties. These include not only the "bridge" words described by Clyne (2003) such as those exemplified above, but also bare forms:

Example 10: French–Alsatian
Ah voila, nitt dass se do **cueillir**, un gehn dann uf d'ander Sit
Yes there you are, they shouldn't pick, and then go to the other side
(Gardner-Chloros, 1991:159)

The French verb *cueillir* is an infinitive – it should be conjugated in the third person plural in order to be grammatical in *either* French (*cueillent*) or Alsatian in this sentence. But the Alsatian infinitive ending *-iere* (e.g. *marschiere*, to march), *is also the third person plural ending*. The French infinitive is therefore a compromise form, as the French infinitive ending *-ir* sounds like an Alsatian *conjugated* third person plural.

5.4.2.4 Double morphology   Double morphology is a further "compromise strategy", whereby morphological marking from both participating varieties is applied to the same words:

Example 11: Turkish–Dutch
POL-EN-lar-a   Hollandaca ders Verdi
Pole-PL-PL-DAT Dutch [people] lesson give/PRET/3S
he taught Dutch to Poles   (Backus, 1992:90)

Myers-Scotton and Jake (2000) claim that the doubling up of certain types of morpheme and apparently not of others confirms the distinctions between different types of system morpheme which they draw in the "4-M" model.

Woolard (1999) argues that such "bivalent" elements, i.e. those which in some sense belong simultaneously to both varieties, should be considered central to an understanding of CS. Whereas they generally "drop out of the analytic account" once they have been acknowledged, they in fact merit analysis in their own right as a "socially meaningful, potentially strategic form of language choice" (p. 9).

5.5   Sociolinguistic v. typological factors

If, as Muysken has argued, different types of CS are found in the context of (a) different degrees of linguistic closeness between the languages and (b) different sociolinguistic circumstances, then it is a priority to find a way of assessing the relative contribution of these factors. The obvious way to do this is to make comparisons between cases where the same pairs of languages are combined in different sociolinguistic settings, and different pairs are combined in similar settings. We could then answer questions such as: How do the two aspects relate to one another? Are the restrictions imposed by grammar the inescapable bottom line, with sociolinguistic parameters merely pushing the patterns towards one set of options rather than another? Or are the social, personal and interactional reasons for CS the primary determinant, grammatical options serving merely as second-order expressions of socially/individually determined choices? Some comparative work was described in section 3.6.2 but a lot more remains to be done.

Gumperz (1964) described a village in India where, through sustained CS, two widely differing languages had all but merged at the grammatical level, lexical differences alone being preserved. Later, in a study in Norway with Blom, at the opposite extreme, two closely related varieties – two dialects of Norwegian – remained functionally distinguished in the community's usage (Blom and Gumperz, 1972).[5] Although Gumperz did not explicitly compare the two cases, such contrasting findings confirm that the degree of typological difference between the two languages involved in CS is not the only factor involved in the linguistic outcome.

Other relevant comparisons have been made. Bentahila and Davies (1983; 1991) showed how different generations in Morocco, educated to differing extents through the medium of French and Arabic, all code-switch but use different proportions of the two languages and combine them in different ways. In the Tyneside Chinese-speaking community, Li Wei (1998a) shows how network patterns affect Chinese–English CS, as did Schmidt (1985) as regards a declining aboriginal language, Dyirbal, and English.

Conversely, we find similarities in code-switching patterns, across different language-pairs, where similar social circumstances obtain: for example amongst close-knit groups of immigrants, CS is often not only very frequent but also

---

[5] Since then, criticisms have arisen to the effect that the two varieties were in fact on much more of a continuum linguistically than Blom and Gumperz implied (Maehlum, 1990). This, however, is separate from the point at issue.

intricate at a grammatical level (Agnihotri, 1987; Cheshire and Gardner-Chloros, 1997; Nortier, 1990).

Third, in cases where there is CS between the *same* language-pairs in *different* sociolinguistic settings, the CS patterns can be radically different. In the German–English data analysed by Eppler (1999), German SOV order is preserved in subordinate clauses, whereas in German–English CS in Australia, a couple of generations down the line, the order shifts to that of English (SVO) (Clyne, 1987:750–751). Basic word order appears to be relatively resistant to change and is not "toppled" until a number of other symptoms of convergence – or dominance of one variety over the other – have manifested themselves. This too could form the basis of a future research hypothesis. Similarly, Muysken (2000) has shown how the manner of incorporation of bilingual verbs varies between Malay–Dutch spoken in Indonesia, and the same combination spoken by Moluccans in the Netherlands.

He cites Huwaë (1992), in which Malay as spoken by Moluccans in the Netherlands is compared with the results of earlier Dutch Malay contact in Indonesia. The more intense contact between the two languages in the Netherlands leads to a different way of integrating the same Dutch verbs into Malay.

Example 12: Bahasa Indonesia/Moluccan Malay
Bahasa Indonesia	*Moluccan Malay*
Saya tidak me-reaksi	**a sing** reageren
I NEG AG-reaction	*I NEG react*

       I do not react   (Muysken, 2000:215)

Such findings contrast with language internal analyses which may lead to incorrect predictions. One such prediction, based on typological considerations alone, is that there could be no CS between languages with radically different word orders (e.g Tamil SOV and Welsh VSO, Sankoff and Mainville, 1986). While this particular contrast remains to be tested, there is in fact no evidence of any such impossibility.

Typological difference is never the only factor determining the outcome of CS. Treffers-Daller (1999) argues that the similar Romance/Germanic pairing of French and Alsatian in Strasbourg and French and Brussels Dutch in Brussels leads to similar patterns of CS despite sociolinguistic differences. The problem is to decide how sociolinguistic differences (e.g. the different status of French relative to the Germanic language in each case) can be weighed against linguistic similarities (see section 2.5).

Halmari hypothesizes that, sociolinguistic forces being equal, languages with a rich morphology would tend to be Matrix Languages since they "bring their inflections along with them" (1997:211). Johanson (2002), on the other hand, points out that typological factors are not decisive in cross-linguistic contacts, viz the multiple influences of Turkic on its differently structured neighbours, and vice-versa. It should be a priority for future research to make systematic comparisons between CS in different settings, taking account of both socio-linguistic and typological factors (LIPPS, 2000).

5.6   Some unconventional proposals

The difficulties of finding a grammatical "formula" to encapsulate CS has led to some unconventional proposals, which lie outside the traditional grammatical frameworks.

5.6.1   "Stand alone" segments (Azuma, 1998)

In an attempt to account for some switches which appeared to violate the MLF, Azuma (1998) suggested that certain chunks, defined as "any segment which can meaningfully stand alone in the speaker's mind", may be switched. Such chunks are accommodated within a new category, the "stand alone category". An extreme example is the word *the* being the only English word in a Japanese sentence, the purpose of the switch being to convey the message that what *the* refers to is unique and matchless. Rather than supporting the MLF model, this type of example points instead to the inadequacy of explanations relying on grammar rather than discourse.

5.6.2   Speaker awareness/education (Pandharipande, 1998)

Similarly, Pandharipande (1998) tries to defend the notion that there are universal structural constraints on CS in the face of her own evidence, from Marathi–English and Marathi–Sanskrit, which shows variation in the degree of convergence within the two pairs, depending on the speakers' *awareness* of the structural differences involved. Her argument, that the strategies for keeping the two languages separate are themselves universal, appears self-defeating, since what is actually shown is that the speakers' degree of education – i.e. a sociolinguistic variable – is necessary to account for the patterns which are recorded.

5.6.3   Clausal chunks (Backus)

Backus (1999; 2003) proposes a different rationalization of certain types of insertional CS which occur within Matrix Language clauses. He suggests that clausal "chunks", or "multimorphemic lexical items", which can be viewed as one idiom, may be inserted in the matrix; sometimes such chunks may be discontinuous, i.e. allow "fiddling" with the tenses and other grammatical elements. These may include plural nouns, verb–object, adjective–noun, etc. collocations, and represent an element which "blurs the distinction between grammar and lexicon".

5.6.4   A grammar for speech?

Brazil (1995) focuses on a stretch of speech which he calls the "increment", proposing this as a speech grammar alternative to the sentence.[6] The increment procedes from the initial state to a target state through simple chaining rules, based on the speaker's perception of what communicative need must be satisfied at the time, without reference to the constituent-within-constituent arrangements of sentence grammars. In order to provide a satisfactory explanation of CS, such a model would, ideally, need to be articulated with the grammatical level, since CS occurs within increments as well as between them.

The MLF itself did in one sense try to break out of the boundaries of grammar by linking the proposed framework to psycholinguistic production and socio-linguistic factors such as markedness, or "rational choice". But the grammatical framework itself, as Muysken argued, accounts less well for some types of CS than for others. Rather than making yet further amendments to it, we should consider from a more general perspective the implications of its fundamental premise, i.e. that one language is always grammatically dominant in CS – for whom is this true? Second, we would need to know what such a statement would "buy" us even if it could be proved.

5.7   Conclusion

Clyne remarked that: "It is a matter of doubt whether the notion of grammaticality can be applied at all to data as variable as that of code-switching" (1987:744). However this does not mean that CS is grammatically arbitrary. Muysken (2000) has suggested, for instance, that similar typologies often lead to CS based on equivalence between structures, whereas conflicting typologies (e.g. opposing word orders) lead to different tactics being employed and different linguistic outcomes (Sankoff, Poplack and Vanniarajan, 1990). Muysken also points out that "The looser the syntagmatic relation is in a sentence, the easier it is to switch" (1995:188).

The difficulty with most models of CS grammar – both alternational and insertional – is that they seek to describe the data in terms of the interaction of discrete systems. The notion of *constraints* and that of *base* or *Matrix Language*

---

[6] Brazil remarks on the obligation "to offer some explanation of how the notion of a sentence has come to hold such a prominent place in our thinking about language". He speculates that this is due to "scholarly concentration, for long periods of history, upon the written word" (1995:227).

both imply that these systems are equated with an external notion of what a language is, i.e. a variety which is the common property of a community. This means that a whole bundle of features, grammatical, lexical, phonological, etc. are stored and employed as a self-contained unit. But CS is of interest precisely because it can provide insights as to how individuals' underlying linguistic competence is *actually* organized, as opposed to how the "languages" which they officially "speak" might, in theory, mesh together. "The phenomenon of CS confronts researchers with the problem of distinguishing between the idea of a *language* as the product of an individual's (grammatical) competence and that of a *language* as an externally defined, self-contained entity" (Le Page, 1989; Le Page and Tabouret-Keller, 1985).

Furthermore, as Jacobson (1998b) points out, several of the main grammatical theories of CS seek to show that universal rules govern the alternation which is observed, differing only as to what those rules are. In so doing they risk losing sight of the role of CS as a mechanism of language change (Winford, 2003). Myers-Scotton's "ML turnover hypothesis" is presented as if one generation speaks A with elements of B, and the next speaks B with elements of A. The "rules" – being universal – do not change, only the order/role of the languages. Yet language change is a gradual process, affected simultaneously by external and internal factors, and such a view cannot account for this gradualness, which is synchronically identifiable as inconsistencies between and within the speakers' output. If CS either "obeys" the proposed constraints or, more rarely, does not, the "deviant" instances remain to all intents and purposes unexplained.

Theories which do attempt to integrate the process of change into their explanations include Boeschoten (1998), who has shown that even within a small immigrant community, CS is tied up with the emergence of new norms. He shows that it can provide a mechanism for grammatical, as well as lexical change, for example by encouraging a preference for structures which show a high degree of congruence between the two varieties. He illustrates this in relation to CS sentences taken from a corpus of second-generation Turkish speakers in Germany (p. 19). Pfaff (1979) had also pointed out a tendency in Spanish–English CS to avoid structural conflict through the increased frequency, in mixed speech, of less popular stylistic options.

The final outcome of language contact is affected by many factors and is inherently unpredictable (Heine and Kuteva, 2005). It may lead to effective convergence of two or more initially separate varieties (Gumperz and Wilson, 1971), but other forms of partial re-alignment, cross-influence or renewed divergence are also documented in different settings. A productive goal for future grammatical studies of CS would be to look at CS behaviour as essentially creative: to identify the grammatical difficulties which code-switchers face within any given language combination and the means which they employ to get round these difficulties – what Sebba (1998) has termed "conceptual work". By examining the techniques which code-switchers employ, we may indeed come across some universal strategies, as may be the case with bilingual compound verbs (Edwards and Gardner-Chloros 2007).

In Chapter 6, we will look at another possible source of universality, i.e. aspects of mental processing and production. In this chapter we saw that independent motivation for the MLF model and the existence of a base language were claimed to be directly related to the notion of psycholinguistic activation (Myers-Scotton, 1993b:46–47). In turn, as we will see, some of the psycholinguistic literature refers to the notion of *base* language, accepting it as part of linguistic orthodoxy (Grosjean, 2000). It is to be hoped that the different sub-branches of the discipline are not building on one another's sand.

Box 6 Code-switching in religious contexts

CS is frequently found in religious contexts, when the language of holy texts comes into contact with vernaculars. The following example is taken from an Orthodox Jewish newsletter, Hakohol, distributed in 2000 to households in North London.

Below are the non-English words in Latin characters, in the order they appear, followed by the phrases in Hebrew, glossed and translated in brackets. Grammatical studies of CS often focus on whether CS is made more difficult – or even impossible – by the differences between the grammars of the languages involved. In this written example, CS occurs despite the different direction of Hebrew and English script (left to right as opposed to right to left).

Halochos – Jewish Laws
Torah – the Hebrew Bible
Chazon Ish – the prename of an important Hassidic rabbi and an authority in religious law, Rabbi Abraham Kerlitz (1878–1953)
Rebbes – Rabbis
Shulchan Oruch – a codex of Jewish law written in the sixteenth century. Literally, 'The set table'.
Shabbos – the Jewish Sabbath, beginning on Friday before sundown and ending on Saturday night after three stars are visible
Shekiyas Hachamo – sunset
Sof Zeman Kriyas Shema – the end of time (of day, permitted) for reading the Shema. (Shema, literally, 'hear': a prayer, which begins with "Hear, O Israel, the Lord our God, the Lord is one")
Tefillah Betzibur – public prayer

brocho – blessing
Talmid Chochom – a wise/learned scholar
Tefillas Haderech – prayer for the journey (recited whenever anyone travels outside a city, any long distance)
Mingham – custom
Birkas Hagomel – blessing of thanks for being delivered from danger
Yotze the brocho – fulfil the obligation of blessing
Shaaloh – a question on a religious matter, to a Rabbi/religious authority

(1)

גוא"צ	ביאת
our redeemer of justice (acronym)	arrival of

בב"א	וירושלים	ציון	ונחמת
Soon in our days, Amen (acronym)	and Jerusalem	Zion	and the consolation

(*... and may we be privileged to witness the – arrival of our redeemer of justice and the consolation of Zion and Jerusalem soon in our days, Amen*).

(2)

לשלום	ותחזירנו
in peace	and you shall bring us back

(*... one includes – and you shall bring us back in peace - a section from the prayer*)

(3)

ומלכות	שם
and kingship	name (of God)

(*... and some say the brocho without – the name of God and reference to God's kingship*)

(4)

העין	מן	נתעלם
the eye	from	vanished

(*... that it is not considered – vanished from sight*)

Important Halochos for the Holidays

With the approach of the holiday season, we would like to point out a number of Halochos, which require particular attention when travelling away from the home and community environment.

Holidays spent in a Torah atmosphere have great benefits for the spiritual and physical well-being of a family. In addition to benefiting from more exercise, fresh air and a break in the daily routine, it is a time when parents can spend time together with their children in a more relaxed atmosphere, enabling parents to have a better understanding of their children's needs and to devote more time to them.

On the other hand, it is of course essential that every aspect of this relaxation be spent as dictated by the Torah. There are many areas of Halocho which apply in holiday circumstances, which we rarely come across during our regular routine, and which we may therefore be unfamiliar with, and require special care. As the Chazon Ish writes in a famous letter, "My Rebbes have taught me that in every move a person makes, he must consider the halochos of the four parts of the Shulchan Oruch."

May we all be privileged to experience a spiritually and physically invigorating summer and return to our regular activities, healthy in body and soul, and may be be privileged to witness the ביאת גוא"צ ונחמת ציון וירושלים בב"א.

Times of Shabbos etc.

Before leaving for one's holiday, it is important to find out the exact times of the beginning and end of Shabbos, Shekiyas Hachamo, Sof Zeman Kriyas Shema, etc. for the place one is going to. If possible, one should find out about possibilities and times of Tefillah Betzibur in the locality.

Travel

It is customary to take leave and receive the brocho of a distinguished Talmid Chochom before setting out on a journey (Orach Chayim Chapter 11o, Be'er Heitev 10 and Mishnam Berurah 28).

According to most opinions, Tefillas Haderech should be recited after leaving town (if one forgot, one can say it later on the journey). There are however opinions that it should be said in the morning, before leaving; each person should follow their own minhag in this matter (See Be'er Heitev 9 and Mishna Berurah 27).

If one is planning to return the same day (i.e. before daybreak of the next day) one includes ותחזירנו לשלום in Teffilas Haderech to include both journeys.

If one travels for a period of a few days, stopping overnight, Tefilas Haderech must be recited every day when setting out on one's journey, after daybreak.

If one travels over sea by boat, Birkas Hagomel must be recited. There are different opinions regarding reciting Birkas Hagomel after travelling over land by plane and it is preferable to be yotzei the brocho by hearing it from someone else. There is also some doubt after crossing the sea by plane, and some say the brocho without שם ומלכות.

When sending luggage, which includes meat, fish, wine, bread, or other foodstuffs to a holiday destination (or anywhere else) with a non-Jew, it must be sealed in such a way that it is not considered נתעלם מן העין, (Yoreh Deah Chapters 63 and 118). If in doubt, a Shaaloh should be asked.

6 Psycholinguistic approaches

6.1. Introduction

A central argument in this book is that CS forces us to consider questions about what a language is, and that such questions are in turn essential to our understanding of CS. These questions are of interest at a psycholinguistic, as at other levels: if we can understand the mechanisms of the processing, decoding, storage, retrieval and production of linguistic material, we may come closer to understanding how language relates to other cognitive faculties. If it can be established that, with respect to any of these aspects, bilingual functioning is in some material way different from that of monolinguals, then there may be a basis for linking this difference to aspects of bilingual speech – for example, for confirming or rejecting the idea that there is always an underlying "Matrix Language".

Psycholinguists have accordingly been intrigued by this opportunity to gain a better understanding of how languages are stored in the brain, as well as production mechanisms, and there is a substantial tradition of psycholinguistic research involving bilinguals.[1] As CS is principally a spontaneous and informal phenomenon, however, studying it in its naturally occurring state is largely incompatible with standard psycholinguistic methodological approaches.

The discussion here of psycholinguistic work on bilingualism, from a non-specialist viewpoint, is based on the idea that CS should be considered from a multidisciplinary perspective. The selection is based on those aspects which have the clearest potential application to understanding CS. In most cases the relevance to natural CS is still more or less indirect, though increasingly the compatibility of theories with the facts of CS is used as a touchstone in psycholinguistic work (e.g. Herdina and Jessner, 2002). There is still a reluctance to straddle the sociolinguistic/psycholinguistic divide, and few cross-references (with the notable exception of Myers-Scotton's work) to the implications of results in one field for theories prevalent in the other (though see Broersma and de Bot below). For example, the parallel between proposals about the

---

[1] As in other aspects of CS, the study of the specificity of individuals who speak more than two languages is not yet highly developed, so most of the work here refers to bilinguals.

bilingual's "language modes" (Grosjean, 1998, 2001) and the sociolinguistic concepts of "audience design" (Bell, 1984), as well as accommodation (Chapters 3, 7), has not, apparently, been explored. Yet looking at the same phenomenon both from a psycholinguistic and a sociolinguistic/interactional point of view could add considerably to our understanding.

The main impediment to such cross-fertilization is the methodological divide. Psycholinguists generally avoid engaging with spontaneous, natural language, preferring to use controlled, experimental data – language elicited in a laboratory, measurable along as many dimensions as possible, and often simplified so as to bring out the role of particular variables in the context of replicable studies. This approach derives from a Western epistemological tradition which encompasses all the major disciplines laying claim to the status of being "sciences"; a discussion of the advantages and disadvantages of such an approach is beyond our scope here.

The "scientific" study of language is of course essential. Psycholinguistic and neurolinguistic research enhances our knowledge of the brain and may extend our ability to treat various disorders effectively. But the demands of the clinical sphere should not prevent communication between psycholinguistics and other branches of the discipline.

Within its own terms, neuro/psycholinguistics seems to be making relatively slow progress – as his parting shot to his 1999 *Neurolinguistics of Bilingualism: an introduction*, Fabbro laments the poor state of knowledge of the "physiology of language". The evidence presented in this chapter suggests that some types of progress might be faster if more account were taken of linguistic functioning in naturalistic settings. *Validity* need not necessarily be sacrificed to *reliability*,[2] and with some imagination, rigorous scientific method could be applied to "real" CS data, collected in natural settings. The fact that this is rare for the time being is reflected in the slightly different appearance of this chapter compared with the others, in particular with respect to the small number of examples from code-switched speech.

6.2   Some methodological issues

6.2.1   Forcing speech into "languages"

The most fundamental of these issues relates to the fact that psycholinguists rarely appear to question whether and why each of the "languages" of bilingual subjects should be seen as self-contained, discrete entities – in this, as we saw in Chapter 5, they are in the company of other types of linguist, such as many of

---

[2] In scientific terms, *reliability* refers broadly to a study's replicability, and *validity* to its relevance to the object of study.

those interested in grammar. Subjects of psycholinguistic studies, almost invariably, are said to speak, say, "English and Spanish", or "French and German", without much consideration as to how the type and nature of their bilinguality might influence the results. There is a dearth of psycholinguistic studies of intermediate phenomena such as dialect or register-shifting, or of subjects who speak an avowedly "mixed" variety such as a pidgin or a creole. Instead, most studies focus on so-called "bilingual" subjects (usually university students) whose mother tongue is a widely spoken and standardized language such as English or Dutch, and who have learned another standard "language", usually limited to French or Spanish, in an academic context. The experiments often involve testing them by requiring them to speak or react to these "languages", so as to investigate the underlying mental representation which these studies purport to be exploring, thus leading to an unsatisfactory circularity in the results. In Kamwangamalu and Li (1991), for example, Chinese–English bilinguals in Singapore had to decide whether ten sentences with Mandarin–English switching were "English" or "Chinese". This begs the question – why should they be either? Furthermore, in natural circumstances such a decision would normally never need to be taken, so the subjects were forced to make a decision whose relevance to their actual behaviour is at best dubious.

6.2.2   Experimental tasks

The tasks given, as in the example above, often bear little relationship to normal bilingual functioning. Azuma (1996) asked Japanese–English bilinguals to switch languages whenever a particular sound was played, while they were speaking "spontaneously". Results indicated that in many cases, they chose to maintain surface grammaticality by delaying the switch until later in the sentence, or by repeating a chunk of what had already been said so as to avoid switching in mid-flow. But their choices in no way resemble those which underlie spontaneous code-switches, since all natural motivation for CS was (a) lacking and (b) supplanted by an artificial one. To this we should add the effect of being observed by academic researchers in an unnatural context, which is hardly conducive to an output resembling their natural behaviour.

Toribio and Rubin (1996) report on a pilot study of CS in second language learners (see Chapter 7). They asked English-speaking beginner, intermediate and advanced learners of Spanish to repeat sentences containing CS, some of which embodied what the experimenters considered to be "legal" code-switches, and some of which contained "illegal" ones. "Legality" was determined by whether the code-switches obeyed the Functional Head Constraint, a constraint of UG, extrapolated to predict where switches "should" occur in bilingual sentences. They found that the advanced learners had a tendency to turn "ill-formed" into "well-formed" switches. The authors conclude that the less competent learners were simply interpreting the CS sentences as English strings, whereas the advanced learners were able to show UG effects distinct from those of the first language. Such an experiment raises numerous questions, not least of which is the fact that, as far as we know, none of these learners was a code-switcher in their everyday life. Consequently, the advanced learners may simply have been trying to demonstrate their competence by "correcting" the sentences to conform to more traditional grammar.

6.3   Areas of psycholinguistic research with potential relevance to code-switching

Psycholinguists divide up language functions into those concerned with (a) the storage and representation of linguistic elements in the brain, (b) the neurological activation and inhibition which determine how these elements come to the surface, and (c) production mechanisms (a sequence summarized in the title of Levelt's (1989) book, *Speaking: from intention to articulation*). Historically, the majority of psycholinguistic studies, as of sociolinguistic ones, were based on monolinguals. Studying bilinguals, however, brings to the fore certain issues of storage and production. The study of bilingual aphasics, discussed below, is a good example: psycholinguists already derive substantial information about language and the brain from cases where monolingual language does not operate smoothly (such as pauses, self-corrections and "tip of the tongue" phenomena); the transitions and dysfluencies involved in bilingual production can similarly reveal aspects of these processes which would otherwise remain hidden. To this one could add that as in other areas of linguistics, one should study the bilingual majority rather than the monolingual minority.

6.3.1   *Separate and joint access to the bilingual lexicon*

The mechanisms for keeping languages separate are one important focus. If languages in the bilingual brain were totally separate, neither translation nor CS would be possible; if they were totally integrated, then bilinguals would presumably code-switch randomly all the time and would not be able to speak monolingually. The question used to be asked in terms of whether there was one "lexical store" in the bilingual brain or two. Much research has now shown that bilinguals can never totally "switch off" one of their languages, and the question is now asked in different terms: how does the bilingual "access" words from their different languages appropriately for the task in hand? Whereas many studies throw light on how this is done at the level of perception – since input can be manipulated experimentally – very little is yet known about production, since it cannot be manipulated in the same way (de Bot, 2004).

The concept of "language tags" is often used in models which attempt to explain this dual ability (Albert and Obler, 1978).[3] One of the features attached to words in the brain is assumed to be the language to which they belong. In such studies, the lexical level has pride of place, i.e. how individual words are stored, connected with one another and with their meanings, and how they dictate the grammatical structures within which they appear in speech. The proposal that this level has primacy is known as the "lexical hypothesis" (Levelt, 1989).

Intensive CS in normal subjects suggests that the varieties are closely inter-linked in the brain, and simultaneously accessible. Decisions as to which words to utter in which language appear to take little or no measurable time (though see the discussion below about phonological aspects of CS).

6.3.2.   Encoding and production

Second, psycholinguists have attempted to determine at what point in the production process the encoding language is selected, which in turn pinpoints the moment when the "decision" to code-switch becomes relevant. Meuter (2005) suggests that the available evidence on activation indicates that all related lexical representations are activated late in the selection process,[4] and that there are four main types of factor relevant to the selection of a language:

(1) global "de-selection" of the undesired language – though we cannot be sure the de-selection is global or whether it only affects the relevant parts;
(2) the effect of proficiency: it has been shown in various experimental tasks that it is more difficult to inhibit the L1 than the L2, but that once that has been done switching back *into* the L1 takes longer than continuing in the L2 (as measured in milliseconds);
(3) the factors that trigger a switch;
(4) the monitoring capacity, which allows the selected language to be maintained.

These processes are obviously largely subconscious, as speakers are on the whole not very aware of their code-switching behaviour, and tend to be sur-prised at their own performance if you play it back to them (see section 3.3.1.2). Since we cannot observe the language production process directly, various models for it have been proposed (see below). Along with the evidence from bilingual aphasia and studies of the localization of languages in the brain, these

---

[3] Defined there as "a feature label associated with each individual item".

[4] Slips which arise during conference interpreting may provide a useful source of data. Simultaneous interpreters, particularly when they are working "bilingually" – i.e. with two languages, both used passively and actively – sometimes accidentally *paraphrase* in the original language instead of translating into the target language. This may imply that the effort which goes into understanding and generally processing the input takes precedence over the decision as to which language to choose for the output. See also the question raised in section 6.6.1.

are the principal areas of psycholinguistics with a bearing on CS which will be considered in the remainder of this chapter.

6.4   Bilingual aphasia

Since experimentation on human subjects is limited for ethical reasons, the study of *disorders* of the language system has traditionally been used as a source of information about the underlying representation of languages in the brain. The recovery patterns of bi/plurilinguals who suffer brain lesions ("aphasias") and lose some of their language abilities as a consequence have been studied and described for over a century (Hyltenstam and Stroud, 1989). By doing so, researchers hope to find out more about the physical location of language faculties and also about their functional interaction in tasks where the use or knowledge of several languages is required (Clark and Clark, 1977).

6.4.1.   A methodological caution

Grosjean (1989) has warned that before drawing conclusions from such subjects, it is essential to have some idea of their premorbid or baseline language habits, otherwise one might, for example, assume that they were code-switching as a result of pathology, when this was in fact their normal mode of speech. Second, Grosjean pointed out the crucial role of specific methodological considerations in the *testing* of bilinguals, such as the need to use a monolingual researcher when testing the performance of bilinguals in monolingual tasks (2000), as a bilingual tester might bring forth responses affected by the subjects' bilinguality. Alongside the question of in what sense the languages are independent entities, Grosjean's admonitions point to experimental pitfalls which may undermine the conclusions of research in this field.

6.4.2.   Brain scanning techniques

In the future, brain scanning techniques such as CAT, PET and MRI[5] may provide further insights regarding storage, activation and production (see Vaid and Hull 2002:343–350). Currently, subjects to whom these techniques are applied are studied in a heavily controlled environment (sometimes placed in a scanner or even wearing a special cap with electrodes), and the type of "linguistic reactions" which are studied consist of brain activity in response to single word stimuli (Green, 2001; Grosjean, Li, Münte and Rodriguez-Fornells, 2003). Some of the conclusions drawn from these studies are, clearly,

---

[5] CAT = Computerized Axial Tomography, PET = Positron Emission Tomography, MRI = Magnetic Resonance Imagery.

informative about language control in bilinguals and potentially relevant to CS, e.g. the finding that bilinguals find it very difficult to completely "turn off" their response to either of their languages. There is also some evidence that linguistic activity is represented in the same cortical areas in balanced bilinguals and in different areas in less proficient ones (de Bot, 2004). However, we are still a considerable way from being able to use these techniques to study spontaneous speech.

6.4.3. Emotional factors

The literature also contains a large number of interesting case studies (e.g. Fabbro, 1999; Grosjean *et al.*, 2003; Vaid and Hull, 2002). For example, there is growing evidence that emotional factors have a considerable impact in how one learns, remembers and uses languages (Dewaele, 2004; Pavlenko, 2004; 2005). Switching to an L2 may serve a distancing function (the "L2 distancing effect") or allow the speaker to avoid anxiety-provoking material, whereas the L1 elicits more personal involvement. Pavlenko (2005) cites the following significant example from a psychotherapy session described by Rozensky and Gomez. The switch from L2 to L1 leads the speaker to become more emotional and to recognize feelings which were not otherwise articulated:

Example 1

P: I don't want to do it. I really don't want to go to the hospital. I've already been to the hospital so many times for tests and everything else.

T: It sounds like your doctor thinks it's important.

P. I know. I know. I suppose I should do it and get it over with but I don't know …

T: Do you have any idea why you are so against the idea?

P: [Silence] I am not sure. I don't know how to describe it.

P: Can you try?

P: It's hard, it's so hard.

T: Can you try it in Spanish?

P: [Tears starting] **No quiero. Tengo, tengo miedo**. [Silence]
    [*I don't want to. I'm, I'm afraid*]

T: **Miedo de que?**
    [*Afraid of what?*]

P: [Crying hard] **Que no voy a salir**.
    [*That I'll never come out*].

(Rozensky and Gomez, 1983:156)

The different emotional roles of the bilingual's languages are also reflected in some studies of bilingual aphasia. One well-known case concerns a multi-lingual patient, who, following a stroke, was only able to talk in a language he had not used for years, French, which had had great sentimental importance in his life, as he had had a passionate love affair with a French woman in his youth.

Example 2
The patient began to speak again two or three days after the fit, but to everyone's surprise he spoke in the beginning only French, first stammering out [a] few words, then successively more and more correctly. His wife did not understand him, and his children with their poor school French acted as translators between their parents. (Grosjean, 1982:229, reporting Minkowski, 1928)

The close connection, which these examples illustrate, between the languages spoken and emotions is likely to prove highly relevant to our understanding of the motivations behind CS. Pavlenko mentions that the effects of switching to or from a mother tongue may also be at least partly to do with pragmatic differences between the languages themselves: Guttfreund (1990) reports on a series of psychological tests administered to Spanish–English bilinguals, of whom half were Spanish-dominant and half were English-dominant. *Both* groups exhibited more anxiety and depression in Spanish, reflecting the fact that showing affect in Spanish may be more acceptable than in English.

6.4.4   Network failures

Information gleaned from bilingual aphasia also has a bearing on the issue of language separation v. conjoinedness. For example, aphasia can result in an *inability to switch* into one of the subject's languages, even though it is clear that comprehension is preserved; alternatively, the ability to speak a language may be preserved while comprehension is missing. It is even possible for both situations to pertain at once: Albert and Obler (1978) report the case of a patient who had Broca's aphasia in Hebrew (i.e. she understood but could hardly speak it), and Wernicke's aphasia in English (i.e. she spoke but could not understand it). There are also reports of stimulation of certain areas of the brain (e.g. during brain surgery under local anaesthetic) giving rise to a flow of language, which sometimes involves CS when the patient is bilingual (Lebrun, 1991; Fabbro, 1999). The speech of brain-disordered individuals, as one might expect, often shows other signs of confusion along with unruly CS, as demonstrated by the patient E.G., who suffered a stroke at fifty-five. He was of Slovene mother tongue, with Italian as a second language, Friulian as a third, and English as a fourth.

Example 3
EXAMINER: What was your job in Canada?
EG: In Canada? **Co facevo la via?** I was working with **ce faccio coi..del..fare, i signori la che i faceva**
             *In Canada? **What I did there?** I was working with **I do with..do..men there who did..***

(Fabbro, 1999:154)

Other types of bilingual disorder which have a bearing on this issue include "alternating antagonism", in which patients are only able to express themselves in one language at a given time; inability to translate between languages although both are clearly understood; and, conversely, "automatic translation", a compulsion to translate everything said in one language into another.

Perečman (1989) lists the types of pathological mixing encountered, including word mixing, root and suffix mixing, blending of syllables, use of the intonation of one language with the lexicon of another, the syntax of one with the lexicon of another or words from one language pronounced with the phonemes of another. She proposed to correlate each of these types of mixing – lexical–semantic, syntactic, morphological, phonological – with the production stages outlined in Garrett (1980). These four stages concern:

(1) conceptual relations established at message level;
(2) selection of words relevant to the sentence, at functional level;
(3) closed-class words selected at positional level, and phonological form assigned;
(4) phonetic form of words specified at phonetic level.

The implication is that the different types of switching observed originate in one of these levels of planning. This would seem to correspond well with the fact that in normal CS, several entirely different types of CS can co-exist in the same conversation and have quite different motivations. Giesbers (1989), discussed in De Bot (1992/2000), similarly suggests that different types of CS are linked to different modules in the language production system. Amongst these, Giesbers identifies unintentional CS ("performance switches"), not motivated by contextual factors or linguistic need but resulting from interference – which he considers "bilingual slips of the tongue" (see example (4)).

Other types of bilingual aphasic behaviour are distinct from CS as such, e.g. the phenomenon of spontaneous translation or language "tagging" (in a different sense to that used above – here it means naming the language of the question instead of replying to the question) (Perecman, 1989). It is important to note, however, that bilingual aphasics do not necessarily mix their languages in a pathologogical fashion, and in some cases their CS shows the same kind of grammatical patterns as that of non-disordered people for whom CS is an everyday mode of speech (Hyltenstam and Stroud, 1989). Marty and Grosjean (1998) found in an experiment that aphasic bilinguals retained the ability to control the language "mode" in which they operated (see discussion of this concept below), in other words to switch to a monolingual mode when addressing a monolingual interlocutor.

The conclusion from the aphasia studies as far as CS is concerned must be that the same sort of disturbances which affect linguistic abilities generally may also affect CS, and *not* that any breakdown in language faculties *results* in CS. Only in the most extreme cases is the CS of aphasic patients significantly different from that of certain non-aphasic bilinguals. The studies therefore support the idea, now prevalent in the sociolinguistic literature, that CS is "just a normal way of speaking".

6.5   Localization and lateralization of the bilingual's languages in the brain

The search for the *localization* of languages in the brain has a long history. The major breakthrough with respect to where specific language *functions* are localized came from the work of Broca (1861), who discovered that the left hemisphere's third frontal convolution was an important centre for language production, and Wernicke (1874/1977), who identified various anatomical pathways, as well as the memory area, for the sound and the motor images of words. Since then, numerous different types of study have confirmed that for a high proportion of right- as well as left-handed people, most language functions are located in the left hemisphere of the brain (Obler, Zattose, Galloway and Vaid, 2000; Fabbro, 1999).

6.5.1   *Different languages, different locations?*

Demonstrating that different languages are stored in different areas of the brain proved much more difficult and controversial. While some believed this to be the case, others argued strongly that the languages are kept apart by neural mechanisms only (Paradis, 1981; Paradis and Goldblum, 1989). Real-life cases are rarely sufficiently clear-cut to give unequivocal support to either position. For example, although the brains of bilingual aphasics are frequently examined post mortem in order to determine the locus of the damage, few patients demonstrate one isolated language deficit (e.g. total loss of one language), such that one could clearly correlate the lesion with the use of that language and that language only.

6.5.2   *Locating the switching mechanism*

Fabbro (1999) does however mention Pötzl's (1925) observation, on the basis of a brain-damaged patient who lost the ability to switch *away* from the language spoken just prior to insult, that *the ability to switch itself* was located in the left parietal lobe (see also Fabbro, Skrap and Aglioti, 2000). Meuter points out the potential relevance of the fact that switching behaviour in general (e.g. the ability to switch tasks) is controlled in the frontal lobes (2005: 363–364). Similar questions arise for classic linguistic CS and switching between different signing systems in the deaf community, or switching between a sign language and a vocal language where speech and signs are produced simultaneously rather than sequentially (Davis, 1989; Ann, 2001).

Pőtzl's observation ties in with a tradition of research in which it was assumed that there was a specific on/off switching mechanism in the brain. In 1959, Penfield and Roberts proposed a "single switch model", which suggested that the activation of one of the bilingual's languages rendered the other inoperable. There followed a series of papers on the "two-switch model", according to which there was an "output switch" for production and an "input switch" for processing incoming language (e.g. Macnamara, 1971). It was proposed that the time taken by the input switch could be measured by comparing the reading times for monolingual texts and for comparable texts containing deliberate CS. The contrived nature of this activity, however, cast doubt over the validity of the conclusions. Neufeld (1976) rightly pointed out that there are different components involved in CS, phonological, lexical, semantic, etc., and that different experimental tasks would call these into play to differing extents. Albert and Obler (1978) argued that the control system of bilinguals is more continuous and flexible than the single or dual switch models suggest, and that neither language is ever totally excluded. This approach has been taken forward by Grosjean and Green among others (see below).

6.5.3   One pattern of lateralization for all?

Albert and Obler (1978) claimed that linguistic functions in bilinguals are, more often than in monolinguals, represented, to some extent at least, in the right hemisphere of the brain. This is held to be the case particularly where the second language is learnt later in life and by more explicit means. Paradis (2000) is, however, strongly critical of psycholinguists' endless revisiting of the lateralization question. He shows that for each study which has found the bilingual's languages to show different lateralization patterns, another can be found to show that the pattern is the same as in monolinguals, or that no clear conclusion can be drawn (Obler et al., 2000).

   This brings us back to the point made earlier, that traditionally, psycholinguistic studies did not take much account of individual differences in bilinguality, though this is now changing (Herdina and Jessner, 2002; de Bot, 2004). Where, exceptionally, some account was taken of these differences, such as the age when subjects started learning their L2, interesting results were obtained. For example, there appears to be a reasonable measure of agreement among researchers that a second language learned after puberty is more likely to be represented, at least to some extent, in the right hemisphere – whereas language functions overall are represented in the left hemisphere. Children who suffer a brain trauma in the left hemisphere before the age of around ten can "relocate" language functions to the right; and in cases of an aphasic lesion affecting the left hemisphere, it may be easier for a patient to recover an explicitly learned language (even one which was never actively used, such as Latin or Ancient Greek), rather than their mother tongue, which was acquired through unconscious mechanisms and is represented in "implicit" memory systems (Fabbro, 1999).

6.5.4   Drawing conclusions from lateralization studies

Even if we were able to show clear, unequivocal patterns of lateralization or localization of the language functions in bilinguals, it remains unclear what exactly this would tell us about bilingual *functioning*. The fact that, in practice, it remains so difficult to pin down the bilingual's languages to different locations in the brain after numerous attempts, implies that bilingual competence is on the whole a well-integrated capacity (particularly in the case of varieties learnt simultaneously as co-mother tongues).

The difficulties of drawing unequivocal conclusions from clinical evidence about the organization of languages in the brain suggests that "languages" as such may be the wrong units to be looking at, and that we should be looking instead at groupings of features, which vary from bilingual to bilingual, and are the building blocks of languages. Sometimes, these blocks may be assembled in such a way as to produce what we identify as a monolingual utterance – though even then we should be aware that what appears to be a monolingual utterance to a monolingual interlocutor may in fact be made up of elements from more than one language. Each of the bilingual's languages is informed and altered by their competence in the other – even one which is no longer used or "remembered" at a conscious level. The fact that such "forgotten" languages are still imprinted in the brain is demonstrated by the fact that in some cases they have been reactivated under altered states of consciousness such as hypnosis (Fabbro, 1999).

6.6   Models of bilingual production

Psycholinguists make extensive use of "models", which are often schematized in the form of diagrams in which the important factors are framed and connected to one another by lines or arrows to show the causal/temporal/implicational relationship between them (see Figure 6.1).

This method of presenting and systematizing theoretical proposals is much less common in other areas of linguistics. As soon as one gets beyond a basic diagram such as Figure 6.1, questions arise as to the exact relationship of the components within the model to one another and also of the model overall to the behaviour which it proposes to schematize. In particular, the type and extent of counter-evidence which renders necessary a revision of such models is an open question.

Several such models have been developed to explain bilingual performance. These have been discussed at length in the psycholinguistic literature and only a highly selective account can be given here (e.g. Kroll, 1993; Fabbro, 1999; Clyne, 2003; Dijkstra and van Hell, 2003). The models are focused on bilingual

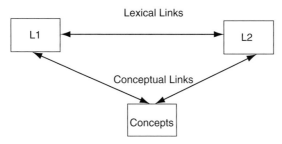

Figure 6.1 Hierarchical model of billingual memory representation (Kroll, 1993: p. 54)

production in general rather than CS, though attendant proposals as to how CS can arise are a useful by-product. Both Clyne (2003) and Fabbro (1999) add their own comments and suggestions – in Clyne's case amounting to an alternative model (2003:213). The main models discussed here are Green (1986/2000) and De Bot (1992/2000) (both reproduced in Li Wei, 2000). Clyne also pays considerable attention to Dell (1986), Grosjean (1998) and Myers-Scotton and Jake (1995). An influential older proposal to explain how lexical items are represented in the brain, with potential applications to bilingual performance, is Morton's "logogens" (1979).[6]

As stated, an overall understanding of bilingual functioning is the aim, but for present purposes, we will concentrate on the types of explanation which this research offers for CS in particular.

6.6.1   Green

An advantage of Green's (1986/2000) model lies in its economy: it accounts for both normal and pathological language behaviour in bilinguals, using the notions of control, activation and resource. Activation is a complex psycholinguistic concept, which depends on such factors as the amount of contact with and use of a language, the level of proficiency, the method of instruction, age of acquisition, etc. De Bot (2004) provides an image to explain activation and its opposite, inhibition, which he likens *not* to an on/off switch but to "holding down ping-pong balls in a bucket of water" – where occasionally, however hard one tries, some will pop to the surface.

Each of the bilingual's languages, and each element within them, has an "activation threshold" which depends on how often, and how recently, they

---

[6] Logogens were said to be "devices that collect evidence for the appropriateness of a word". Information which activates logogens originates in the cognitive system. Each logogen has a threshold. When the collected bits of evidence exceed the threshold, the logogen "fires", i.e. is ready for use.

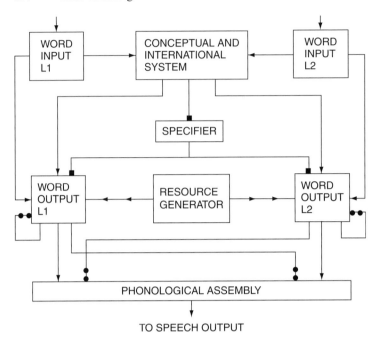

Figure 6.2 An inhibitory model for a bilingual speaker within the control, activation and resource framework (Green, 2000: Fig. 16.2)
Notes: →, flow of activation; ─■, control instructions; →→, resource input; ─●─●, inhibitory control.

have been used (Fabbro, 1999). The activation level for comprehension is lower than that for production, which, as Green explains, is why some aphasics can still understand a language, though not speak it (the same applies in normal subjects when presented with a second language which has gone "rusty") (see Figure 6.2).

However, Dijkstra and van Hell (2003) point to various questions inherent in the "activation" metaphor. Does it imply that there is an active representation of the language *as a whole*? How can a language be activated without actually being used? To what extent does activation depend on "top-down" – i.e. contextual – factors?

The converse process, "inhibition", is the process whereby, a given word having been selected, the possible alternatives are suppressed, including, in bilinguals, words in the other language. Similar processes in monolinguals presumably suppress words from the wrong register or in the wrong dialect. Experimental evidence suggests that bilinguals are only partially able to inhibit the activation of one of their languages in selective word recognition tasks. Dijkstra and van Hell therefore advocate the activation metaphor being applied in a well-specified and testable way only.

Green writes specifically about CS (1986/2000:414), so we will look at what he says in some detail:

In the case of code-switching, there need be no external suppression of L2 at all; at least in the simplest case, such as continuous word association, the output can be free to vary according to which words reach threshold first. Indeed in this circumstance, mixing languages is certainly no slower than producing associations in only one language ... *In the case of normal speech a word cannot be produced unless it fits the syntax of the utterance. Accordingly, for example, an adverb will not be produced in a slot requiring a noun. Switches then will obey the syntactic properties of the two languages although no special device or grammar is required to achieve this goal. Code switches most often involve single words, especially nouns ..., though ones involving phrases or entire clauses also occur. In these latter cases, we suppose that structures from L2 reach threshold earlier. Since any words produced must meet the structural conditions, such a scheme predicts that code switches will preserve the word order in both languages.*

The second part of this passage, which has been italicized, raises certain problems if one looks at it in a wider – i.e. not purely psycholinguistic – framework.

First, in what sense is it true that a word *cannot* be produced unless it fits the syntax of a sentence? This statement seems to stem from theoretical linguistics. What is meant by the word *cannot*, since we know that this *does* happen? As we have seen in Chapter 5, speakers *do* violate grammatical rules. The shifting of a word from one syntactic category to another, also said to be excluded, is a productive technique both for monolinguals and bilinguals.

The idea that CS requires no further grammatical apparatus beyond that provided by the two existing languages (the "null" hypothesis) has been discussed in section 5.3.2.2. It leaves out of account the creative and innovative devices which particularly characterize CS (e.g. new operator verb constructions, see Chapter 5). Why should the techniques for doing this not be considered part of linguistic competence? The assertion that code-switches most often involve single words is true in some communities but not in all, and cases have been reported where inter-clause or inter-turn switching is more common (see section 4.4.1). The last sentence of the quotation is again derived from the grammatical work on CS, in this case Poplack's work on constraints (to which Green refers). There are in fact numerous cases, as we have seen in Chapter 5, where CS does *not* preserve the word order in both languages. The model is focused on the individual only, and an idealized individual at that. It does not cater for the many variations in CS behaviour which sociolinguists have demonstrated.

To what extent is Green's model still helpful to our understanding of this phenomenon? The idea that when speaking monolingually, bilinguals are *inhibiting* one of their languages is widely accepted, and accounts for involuntary switches – failures of the inhibitory system. The system slips when the speaker is tired, stressed, etc., as bilinguals will attest and psycholinguists have pointed out (Javier and Marcos, 1989).

Example 4

An old lady speaking to a monolingual French-speaker in Strasbourg was recounting a story, and in the middle of the story, which was told entirely in French, she slipped in the phrase *un dann hab 'i g'saat..* (and then I said) in Alsatian before carrying on with her (self-) quotation in French. (Gardner-Chloros, 1991)

Her inhibition system had failed for that short, framing clause, and she had switched exactly as she would have done had she been speaking to a member of her bilingual, code-switching network. Matras (2000b) suggests that connectives may be particularly subject to such non-volitional switching, and that this in turn may lead to specific language changes.

The aspects of activation which are basically "intention-neutral" – e.g. based on frequency of use, "availability" of particular words, etc. must be balanced with the fact that much of CS has a clear function, discourse-related or otherwise (Auer, 1998b). Green does not explain how "deliberate" activation relates to the more mechanical kind, in which whichever word "reaches threshold first" is used. What happens in case of conflict between the two types, i.e. when a word comes more easily to mind in one language or is in the language required by interlocutor-related factors, but is in competition with a more suitable equivalent in the alternative language? What determines the outcome of the battle between conflicting activations? An answer may lie in the "specifier" in the node above – a unit which specifies which language should be spoken and whether the subject should code-switch or translate, i.e. operate between the two systems – but so far the role of the specifier remains somewhat mysterious. The problem is reminiscent of the conflict between languages as indexical of social factors and languages as conversational and pragmatic tools (section 4.2.4), and goes to the heart of the difficulties in analysing CS.

The final element of Green's model, which was added to his earlier version, is the notion of "resource". This idea "makes explicit the fact that a system needs energy to operate" (1986/2000:412) and, as can be seen in Figure 6.2, the "resource generator" occupies a central position relating to word output in each of the languages and putting in the necessary "energy" before the final phonological assembly. The use of this concept allows a bridge to be made between studies of normal and brain-disordered speakers: in various disorders the language system may not be lost, but the patient may simply lack the necessary resources to activate it. Recovery implies a renewal of the resources which power activation and inhibition.

6.6.2   De Bot

De Bot (1992/2000) set out to make the minimum possible number of adaptations of a well-known model of monolingual production by Levelt (1989), so as to make it adequate for bilingual production. Rather than offering a

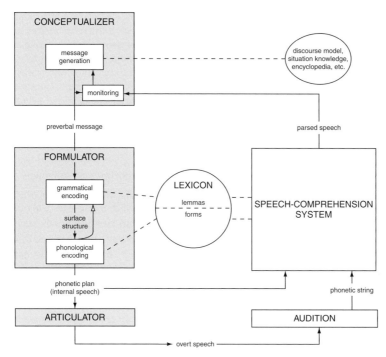

Figure 6.3 Levelt's speech production model (Levelt, 1989: Fig 1.1.)

diagram of his own, he reproduces Levelt's Speech Production Model (see Figure 6.3), and discusses in what ways it needs to be adapted. Supplementary information is taken from De Bot and Schreuder (1993), which particularly concerns CS.

The model includes a "Conceptualizer", in which intended meaning is planned and converted into "preverbal messages"; a "Formulator", where this message is converted into a "phonetic plan": this is where the appropriate lexical units, grammatical and phonological rules are selected; and an "Articulator" which converts this plan into actual speech. At the Formulator stage, a distinction between two aspects of a lexical entry is relevant: on the one hand it consists of a "lemma", representing the meaning and syntax of the lexical entry, and on the other hand the "lexeme", its morphological and phonological form.

Levelt's proposals as to how speech goes through the various planning stages before emerging on the surface is one of the main models in the field. Its extension by De Bot to bilingual production increases its potential applications and testability. However, what exactly *is meant to be happening* at each of these stages is not transparent, and raises again the question of the exact status of such models. As De Bot writes:

In order to try to clarify the workings of this model I will illustrate the various components by using an example. Imagine we want to say: *The train from Amsterdam arrives at platform four.* We know from our knowledge of the world that trains regularly arrive at platforms and stop there, and that there is more than one platform. The communicative intention is pre-processed in the conceptualizer, after which the contextual information is passed on to the formulator in manageable chunks in the preverbal message. *How this information is passed on is not exactly clear. It is possible that we have some sort of mental image of trains, platforms and arrivals which is then transformed into interpretable information.* (1992/2000:424).

De Bot goes on to adapt the original model. First, he gives two possibilities: either there is a separate formulator and a separate lexicon for each language – which makes it difficult to see how CS could take place – or there is one large system storing all the information, "linguistically labelled in some way", about the different languages. The problem is then to understand how bilinguals keep their languages separate. De Bot refers back to the early research which posed this question in a very stark form (Kolers, 1963), and to more sophisticated recent hypotheses about various types of "sub-sets" of linguistic elements described, for example, by Paradis (1987). He comes down for an intermediate solution, i.e. that the systems are partly unified and partly separate, depending on the closeness between the languages and the speaker's own proficiency in each. Links between elements are strengthened through continued use, and in general, those between elements of a single language would be stronger than between those in different languages. In the case of regular CS, however, interlingual links could be just as strong as intralingual ones. De Bot's conclusion is that the lexicon and phonological information are stored together, but that the formulator is language-specific. Separate lemmas are necessary since these carry the syntactic information for correct formulation in each language. De Bot and Schreuder (1993) suggest that "language" is one of the characteristics of a lexical element used in the retrieval process: "In other words, in some settings words from the other language can act as the next best solution to a word finding problem, much in the same way that a near-synonym or a hypernym can serve as such" (p. 201).

De Bot agrees with Giesbers (1989) and also with Poulisse (1997) – whose work concerns L2 learners – that CS as a "speech style" is made up of "performance switches" which are the "result of form characteristics being more or less randomly linked to lemmas in the surface structure" (1992/2000:438). Such switches contrast with those initiated at different levels in the production process, for example those which are "triggered" by words which are similar in form in both languages, or those which are due to unequal command of the two languages, or lack of immediate availability of the required word in one of them. An explanation is offered for cases where CS appears to be entirely "non-deliberate", such as that of Dutch immigrants in the USA or Australia who, after living for decades in an anglophone environment, have difficulty speaking Dutch and keep slipping back into English, often at the point where they encounter words which are similar or identical in both languages. De Bot and Schreuder (1993) suggest that this is a case of Dutch being very weakly activated (through disuse), whereas elements from the second language, English, are so highly activated that they cannot be inhibited (see also Clyne, 1991a; 2003). De Bot admits, however, that it is not always easy to draw clear lines between the different types of CS, echoing the difficulties faced by sociolinguists in classifying switches according to their likely type/origin/motivation (see Chapter 3).

To sum up, De Bot, based on Levelt, claims that macro-planning (in the conceptualizer) is not language-specific, that bilinguals have a single lexicon and a single articulator, and that lemmas are linked to various form-characteristics of words. As the production process advances, the preverbal message contains information about the language in which parts of utterances are to be produced. Finally the relevant language-specific formulator is activated. Kecskes and Moyer (2002), in their "Ethno-conceptual model", add that culturally specific concepts are also already present at the conceptual level which activates the use of lexical items. CS is therefore not simply a syntactic phenomenon, but the outcome of individual choices which are conceptually motivated, as well as contextual constraints. At a linguistic level, as a result, conceptually congruent but grammatically different elements may be interchangeable. They use this to explain a number of examples showing English verbs used with the subcategorization rules of their Spanish equivalents (2002:13).

Clyne's analysis of the psycholinguistic models supports a model in which material from both languages is stored jointly, but with elements from the same language being more closely linked. He also believes that "Various contact phenomena support inhibition of the less active language" (2003:242). De Bot concludes by pointing out that "the empirical basis for an evaluation of a bilingual production model is rather small at the moment" (1992/2000:442). His use of the literature implies, however, that he is open to testing the model against naturally occurring data. If this happens, it could provide a useful underpinning, in psycholinguistic terms, of analyses based on data collected for sociolinguistic purposes.

6.6.3. Myers-Scotton and Jake: testing theories on naturally occurring data

Myers-Scotton and Jake (1995/2000; 2001) were mentioned in Chapter 5 because, unusually, their work represents an attempt to straddle grammatical and psycholinguistic concerns. The 4-M Model and Abstract Model attempt to follow through Jackendoff's (1997) proposals on the role of the mental lexicon in connecting a theory of grammar with language processing and production. Along with very few other studies (e.g. Karousou-Fokas and Garman, 2001;

Broersma and de Bot, 2006), they use naturally occurring CS data to test their hypotheses.

In explaining their "4-M" Model, and in putting forward the CP as a unit of analysis (see section 5.3.3), Myers-Scotton and Jake remark that the conceptual level is not made out of syntactic units, but that instead "Intentions activate language-specific semantic/pragmatic feature bundles", which in turn interface with language-specific lemmas (2001:87). The problems involved in verifying such a chain of events have been alluded to above. What is new here is that morphemes are said to fall into four psycholinguistically distinct types (content morphemes and three different types of system morpheme), whose different roles in language production explain various "asymmetries" in existing data-sets – for example, the near-absence of full English noun phrases in a Spanish frame, or the difficulty of inserting English verbs in an Arabic frame. It is unclear how the system copes with intra-linguistic variations in the patterns.

Karousou-Fokas and Garman (2001) revisited these proposals in relation to bilingual conversations recorded among twenty-four Greek–English bilinguals. They accepted that there is a fundamental processing distinction between open- and closed-class items, but chose another segmentation unit for discourse, the "text unit", different both from the utterance, which relies partly on the tone unit, and from the CP, which is more grammatically defined, to analyse their naturally occurring CS. Significantly – and this is an important innovation – they compared the number of instances of CS in different grammatical positions with the absolute number of these positions in the data. Their results showed that the "text unit", along with the onset of a new turn, were both powerful switching positions in their data. The only boundaries to actually resist CS were word-internal ones. This can be seen as part of an ongoing search for the surface linguistic units which best correspond with code-switching (see Backus in section 5.6.3). Planning, on the other hand, can take place in a language other than the one currently being spoken or comprehended – "Both languages can be equally operative during the planning process" (p. 65).

6.6.4   Grosjean

Grosjean (1982) was a pioneer among psycholinguists in considering bilingual-ity to be the norm and for being interested in it for its own sake. As such, he is particularly attuned to methodological issues which vitiate psycholinguistic research with bilinguals (see section 6.4.1). A major contribution lies in his development of the concept of language "modes", which links in with a number of findings about bilingual processing. The basic proposal is that bilinguals are able to function either in one of two (or more, in the case of trilinguals) monolingual "modes", or alternatively in a bilingual mode. These modes are on a continuum, and where the individual is situated at any given moment

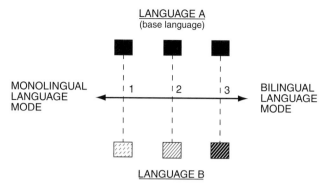

Figure 6.4 Visual representation of the language mode continuum. The bilingual's positions on the continuum are represented by the discontinuous vertical lines and the level of language activation by the degree of darkness of the squares (black is active and white is inactive). (Nicol, 2001: Fig 1.1.)

depends on the state of activation of each language (see Figure 6.4). This activation is a function of context, interlocutor, topic and other factors.

The implicit assumption is that, at any given time, one language is the "base" language and thereby "governs processing". Myers-Scotton cites this work as the origin of the Matrix Language Frame model, and given the propagation of this concept, it is important to consider on what it rests. "(1) the pre-eminence of one language over the other during language processing by bilinguals; (2) the distinction between the behavior of system and content morphemes in speech errors; (3) other distinctions regarding these morphemes in patients with Broca's aphasia; and (4) the possibility of each language having its own direct access to a common conceptual store during CS production" (Myers-Scotton, 1993b: 46–7). The base language is therefore a hypothesis designed to explain a range of disparate findings from psycholinguistic experiments, such as the fact that when English words were embedded in French sentences, French–English bilinguals showed a delay in recognizing the English words: "Of interest is the 'base language effect' (i.e. the first reaction of subjects is to think that the language of the word is the context (base) language, *or what is called the ML here*"[7] (Myers-Scotton 1993b: 47). But there are other possible alternative explanations for this finding, such as that French texts with English words inserted in them may have been an entirely new experience for the subjects and caused a degree of old-fashioned confusion. Reading texts in two languages has been found to take longer than reading texts in a single language – although in some circumstances frequent switching can apparently neutralize the problem. Dussias (2001), also measuring reading comprehension time, found that

[7] My italics.

frequent CS in a corpus was easier for subjects to process than infrequent CS. There is more to this argument, and the degree of activation must be tied in with the degree of proficiency; but as we have seen above, activation is a multifaceted concept which has several origins, both external and internal to the speaker, and does not operate in a blanket fashion.

Grosjean allows for the base language to change frequently when the speaker is in the bilingual mode (how frequently is not discussed). This means, in terms of Figure 6.4, that a fourth position is not allowable, viz. one where a bottom square, for language B, is also black, i.e. fully activated. Grosjean does allow for both languages to be equally activated in simultaneous interpreting (where one language is activated receptively and the other for production), or in certain experimental tasks, e.g. where subjects are told that the verbal stimuli they are given belong to either language, but does not explain why it is exclusively in such cases that equal activation is possible.

The concept of *language mode* and the question of one-at-a-time v. dual activation are two sides of the same coin, and Grosjean (1997; 2000) reports on a variety of experiments, carried out both by himself and by others, where the notion of *language mode* is put to the test directly or indirectly. The concept is found helpful in explaining a variety of experimental findings, of which only two examples will be given here.

(1) In a laboratory-based study, Grosjean (1997) manipulated the language mode of French–English bilinguals, who were told they were taking part in a "telephone chain" designed to test the amount of information that could be conveyed from one person to another. They had to retell French stories, containing English code-switches, to three different interlocutors, who were not actually present but who were described to the subjects by means of biographical sketches. The first was described as having a strongly francophone background, the second as having a more mixed anglophone/ francophone background and the third as having a balanced linguistic back-ground, i.e. using both French and English regularly. He anticipated that the subjects would be in an increasingly bilingual mode with each of these three imaginary interlocutors respectively. As expected, it was found that the number of code-switches into English varied significantly depending on which interlocutor was being addressed. In fully bilingual mode they hesi-tated significantly less. Grosjean concluded that the concept of language mode helps to predict the extent and type of CS.

What the experiment shows is that, having as far as humanly possible excluded all other factors which could influence the outcome, and in the absence of any other discernible influences, bilingual subjects adapt the balance of their bilingual output in order to fit in with characteristics of their interlocutor. What the experiment cannot tell us is what these subjects would have done in real-life situations. Faced with a real, visible interlocutor, whom one might or might not empathize with, and given a lack of external pressure – unlike in the experiment – to speak a particular language, what language choices would these speakers have made? We do not know whether they code-switch in their daily lives, and we are unaware whether the different modes are representative of variations in their natural speech patterns. In any real situation, speech accommodation would be one of the relevant factors, but we know this to be a very complex aspect of behaviour (Giles and Smith, 1979). The results obtained can only tell us what happens in the rarified context of the experiment, and the relationship of those results with real-life performance remains uncertain.

(2) The second experiment concerns the phonology of CS, an under-investigated area. According to Grosjean, various experiments have shown a "base language effect" during the perception of CS, that is to say that "there is a momentary dominance of base language units (phonemes, syllables, words) at code-switch boundaries that can, in turn, slightly delay the perception of units in the guest language" (Grosjean, 1997:236) – it might in fact be more appropriate to describe such effects as "carry-over" effects rather than "base language effects" so as to avoid prejudging the base language issue. Despite the reported "momentary dominance of base language units" in perception, this effect was not reproduced in the productive sphere. Grosjean and Miller (1994) found no phonological "carry-over" from one language to another in a code-switched condition when bilingual subjects had to pronounce various English and French phonemes. For example, they pronounced the stop consonants /p/t/k/ differently depending on which language the word was in, just as they did in monolingual mode (though see MacSwan (2000) and Botero, Bullock, Davis and Toribio (2004), who did find some phonetic effects in the immediate environment of code-switches, as well as some convergence in VOT[8] values).

Finally, a caution about the language mode hypothesis has been issued by Dijkstra and van Hell (2003) who tested it in relation to trilinguals. The hypothesis assumes strong sensitivity to top-down context factors, which can change in a gradual manner depending on the environment (Grosjean and Soares, 1986). In an experiment where Dutch–English–French trilinguals had to perform word-recognition and lexical decision tasks in a monolingual Dutch context, their performance was significantly faster when the Dutch words had cognates, even if these were in their L3, French. The language mode, and the external activation on which it depends, seemed to have no effect on

---

[8] Voice Onset Time is a measure of the way in which the vocal cords operate when different phonemes are pronounced, and is characteristically different from language to language:"The duration of the time interval by which the onset of periodic pulsing either precedes or follows release" (Lisker and Abramson, 1964:37).

performance in this case; the authors therefore argue for the notion of activation to be applied in a highly specified and testable way in the future.

The concept of "language mode" developed by Grosjean is a useful way of describing the fact that many bilinguals, or at least those who have the opportunity to speak their languages in separate contexts, can be in a more or less bilingual "frame of mind" at a given moment. It is not surprising that asking them to perform tasks requiring bilingual skills – especially ones which would never be called upon in their normal lives – causes a certain brief delay or surface dysfluency, though the Dijkstra and van Hell experiment described shows that such an effect cannot always be detected. What is not altogether clear is what kind of repercussions the hypothesized "base language effect" has on bilingual performance and whether such effects go *beyond* the immediate "mind-set" which affects minute-by-minute behaviour.

Simultaneous interpreting is unlikely to be a unique instance of both languages being equally activated, and the conclusions of Karousou-Fokas and Garman (2001), described above, support the possibility of dual activation. Finally an electrophysiological study of reactions to Spanish–English CS showed that, under some circumstances at least, processing a code-switch may entail less disruption than processing an unexpected item in the same language (Moreno, Federmaier and Kutas, 2002).

6.7   Conclusion

In this chapter, we have reviewed some of the psycholinguistic work relevant to CS, highlighting some problems with extrapolating from the experimental to the real situation. Naturally occurring CS has been very little studied from a psycholinguistic perspective, although at least some psycholinguistic measures (e.g. VOT) can be applied to it. A recent psycholinguistic experiment put to the test Clyne's (1967) notion of "triggering"[9] and found that CS was significantly more frequent in the vicinity of a cognate (of which most were proper nouns) (Broersma and de Bot, 2006), thereby confirming the validity of Clyne's analysis; unusually, the data used was a corpus of self-recorded, informal conversations involving three Dutch–Moroccan Arabic bilinguals.

There is a lack of comparative psycholinguistic work which could help account for the variations found within CS, though some models (de Bot, Green) do attempt to account for CS which is due to competence problems and failures to control the languages properly. So far, findings fail to throw much light on the processes, whether externally or internally driven, which underlie CS in conversational contexts, though Green's model, which allows,

---

[9] According to Clyne (1967), certain words, particularly cognates, are liable to "trigger" a switch into the other language.

under some circumstances, for words to reach the surface regardless of language, is potentially compatible with "switching as an unmarked choice" (Myers-Scotton, 1983; Myers-Scotton and Jake, 2001). Notions of inhibition and activation contribute more to an understanding of apparently random, and lexically driven, CS than to that which translates conversational purpose, and as we have seen, the relationship between bottom-up (or internal) activation and the top-down (or external) kind is still under investigation. Meuter (2005) has pointed out that both activation and inhibition should be seen as more complex phenomena than they have so far. As an example of that complexity, experimental evidence shows that, generally speaking, it is harder for bilinguals to inhibit their L1 than their L2; however, perhaps due to the greater inhibition effort required, switching back from a weaker L2 to the dominant L1 is more demanding than vice-versa. Furthermore, calculations of the "cost" of switching must be related to specific tasks, as they are not the same, for example, in naming and in comprehension tasks.

The possibility of "dual activation" is only considered in a minority of studies (e.g. Karousou-Fokas and Garman, 2001). Yet single or competing activation begs a number of questions in relation to fluent bilingual CS. Highly mixed varieties described by sociolinguists such as Boeschoten (1998), Meeuwis and Blommaert (1998) and Gafaranga (2005) could lead to a reconsideration of the base language paradigm which is associated with single activation. As Tracy (2000:28) put it, the coactivation of dual systems is a normal phenomenon, visible in the interpretation of irony, metaphor and ambiguity: there may also be "cognitive levels of abstraction where requirements of individual grammars can be more or less playfully suspended, possibly not unlike what we, as linguists, do all the time when we (voluntarily, to be sure) create ungrammatical examples" (p. 29).

Such coactivation is discernible when a fluent French–English bilingual remarked "That's a bit *ridiculeux*", knowingly using a form which is neither "French" nor "English" (English *ridiculous*, French *ridicule*) – though it was given a French ending – and thereby implicitly mocking his own fake CS (unpublished example). The choice of educated – and usually non-balanced – bilinguals for psycholinguistic experiments tends to minimize such manifestations. Where production, unusually, is the focus of attention, most utterances are assumed to be the product of a sequential single-system output, i.e. to be fairly clearly assignable to one language or another. Compromise forms, "bare" forms and "covalent" elements are rarely even mentioned in the psycholinguistic literature (Woolard, 1999). We should look forward to psycholinguistic studies of CS where the concept of separate and discrete "languages" is not taken as a given, and where such elements are central, rather than peripheral, objects of study.

7 Acquiring code-switching: code-switching in children (and L2 learners)

7.1 Introduction

As was the case in earlier chapters, the preference for an interdisciplinary approach makes it necessary to be highly selective within the various contributing research traditions. The considerable literature on both monolingual and bilingual child language acquisition which is relevant to the issues discussed here, cannot be summarized in toto and the reader is referred for further background information to Fletcher and MacWhinney (1995), Bialystok (1991) and de Houwer (1995). As in the psycholinguistic studies, a number of issues addressed in the literature on bilingual children have a bearing on CS, whether or not children's CS is the topic of the research as such.

One such example is that of the *critical period hypothesis*, on which there is a large number of publications. This hypothesis states that there is a "critical period", generally thought to end at puberty, during which children can acquire full native competence in their mother tongue. Children who suffer accidents, illnesses or deprivations affecting their language development *prior* to this critical stage are generally able to recover full linguistic functioning, whereas those who suffer such traumas beyond this point may never be able to do so. Similarly, second or third languages can usually be acquired with full native-like competence by young children, but there is evidence that this ability also declines with age, i.e. there is an – admittedly less crucial – *critical period* for acquiring further languages as well (Hamers and Blanc, 2000; Johnson and Newport, 1989). Issues to do with maturation of the brain and lateralization form the backdrop to this discussion (see section 6.5).

If learning a second language is qualitatively different from a certain age onwards, then it is possible that CS by early simultaneous bilinguals is also qualitatively different from that of later second language learners. Unfortunately, there is as yet limited research on CS in L2 learners (though see Poulisse and Bongaerts, discussed below) and a lack of direct comparisons with double L1 bilinguals. We do have evidence, however, that adults can learn to code-switch late in life – several of the examples in Chapter 3 are taken from adult migrants who "acquired" CS along with their acquisition of the

L2 (see section 3.3.2). CS can also result from *attrition* of one of the speaker's languages, as with the elderly Dutch and German speakers in Australia described by Clyne (see section 5.3.3.1.1). Interestingly, it can also be used extensively by speakers who are not very fluent in one of the languages, when the indexical value of that language is an important part of their identity. Besnier (2003) illustrates this phenomenon among Tongan "Leitī", a category of males who adopt numerous traditionally feminine characteristics and orient their lives towards a "modernity" which, for them, is symbolized by the use of English.

Research on bilingual children is generally carried out with little reference to studies of bilingual adults. Some mention is made of the psycholinguistic models discussed in Chapter 6, and occasional references are found to studies of adult CS in a sociolinguistic context, usually in order to point out that the mixing encountered in bilingual children is a completely different phenomenon. Once again, the insights to be derived from comparative studies are underestimated. From the point of view of an understanding of CS, studies of bilingual children provide many important insights. Numerous studies have been carried out, documenting children's CS in a comprehensive way. Our knowledge in this area is therefore rather solidly based. To give one brief example, many bilingual children are reported as producing words containing morphological mixtures and mixed two-word utterances between around one and two-and-a-half, even when the languages are presented to them in separate contexts. There is usually a steady decline in such mixtures thereafter (Hamers and Blanc, 2000; van der Linden, 2000; Vihman, 1985; Tabouret-Keller, 1969).

7.2   Issues in child bilingualism

7.2.1   Characteristics of bilingual children

The subjects of child bilingualism studies are not generally typical of the population at large. The majority are "elite bilinguals", in many cases the offspring of the linguistic researchers or their acquaintances, studied longitudinally over a period of months or years in the family context (Leopold, 1939–1949; Taeschner, 1983; Fantini, 1985; Saunders, 1982; Deuchar and Quay, 2000). The advantage of this method is that the child's speech is thereby recorded in a natural setting, with access to someone who fully understands what they mean. The disadvantage is that the children are likely to be at the top end of the scale, both cognitively and socially (for a discussion of the particular features of such bilinguals, see de Mejía, 2002). We lack studies of ordinary, working-class children brought up in native plurilingual environments, who constitute the majority (exceptions include Zentella, 1997; Tabouret-Keller, 1969).

Among these well-educated, middle-class bilinguals, there are a number of variations: each parent speaking their (different) mother tongue to the child;

both parents speaking one language and the environmental language being different; both parents speaking a language which is not their mother tongue to the child, but speaking their mother tongue to one another, etc. (Romaine, 1995). Each of these situations leads to different degrees/types of separation of the languages in the child's input. This is important because one of the main factors which we need to know about in order to understand the linguistic behaviour of bilingual children is what type of input they receive from their parents or carers. Most of the studies referred to below concern the development of early simultaneous bilinguality, but the variety of input – and outcomes – is all the greater when one also takes account of consecutive bilinguality. For a discussion of the differences, see Hamers and Blanc (2000: 65–72).

Most of the bilingual children whose development is described in the literature are presented by their parents with two languages which are deliberately kept separate, at least up to a point. The extreme version of this policy is known as Grammont's Law (1902), which advocates each language being spoken on an exclusive basis by each of the children's carers. More recently, this principle has become known as OPOL – One Parent One Language (Barron-Hauwert, 2004). Children whose parents decide to "manage" their children's bilinguality in this way are the majority of those described in the research literature, but they are undoubtedly in a minority of bilinguals worldwide. However, parents who claim to be strict followers of OPOL often turn out, when their speech is systematically observed, to be subconsciously code-switching in spite of their best intentions (Lanza, 1997; Juan-Garau and Pérez-Vidal, 2001; Goodz, 1989). The underlying basis of the belief that OPOL is the best way to bring up bilingual children is that, in many cases, it is the children's ability to *keep the languages separate* which is valued, rather than their ability to exploit the interaction of the two varieties. As Lanza puts it, "Bilingual awareness is implicitly defined as formal separation of the two languages" (1992).

Most of the studies concern children whose languages are relatively closely related (exceptions include Gawlitzek-Maiwald, 2000; Mishina, 1999; Vihman, 1985). This limits the opportunity to observe what happens in cases of structural conflict between the languages. Ideally, we would want to carry out comparisons between children learning more or less distantly related language pairs in order to test the effect of the linguistic factors proper on CS (the same is true of adults – see Chapters 5 and 6).

7.2.2   Some problems with studying children's code-switching

Most child language studies involve an assessment of the role of input from adults, carers and the environment generally on the child's learning and linguistic choices. In the case of bilinguals, and of CS in particular, the question of what is learned and what is the result of more or less spontaneous development is particularly crucial, so we will come back to this issue in section 7.7 below.

Another, related challenge in the study of children's CS is to sort out developmental from non-developmental issues. The mixtures produced by children in a bilingual environment alter in type as they grow up, owing to their maturing metalinguistic capacities, as well as their increasingly sophisticated linguistic competence. Several studies (e.g. Meisel, 1989) state or imply that the early manifestations of mixing found in such children are of a quite different nature to "adult CS", and that, whereas the latter is a matter of pragmatic competence, the former is a function of the child's developing language system and incomplete differentiation between the two varieties. Some of the evidence we will discuss does show children's CS patterns changing over time in response to increasing linguistic sophistication. But there are *degrees* of purposefulness in adult CS as well as that of children. CS in adults can be related to uneven competence in the two varieties, and is therefore not always a manifestation of pragmatic intent (see section 1.1, example 2).

In fact, any assumption that adults can "distinguish two systems", whereas children cannot, needs to be examined critically. *Some* adults can do this in formal or experimental tasks, or under particular circumstances of production, but not every instance of CS entails that the speaker can make such distinctions (see section 4.2.2.2). Both sociolinguistic and psycholinguistic studies described in previous chapters suggest bilinguals' ability – or desire – to separate their languages depends on many factors, including their education, the norms of the community where they live and the type of conversation.

It is doubtful whether there is, or could ever be, a reliable way, in adults or in children, of distinguishing "deliberate" from non-deliberate CS except in a small minority of cases (for example, those involving self-corrections or certain types of flagging). At one end of the scale, some instances of CS appear to be "slips of the tongue", and at the other end of the scale, some switches have a very clear conversational function, for example addressee specification, or following the *we code/they code* pattern (see section 3.5.1.). In between the two extremes lie the majority of CS utterances, where it is unproductive to ask the question *Why?* and expect to find an answer based on personal intentions. The "reasons" have to do with the patterns we are exposed to, with conversational factors and with our psyche. At most, one can say that there is a "scale of deliberateness" which can be applied to CS, whatever the speaker's age, but that with the exception of the extreme ends of the scale, placing individual examples on points along it remains a matter of (occasionally enlightened) conjecture.

7.3   Terminology again

By a certain age, bilingual children acquire the ability to code-switch for the full range of functions used by adults, but, until that stage, the mixtures which they produce are related to their linguistic development and to the degree of their awareness that there are two varieties in their environment. It has therefore been argued that it is more appropriate to use a different term, such as "mixing", for young children's alternations (Meisel, 1989).

As with adult CS, studies of bilingual children often begin by explaining how various terms will be used. While CS is, in this field too, a commonly used term, several authors refer instead to code-mixing, or even just mixing (Boeschoten & Verhoeven, 1987; Paradis, Nicoladis and Genesee, 2000), and as with adult CS, the lines between its different manifestations are drawn in different ways. Meisel (1989) defined "mixing" as the fusion of two *grammatical* systems, and CS as a skill in the bilingual's *pragmatic* competence (p. 36). Others (e.g. Comeau, Genesee and Lapaquette, 2003) use "code-mixing" as the generic term. Perhaps as a way of avoiding these endlessly repeated terminological debates, the various contributors in Döpke (2000) refer mainly to "cross-linguistic structures".

The effort to draw clear lines between different sub-categories of CS faces the same difficulties in children as we discussed in relation to adults in Chapter 1. On the whole, child language researchers have adopted a more pragmatic approach than sociolinguists, using terms such as mixing, code-mixing or code-switching fairly loosely, and specifying what phenomena they are focusing on in the particular study, e.g. lexical mixing. Many studies are concerned with the earlier stages of acquisition and consequently with "mixing" at the one- or two-word stage, or even with phonological separation and mixing before that (Deuchar and Quay, 2000). Some authors refer to "borrowing" in children, but use the term in a different sense to the sociolinguistic studies, where it has a diachronic dimension – although, as we have seen, the usage there is far from consistent. In child language, "borrowing" tends to be used in relation to the early stages, when children use words from either language because they lack translation equivalents (Genesee, 1989). Code-switching for lack of alternative also occurs in adult speech, whether the word is temporarily unavailable for processing reasons or because it has never been acquired. Other terms which occur include "interference" and "loan-blending"; the latter refers to using a word from the lexicon of one language and adapting it morphologically to the other language, and is considered perfectly systematic by some authors (e.g. Hamers and Blanc, 2000:58), whereas for others, who subscribe to the free morpheme constraint (see section 5.3.1.2), it represents an aberration. Examples include such phrases as *Ich hab ge-**climbed up*** 'I have climbed up' with the German regular participle prefix *ge-* added to the English participle *climbed*, spoken by a two-year-old (Tracy, 2000); and *I say we don't go to trou-s in France anymore*,[1] spoken by a twelve year old (unpublished example). *Trou* was pronounced with French phonology but with the -s of the plural sounded as in English.

Terminological mismatch, along with the fact that the child studies generally focus on a significantly different type of production to the adult ones, should not deter us from considering their relevance to issues addressed elsewhere in CS. First, we have seen how one type of bilingual behaviour merges in with another (section 2.2.4), and what is relevant to one type of bilinguality is often relevant to other types as well. Second, as the old saying goes, "the child is father to the man". Adult code-switchers develop out of child bilinguals (as do adults who keep their languages separate, of course), and although adult CS may result from social conventions which an individual speaker encounters relatively late in life (as in migration), the seeds of the ability to code-switch are planted in childhood. There is therefore much to be said for trying to understand the "ontogenesis of bilinguality", to use Hamers and Blanc's term (2000). For example, if bilingual children, from the earliest stages, can separate their two languages as and when necessary, it is easier to understand how, later on, the ability to manipulate the two varieties in different circumstances might be a subconscious skill.

7.4   One system or two – the wrong question?

For the terms "mixing" or "switching" to be meaningful, there must be two identifiable, separate entities to mix. As with adult CS, we must bear in mind the difference between the observer's point of view and that of the speaker (see section 1, example 1). The adult's observation that a child's utterance contains elements of, say, Japanese and elements of French, may not correspond with any dichotomy from the child's point of view. There is no a priori reason why a young bilingual child should be aware that the words, expressions and sentences which they hear around them are labelled as separate "languages" in the outside world.[2] This does not imply unawareness of the *differences* between the varieties they hear. As we will see, this awareness has been detected from the earliest age. But being aware of the differences – and able to reproduce them – is not the same as having internalized rules as to what can be combined and what

---

[1] A *trou* – literally a 'hole' – is a term used to mean an isolated place where nothing much happens. The speaker was complaining about a long – and, to him, pointless – car journey through France.

[2] This is separate from the issue of when children acquire the adult names for languages. Some children use names like "Mummy's language" and "Daddy's language" before they acquire language names, but the point here refers to the early stages before any such labelling is found.

should be kept separate. This more metalinguistic ability, which includes the learning of norms appropriate in the environement, is likely to proceed at a different pace (Tabouret-Keller, 1969).

7.4.1   What does "mixing" mean in children?

Children from the youngest age can discriminate between patterns. They have the ability to pick up co-occurrences, e.g. of French phonemes with French words, and will tend to reproduce those co-occurrences. If this were not the case, the "mixing" which has been identified in young bilinguals would be more extreme than it is usually found to be. One might wish to make a distinction between mixing and simple confusion. The latter might depend on many factors, notably the particular language combination which is involved. For example Paradis (2000) suggests that the relatively variable word order in Dutch and German explains why some studies using these pairs have found transfers due to confusion between the two, and Schelletter (2000) shows how the contact situation motivated a German–English bilingual child to analyse negation in both languages along the German – more adverbial – model. Meisel (1989) refers to the fact that children sometimes use translation equivalents as if they were synonyms as a symptom of "fusion".

Certainly at the one- and the two-word stage, i.e., in practice, well into the child's third year, it is not possible to talk in terms of a "base language", as many two word utterances consist of one word from each language, such as *où car*? 'where car?' from a French–English bilingual two year old (Genesee, 2001:155). Even when the child's sentences begin to include more morphemes, the "language of the conversation" criterion and the morpheme count criterion are often in conflict: "There may well be utterances without a 'definite language' but rich in multiple representations instead" (Tracy, 2000:21).

An extended example from this study, along with a selection from Tracy's commentary, illustrates several typical aspects of mixing in young bilinguals. The child, Hannah (two years, three months), a German–English bilingual, is trying to get her mother to help her strap her doll into her buggy. This example is reproduced as in the original text deliberately without signalling the language changes with a different font etc., as the distinction between the languages forms the subject of the commentary; therefore only a gloss has been added (\ signals falling intonation).

Example 1
(a) die dolly [ənstræpən] \
     the dolly strap-in INF
(b) die dolly [əntræp] \
     the dolly ..trap

(c) dəs eins-[straːp iːn] die puppe \
    it in- strap in the dolly
(d) die ein-[straːp iːn] die dolly \
    it in strap in the dolly
(e) die mama helf mir [tap] it [iːn] \
    (the) mummy help me strap it in
(f) mama (=voc.)   [tʰap] it [iːn]\ die dolly \
    mummy [=voc.] strap it in \ the dolly

The child starts with what looks like a German VP, (a)–(b), with the verb in the latter case already on its morphological way to an English infinitive, the form required for the English constructions with which she ends up in (e) and (f). In (c) and (d) we witness some blending of both German and English with respect to syntax and morphology. Throughout, the long vowel of *in* appears to retain phonological properties of the separable German particle *ein* (including stress).

Note that *strap* is not a verbal stem in German, but this is an accidental, not a systematic gap. Also, in this particular instance, there is no other equivalent German expression with the separable prefix *ein*. The most idiomatic translation for the set (a) to (f) into German would require *anschnallen* (or *festschnallen*), and actually, for all we know, the *an* might well be on its way in the "grey", ambiguous onset of the first syllable of the verb in (a) and (b). On top of the contrast involving the positioning of the verb with respect to its complement (OV *vs.* VO) and the contrasting morphological design of an English v. a German infinitive (stem +Ø v. stem + -*en*) there is, then, from the child's perspective, an additional conflict involving a (virtual) German particle verb (*einstrappen*) and an English phrasal verb (*strap in*). The overall tentative pattern shows two things: uncertainty about the home base of the verb and, nevertheless, expertise in conjuring up the contexts appropriate to both languages, with the blends in (c) and (d) offering us a particularly good glance at online competition and conflict resolution. This resolution is not a permanent option for the child's grammars, which can contain only VO *or* OV. It is impressive how early bilingual children become experts at handling what they perceive to be crucial design features of each language. (Tracy, 2000: 30–31)

The interesting thing about this example is that although the child is mixing her languages at different levels, as Tracy points out she is clearly aware of various differences between the two languages. For example, she has a translation equivalent for *the dolly* 'die Puppe' and she is aware of English word-order rules (line (e) as opposed to the rest). Even if we describe her as having "two systems" here – which seems a pointless oversimplification – she seems more concerned with how to combine them, so as to maximize her resources, than how to separate them. As Meisel (2000) remarks, the question of whether the child is applying one system or two cannot be separated from the question of when grammatical processing starts – i.e. when it takes over from the semantic/ pragmatic principles which, it is generally assumed, serve to organize early child language.

More recent studies have tended to incorporate the "hypothesis of independent development" (Genesee, 1989) and to address detailed questions regarding the type of separation or interaction between the languages. For example, Yip and Matthews (2000) use both quantitative and qualitative methods to examine syntactic transfer effects from Cantonese to English in their bilingual son between the ages of one and six. They support the idea that two systems are developing independently, but do note a number of transfer effects from the dominant language, Cantonese, to English. By contrast, Juan-Garau and Pérez-Vidal (2001), observing a Catalan–English boy in similar circumstances (OPOL was practised in both cases), found that the aspects of word order which they were observing (notably subject realization) developed quite separately with no transfer being evident. More comparative research is needed to establish under what linguistic and other conditions transfer phenomena are present or absent in bilingual children's speech.

7.4.2   Discrimination in receptive and productive abilities

7.4.2.1 Receptive   Various experiments show that babies are aware of differences between languages from the earliest age. Thanks to a technique which conditions the infants to turn their head in response to a change in continuous auditory stimulation, it can be shown when they are differentiating between different languages spoken in their environment (Bosch and Sebastian-Gallés, 2001). Various studies have thus been able to show that babies from a few days to a few months old can discriminate the sounds of their mother tongue from those of another language (Hamers and Blanc, 2000). Children brought up in a bilingual environment are, it would seem, better at discriminating between their own language and another, totally unfamiliar, language than children brought up monolingually (Eilers, Gavin and Oller, 1982). The ability to discriminate is based on the characteristics of the signal itself – whether or not the parents are practising OPOL is secondary.

7.4.2.2 Productive   As regards production, even before children produce their first word, their babbling differs depending on the language of their interlocutor (Giancarli, 1999). Maneva and Genesee (2002) found that 10–14-month-old bilinguals babbled in different phonological patterns with their French-speaking father and English-speaking mother. This being so, it is not surprising to find that when they start speaking, bilingual children adapt to the language of the interlocutor. As they progress, there is increasing separation of the varieties according to the interlocutor. Growing awareness is demonstrated by the fact that children start *asking* for translations, which seems to occur around the age of two (Hoffmann, 1991; Vihman, 1985). However, considerable inter-individual differences have been noted in the level of bilingual awareness and therefore in the amount of mixing which takes place (Arnberg and Arnberg, 1992; Genesee, Nicoladis and Paradis, 1995). For example,

Morita (2003) describes the development of two Japanese siblings living in the USA. One avoided using Japanese terms of address, which are far more complex than the English system, until he was able to deduce the right forms from his mother's input. The other got round the problem by using English *you* in Japanese utterances.

Recent studies often take as their starting point the contention in Volterra and Taeschner (1978) that, in the earliest stages, children exposed to two languages have a "single system", which they then gradually learn to differentiate. Volterra and Taeschner identified three stages: first, a single lexical system including words from both languages; second, two lexical systems but a single set of syntactic rules; and finally, differentiated lexical and syntactic systems. This "single system" hypothesis was supported in various forms by other authors around the same time, e.g. Vihman (1985) and Redlinger and Park (1980). An interesting parallel may be drawn with the psycholinguistic explanations of CS in terms of a single-switch system, which were then replaced by a dual, and finally by a more complex and differentiated set of procedures (see section 6.5.2).

Over the last twenty or so years, the "single system" hypothesis has been criticized on several different counts. It is only possible to give a selection of these discussions here, and we will concentrate on three major case-studies, namely De Houwer (1990), Lanza (1997) and Quay and Deuchar (2000). As De Houwer points out, it is far from clear what type of evidence would be adequate to confirm either a single-system or a dual-system hypothesis (1990: 49). Such a discussion is subject to the same ambiguities as those which surround the use of the term "language" (see Chapter 1).

(1) De Houwer's subject Kate, a Dutch–American English bilingual, was observed from 2;8 (two years, eight months) to 4;0. Although her CS was found to be skilled and smooth, in the earlier stages of the observation, Kate did occasionally address monolinguals in the "wrong" language or code-switch inappropriately. Interestingly, her self-repairs increased dramatically in both languages at the same time – including the "repairing" of inappropriate switching, at the age of 3;1 to 3;8 (1990:113). While De Houwer considers that there is a maturational element involved, as evidenced by the relatively sudden onset of the self-repairs, she also stresses that plenty of evidence was found for *separate* morphosyntactic development, similar to that in monolingual children, in both of Kate's languages. The latter finding confirms results from a group study by Kessler (1971), who remarked that: "Structures common to two languages are acquired in approximately the same order and at the same rate by bilingual children … The sequencing of specific structures is dependent on the extent of linguistic complexity, describable in terms of case grammar relations … The most linguistically complex structures are those acquired last" (pp. 93–94).

Döpke (2000), however, points out that just because the vast majority of structures produced by bilingual children are acquired in exactly the same way as by monolingual children, this is not a reason to ignore the cross-linguistic structures, as they can still be systematic, as opposed to "performance errors" (see section 1.8).

(2) Lanza (1997) studied two two-year-olds simultaneously acquiring English and Norwegian. Various differences appeared between the acquisition patterns of the two children, one being only slightly dominant in Norwegian, the other more markedly so. One family practised OPOL, the other used more CS. As far as the formal aspects of the children's mixing were concerned, Lanza found that, in the early stages, the children's dominance in Norwegian expressed itself in the fact that they used a considerable number of Norwegian function words with English lexemes, but not vice-versa. Bolonyai (1998) found similar linguistic evidence of the dominance of one language over the other in a Hungarian child who moved to the USA. As English became more dominant, she claimed that a "turnover in the Matrix Language" had occurred (see section 5.7).

Dominance in one language does not, however, always lead to such a pattern. An English–French bilingual three-year-old used lexical importations from his dominant language, English, in sentences whose grammar was entirely French, as in: *Ne me* scrabbe *pas comme ça – où est le* sponge *de Nicolas*? 'Don't scrub me like that – where is Nicholas's sponge?' where 'scrub' and 'sponge' were pronounced as French words (unpublished example). Using the English words presumably seemed a better solution than not expressing his desired meaning at all. Many adults also get away with doing this and are probably well enough understood, thanks to the redundant quality of language. A parallel can be drawn here between individual bilinguality and group/community bilingualism. Thomason (2001) asserted that, on the whole, it is the minority group which becomes bilingual and adopts features from the dominant group (see section 2.2.1), but that the majority sometimes also contribute to language change in the minority language. This child's use of his stronger language (English) in the context of his weaker one (French) can be likened to this process at an individual level. Multiple factors are always at play and the pattern of mixing depends, among other factors, on exactly where the individual bilingual's lacunae lie.

Overall, Lanza found the most significant factor in the separation or mixing of the two languages to be the type of bilingual context which each of the parents encouraged. Thus the little girl, Siri, did more mixing with her father when speaking Norwegian than with her mother when speaking English, *even though she was dominant in Norwegian*, because Siri's mother's strategies discouraged mixing. The fact that the children in her study were *able* to differentiate the two languages did not preclude mixing in certain situations. These results are confirmed by numerous reports (Genesee *et al.*, 1995; Mishina, 1999; Shin and Milroy, 2000).

(3) Crucial evidence about children's ability to discriminate is provided in various studies of infant and child phonology. Deuchar and Quay (2000) investigated Voice Onset Times[3] and other phonological differentiators in an infant acquiring English and Spanish, and found an ability to differentiate from the earliest stages. Further examples include:

- Brulard and Carr (2003), who report that a French–English bilingual child used strategies identical to those of monolingual children both in French and English words from the earliest stages of his producing words (reduplication in French and consonant harmony in English);
- Gut (2000), who detected no cross-linguistic influence in the acquisition of question intonation of a German–English bilingual child between 2;5 and 4;3.
- Johnson and Lancaster (1998), whose study of a Norwegian–English bilingual boy found that, although his phonemes differed from those of monolingual children in both languages, overall he clearly distinguished sound production in each one.

As Deuchar and Quay (2000) are at pains to point out, a bilingual child is only in a position to respond differently in the two languages *once translation equivalents have been acquired*. Before that stage, it is pointless to think of there being any "system" as such, even less two competing ones. As in the case of the children observed by De Houwer and Lanza, their study showed that the language of two-word utterances was matched to the linguistic context – with a few exceptions in the form of words which were used indiscriminately, despite context (e.g. *more* and its Spanish equivalent, *más*). From the point of view of syntax, in a longitudinal study of two German–French bilingual children, Meisel (2000) found that they applied different word order in the two languages as soon as they started to produce multi-word utterances.

So rather than focusing on the question "Is there one system or two?", as Deuchar and Quay suggest we should concentrate on *how and when differentiation occurs* in the child's language. This varies according to the aspect being considered (lexis, morphosyntax or phonology), and probably, as we have seen with Lanza, in accordance with the dominance of one language over another. There is no point in describing children's utterances as mixed when the child has no choice because they have not yet acquired the translation equivalents.

---

[3] See Chapter 6, footnote 8.

The case-studies therefore concur on a number of crucial points. There is considerable evidence that even very young children are able to differentiate between languages. Allowing for individual variations, which occur in monolingual children as well, the bilingual children studied learned each of their languages in the same way and at the same rate as their monolingual counterparts. Finally the tendency to mix or not to mix, after the very early stages, is partly individually determined, regardless of similar input.

7.5   Do children obey constraints?

In section 5.3.1, we saw that the constraints on CS which have been identified are not categorical, but merely reflect tendencies which develop in particular circumstances. If there are no absolute grammatical constraints on adult CS, then this is probably the wrong question to ask for children also. However several authors have addressed this question in relation to children, and as in the case of adults, the conclusion depends on the particular data-sets which are examined. Genesee (2001) concluded from a survey that children's CS obeys the same constraints as that of adults. Vihman (1985; 1998) found that most of the constraints implied by Myers-Scotton's MLF model are observed in her corpus, though she remarks on a few inclusions of system morphemes from the embedded language with grammatical agreement in Matrix Language. On the other hand, Bader and Minnis (2000) give examples from an Arabic–English child violating Poplack's constraints. Tracy (2000:19–20) gives examples of many instances of child language where a base language cannot be assigned, for reasons outlined in section 7.4.1 above.

Few of these studies directly compare children's speech with that of the adults in their immediate community (though see Mishina, 1999). Such information would seem highly relevant to understanding the nature of such constraints, if they exist, and to whether they are universal/inborn or the result of input. More studies involving both adult and child CS would therefore be welcome in the future.

7.6   The role of input

More specifically, the role of linguistic input in children's acquisition is crucial. The Chomskyan position that language is an innate human faculty finds support from what is known as the "poverty of stimulus" argument, meaning that the language heard by children in their environment is generally a far from perfect model, yet all normal children nevertheless manage to acquire full grammatical competence in their mother tongue by the time they are a few years old. De Houwer (2009) points out that the study of bilingual children confronts us particularly starkly with the question of what role input plays in child language acquisition. For example, how, and to what extent, is non-balanced input in each of the varieties reflected in the child's own competence?

"Elite bilinguals", as we have seen, are often actively discouraged from mixing their languages by their carers. However, we know that, in a mono-lingual context, explicit adult corrections of the child's language are more or less ineffective in the early years (De Villiers and De Villiers, 1979:108–111). Furthermore, the injunction to use only one language at a time could only have an effect on children to the extent that they were *already consciously aware* of speaking two different languages. The gaining of such awareness is a gradual process, as Taeschner (1983) illustrates: whenever her German–Italian bilingual daughters addressed her in Italian, she would reply: *Wie bitte?* 'Pardon?' in German, in order to get them to repeat what they had said in German. This policy was effective at first, but broke down when the girls realized that their mother understood Italian perfectly well.

Various studies, notably Lanza (1997), emphasize that each parent conveys, through their discourse practices, what proportion of each language is expected, and whether CS is acceptable; the extreme version of this being the OPOL policy. Deuchar and Quay (2000) relate in statistical terms how much of each language the child in their study is exposed to. But they rightly point out that language separation by the parents is not necessarily the sine qua non for the children to learn separation. Eventually, children pick up norms of the society where they live; the question is how/when they become sensitive to these norms and able to reproduce them.

Comeau, Genesee and Lapaquette (2003) claimed that many studies were inconsistent or inconclusive regarding the effect of parental mixing on children. They therefore tested six bilingual children (average age 2;4) in a carefully designed experiment where bilingual assistants deliberately manipulated their own mixing rate. In almost all cases, the children adjusted to match their interlocutors on a turn-by-turn basis. They concluded that an earlier study of parent–child interaction, which showed no correlation of this type, was flawed – observing a child with their parent, as in the earlier study, may not be ideal because their behaviour may be affected by socialization patterns within the family which are not obvious to an observer. Goodz (1989; 1994), who carried out another group study, longitudinal this time, of seventeen French–English bilingual children, also found the children's mixing to be related to mixing by parents. The ability of even very young children (2;4 to 2;7) to adjust their rate of CS to that of their interlocutor was again tested experimentally and found to be significant, even when this meant adjusting their speech to use a higher proportion of their weaker language (Comeau, Genesee and Lapaquette, 2003). Genesee (1989) aptly points out that such results weaken the argument that children's mixing reflects an undifferentiated language system.

One important aspect of input is which particular language combination the child is presented with. Paradis (2000) has suggested that the various studies focusing on Dutch–German acquisition may have highlighted the effects of cross-linguistic interaction, as both languages have a relatively variable word–order and are, of course, closely related, thereby potentially causing confusion. Conversely, Sinka (2000) found that Latvian–English bilingual children mixed mainly at the lexical level, and suggested that the very different typological characteristics of the two languages enable the child to separate the two language systems at an early stage and so to produce language-specific structures. Vihman (1985) claims that certain aspects of children's switching may be related to qualities of the languages themselves. She ascribes her son's use of English function words to the fact that they were simpler and more salient for him than Estonian ones (see the notion of "atttactiveness" in language change, section 2.4). Juan-Garau and Pérez-Vidal (2001) stress the need to look at the interplay of parental input and the child's own pragmatic/linguistic development in order to understand how the child's CS decreases with age – though Meisel (1989) had talked of a U-shaped curve: lots of mixing to start with due to limited competence in the two languages, then fewer mixes as competence increases, then finally the acquisition of adult-like CS abilities.

One of the few studies of a working-class child being socialized in a family and a society where CS is the unselfconscious norm is Tabouret-Keller (1969). By the age of six, her subject, Line, was code-switching between French and Alsatian in a manner quite in tune with that of the adults who surrounded her. This is doubtless representative of the majority of bilingual children worldwide, whose repertoire is shaped by a combination of parental input and, increasingly as they grow up, by all the parameters of their own community's plurilingual behaviour. As Zentella (1997) points out, sub-groups within the community also create their own language and their own repertoire and do not merely reproduce those of the preceding generation: "When Paca, Lolita, Isabel, Blanca and Elli speak, they reflect their partic-ipation in particular ethnic, racial and class networks via their standard and non-standard Puerto Rican Spanish, AAVE, and lower working class and standard New York English, and those dialects tend to influence each other" (p. 271). Just as Zentella remarks in this context that a purely quantitative sociolinguistic approach risks missing the individual and group meaning of Spanish–English switches, so the rather "asocial" approach adopted in many studies of child bilinguality is likely to underestimate the active creation of meaning by children with the basic elements provided by the bilingual models around them.

7.7 Pragmatic uses of code-switching in children

Lanvers (2001) found socially determined CS at a very early age, as well as CS for discourse functions such as emphasis or appeal to the adult. The most frequent CS was classed as "developmental" and was due to lexical gaps. A number of researchers have found CS to be a function of addressee from an early age as well as developing further functions over time (Jisa, 2000; Ervin-Tripp and Reyes, 2005).

Halmari and Smith (1994), in a study of two Finnish–English bilingual sisters aged 9;2 and 8;1 living in the USA, found that 74 percent of their switches occurred when "negotiation talk" started. They noted that particular features co-occur with negotiation, even when English was used for this function instead: voice quality changes, interrogatives, imperatives, etc. – showing CS to be a part of register shift. Shin and Milroy (2000) showed how Korean schoolchildren in New York not only adapted their language choices to the preferences of their interlocutor, but also used CS to negotiate the structural organization of the conversation.

Cheng (2003) carried out a group study involving sixty Malaysian preschool children, twenty-eight Chinese and thirty-two Malay. Code-switching in this group was linked to a variety of discourse strategies. Cromdal (2001), who observed children at an English school in Sweden, found that CS was mainly used as a way to resolve overlaps in the discussion, a change of language enhancing the second speaker's chance to take the floor.

7.8 Cognitive effects of code-switching

There is a large literature on the cognitive effects of bilingualism (see for example Cummins, 2003), but, apparently, little work on the relationship of CS to cognitive development. Vygotsky (1934) believed that language and thought started developing separately, and that language contributed only subsequently to the development of cognitive structures. Early bilingual experience – and, possibly, CS a fortiori – could in theory thereby encourage greater cognitive flexibility, through the greater use of the self-regulatory functions of language (Peal and Lambert, 1962:14). Diaz (1983) pointed out, however, that this involves various assumptions: (1) that bilingual children are thinking verbally in performing non-verbal tasks; (2) that they switch from one language to another *while* performing these tasks; and (3) that the habit of switching improves performance. None of these have been demonstrated yet.

Döpke suggests that the tension between the two systems which bilingual children have to process has a positive role in their language acquisition. She derives this from the fact that the bilinguals whom she studied chose the structures common to their two languages (English and German) with greater frequency than monolingual children (2000:94), which shows that they (a) noticed and (b) were able to exploit the contrast between the two (see also Hulk and Müller 2000:229). Similar observations, as we have seen in Chapters 3 and 5, have been made with regard to adults. While this is not the product of CS as such, but rather of bilinguality, it seems likely that an environment where CS is common would reinforce the sense of contrast and encourage this process further. Sinka (2000), mentioned above, who studied children's CS between two typologically very different languages, Latvian and English, considered that the different nature of the two languages enabled the children to separate the two systems at an early stage and to produce language-specific structures. Accordingly, the mixing observed was mainly lexical. Various studies have shown that bilingual children have an enhanced ability, compared with monolinguals, to deal with abstract concepts, which, it is thought, may be a by-product of the early necessity to separate the signifier and the signified (Hamers and Blanc, 2000).

7.9   Group studies

Many of the important studies in this field are individual case-studies, as we have seen above, but there are also a number of group studies, often longitudinal, which reinforce the results obtained. Together, they give an opportunity – as yet insufficiently exploited – to study the range of individual differences in various aspects of bilingual acquisition.

Lindholm and Padilla (1978) studied eighteen Spanish–English children aged 2;0–6;0, and found that the switches observed served both sociolinguistic and communicative strategies. Redlinger and Park (1980) observed four bilingual children (two German–French, one German–Spanish, one German–English) aged 2;0 to 2;8 and found that with increasing MLU[4] values, the percentage of mixed utterances decreased. Köppe and Meisel (1995) studied five French–German bilinguals aged approx 1;0–4;0, and Meisel also drew for several of his publications on the results of the DUFDE Project, which involved observing children with one French and one German parent. Kessler (1971) studied twelve Italian families with children aged 6;0–8;0, living in Philadelphia. She found that, while bilingual children's language development

---

[4] MLU (Mean Length of Utterance) is a measure of the average number of morphemes in children's utterances, which serves as an indicator of linguistic development.

closely followed that of monolinguals, they tended to acquire structures common to the two languages more readily (see Döpke above).

7.10   Code-switching in the classroom

While many children worldwide are exposed to two or more languages in the home, many are also confronted with a second language at school, or take part in some form of bi- or trilingual education, through design or otherwise. De Mejía (2002) has described elite bilingual education, where, in spite of the prevalence of purist attitudes in many contexts, much CS nevertheless occurs. De Mejía (2002) and Lin (2001) give extensive examples of the use of CS in bilingual school situations, the first in Colombia in private English–Spanish immersion schools where CS is accepted, and the second in Anglo–Chinese secondary schools in Hong Kong where it is officially frowned on, but is nevertheless flourishing. In multilingual Singapore, CS is also an important tool for children in the learning process. Both positive and negative views of CS in education have been expressed.

Martin-Jones has carried out extensive research on classroom CS (1995; 2000) and has demonstrated what a widespread phenomenon this is, and the variety of purposes it can serve. It may for example reflect language practices outside the classroom; serve as an inclusive strategy where pupils are of varying language competences; serve to encourage pupils' acquisition of an L2 by ensuring that they understand at least part of what is said without difficulty; and so forth.

Martin (2003) illustrates classroom CS in Brunei between Malay and English, but also between different varieties of Malay – Brunei Malay, Colloquial Brunei Malay and Bahasa Melayu – especially among the young. Such switching involves moving along a continuum rather than categorical switches, and this is reflected in classroom discourse between teachers and students like that in example 2. This owes its existence equally to pedagogic and discourse-structuring reasons:

Example 2

T: Now carbohydrate …**kalu kamu makan**
                if you eat
    mandangar tu tadi cakap teacher
    listen to what I've just been saying
    if you eat too much of these food. **Apu maksud** teacher **sana..apu maksud**
    teacher
                    what's my meaning here?
    kalau makan terlalu banyak
    if you eat too much

S: **jadi lampuh**
    get fat

T: **apanya kata** teacher **tadi**
    what did I say just now?

S: **mambari lampuh**
       get fat
T: it is not good for your
SS: teeth
T: for your ..health..for your health. not good for your health..you will become very
SS: fat

(Martin, 2003:78)

Similarly, Cleghorn (1992) shows how teachers in primary level science classes in Kenya convey ideas more effectively when they do not adhere to an English-only instruction policy. Merritt, Cleghorn, Abagi and Bunyi, (1992) list four major factors which account for CS in the classroom: (1) official school policy; (2) cognitive concerns; (3) classroom management concerns; and (4) values and attitudes about the appropriate use of the languages in society at large. For an African perspective see the papers in Rubagumya (1994). Further studies include Hurtado (2003), Foley (1998), Camilleri (1996), Garrett, Griffiths, James and Scholfield, (1994); and Garrett, Griffiths, James and Scholfield, (1994).

A glimpse of classroom CS in action is provided by McCormick's notes, taken while observing a class in a school in South Africa in an area known as District Six:

Two children were quarrelling in Afrikaans about their fathers' work. (The fathers are fruit and vegetable vendors.) A child intervened in English and the teacher redirected the comment to the group as a whole, using English. Then, in both languages, she invited responses from the other children. She asked, among other things, whether they knew a traditional vendors' rhyme which was in Afrikaans. One of the quarrelling children was encouraged to sing it. An interlude of physical exercise followed. It was directed in English. Then a child started telling a story in English about how he had been bitten by a spider. He used the word "bleed" instead of "blood": and then the bleed came out. "The teacher supplied the orthodox phrase but did so without drawing attention to the correction: "Oh! So the blood came out!" Several children started talking at once about spiders, some in English and some in Afrikaans. The teacher picked up some threads in Afrikaans but the next child to hold the floor did so in English. He was shy and she encouraged him in English. She was then distracted by an upheaval in one corner of the classroom and asked one of the children in Afrikaans what was happening. (McCormick, 2002:141)

While the informal framework which prevails with this young class may be particularly conducive to relaxed CS, the latter clearly serves a number of important functions in differentiating between types of discourse and in allowing the teacher to fulfil different roles, from directing attention to including shyer members of the class.

7.11   Code-switching in second language learners

CS has not been very extensively investigated in relation to L2 learners, though see Poulisse (1997), Dewaele (2001) and Poulisse and Bongaerts

(1994). Poulisse and Bongaerts (1994) tie in learners' CS with language production issues as described in Chapter 6. They make the point that for a beginner L2 speaker, the L1 has a much higher "resting activation" than the corresponding word in the L2 (see section 6.6.1). They looked at "unintentional" (i.e. non-flagged) CS in Dutch schoolchildren learning English, and found that this consisted principally in the insertion of L1 function words in L2 (English). Poulisse and Bongaerts claim this to be a result of processing considerations and in particular claim it provides support for the "spreading activation model" (Dell, 1986). In an interesting reversal of the sociolinguistic and grammatical findings, they point out that content words, being chosen with greater care, are less likely to be switched. However it seems unlikely that this pattern would be repeated in such a way as to confirm that this was a universal for second-language learners. Other cases of code-switching by speakers with very uneven competence – while they might not be in the same specific situation as these learners – have produced quite different results.

Lüdi (2003) also discusses whether L2 learners code-switch. He points out that it is a well-known communicative strategy for non-native speakers to use their L1 (or another language) to get round communicative stumbling blocks, a phenomenon which he calls *translinguistic wording*, but that balanced bilinguals use this strategy also, as even they are bound to have some lexical gaps. Such phenomena are generally flagged by dysfluencies and hesitations. At the same time, learners may "code-switch" in the same way as balanced bilinguals when they alternate fluently between their L1 and L2, in particular when they are speaking their L2 and need lexical elements from their L1, as in example 3, from a native speaker of German/non-native speaker (NNS) of French,:

Example 3

NNS: et il y a un petit moteur oui oui qui tire le cocon et il y a la **vorrichtung**
      *and there is a little motor yes yes that pulls the cocoon and there is the **device***
      il y a de grands **mast** de **stahl**
      *there are tall **masts** of **steel***

(Lüdi, 2003:178)

Lüdi's point that there is a continuum between CS and *translinguistic wording* is well taken; however, his suggestion that CS can be meaningfully explained with reference to the notion of Matrix Language is subject to the problems which have been discussed in Chapters 5 and 6. Finally, in a study of Igbo-Nigerians learning Italian, Goglia (2006) points out that learners whose native varieties involve unmarked CS may well transfer the switching habit to the language they are learning, thereby increasing their resources in that language.

7.12   Conclusion: code-switchers or code-breakers?

The conclusions we can draw from studies of bilingual language acquisition are complicated by the fact that children can be presented with two (or more) linguistic varieties in so many different configurations. Different methods of observation, appropriate for different ages and circumstances, are also partly responsible for the variety of results obtained. These factors mean that comparability between the studies is an issue. It is not surprising that widely different results are found with respect to many of the questions asked, such as whether children transfer elements from their dominant language to their weaker language only or whether the process is two-way. Also, as with adults, there appear to be no studies yet of CS in relation to personality and cognitive style, although there are strong indications that these affect the quantity and type of CS. Children also vary in the extent to which they pick up, or care about, linguistic purism on behalf of their carers.

The question which runs through this book, i.e. what "a language" is, and how CS can help us to answer it, is powerfully raised by studies of bilingual children. Many researchers initially designed their studies round the issue of whether bilingual children started off with one system or two, by which they meant, what type of awareness did the child have that the input they heard around them was derived from two separate sources, and to what extent could they reproduce this distinction? As soon as one glosses the question thus, it becomes clear that the question is an impossible one. As De Houwer (1995) asks, why should a bilingual child expect everything they hear to come from a single system? Still more to the point, what would lead us to think that this is the type of question children ask themselves?

Bilingual child language acquisition is an "automatic" process requiring no specific or conscious effort by the child. This differentiates it from adult L2 acquisition and makes it more similar to monolingual acquisition, where it is widely believed that children are born with a set of innate principles, such as Universal Grammar (UG) (Chomsky, 1981; Pinker, 1994). Clearly, if this is correct, then the capacity to learn several languages must be equally "hardwired". One aspect of this innate capacity is the ability to identify co-occurrences at many different levels. Thus children acquiring a pidgin as a first language – and, according to the classic definition, thereby creating a creole – are faced with elements which, from their parents', or from other adults' points of view, emanate from two different "languages", but which for them are part of a single one. Adone (1994) has shown how children learning Mauritian Creole "recreolize" their language, i.e. follow several of the predictions in Bickerton's "Bioprogram" (1981). They thereby deviate to some extent from the input they receive – this input being already more variable than in a focused language situation.

Children exposed to standard, focused languages, on the other hand, are either presented with two sets of input which are systematically kept apart in their environment (as in OPOL), or, more commonly, which are kept apart *at certain times* or *by certain people*. They are sensitive to how those groupings operate, be they lexical, grammatical, phonological or simply related to dialect or register, and most acquire the capacity to produce the varieties separately as well as to code-switch. No-one has yet systematically investigated to what extent children brought up *only* with diffuse or code-switched varieties are nonetheless able to speak the contributing varieties in a more focused or "monolingual" fashion if required.

Much more fundamentally even than being language learners, children are code-breakers, i.e. detectors of patterns. The fact that adults – especially highly educated ones – call some of those patterns by a language name, be it English or Navajo, is less of a concern to them than figuring out in what configurations it is (a) possible and (b) common to use them. They are sensitive from an early age to contextual factors, which suggests that, despite criticism of the concept (see section 6.6.4), Grosjean's modes could be useful for research on bilingual children.

This chapter ends with a reference to some of the points made by Tracy (2000) in her paper "Language mixing as a challenge for Linguistics", as these go to the heart of the issues which have preoccupied – or should preoccupy – researchers in this field. The first is an injunction, in analysing mixed productions, to avoid what she calls "the daisy principle" – i.e. the "picking off" of each word or morpheme in the child's output as belonging to one language or the other. Even more so than with adults, many cases are ambiguous or simply not assignable to a particular language – in any case, as we saw, the distinction is meaningless until we are sure that translation equivalents have been acquired. Second, Tracy points out that the fact that closed-class items are, at least in some data-sets, the most frequently switched items (e.g. Poulisse and Bongaerts, 1994) represents a challenge to widely accepted grammatical predictions – and common expectations – about CS.[5] Third, she communicates the idea that in "learning to mean", children learn, among other things, that meaning may arise from contrasts and juxtapositions, of which code-switches are one example: "It is the conflict between different representations which points to the actual message." Last, while formal equivalence may be maintained in language mixing, this could be a simple outcome of the fact that "coactivated parallel formats strengthen each other more than divergent patterns". Appropriately enough, she compares the code-switching child, such as the child with the

---

[5] This point is not negated by the more detailed predictions of Myers-Scotton and Jake (2000) about the different *types* of closed-class item and their role in production (see section 5.3.4.1.2). The issue here is more general, to do with the oddity – and idiosyncrasy – of such a pattern.

doll in example 1, with a linguist, testing the limits of language (Tracy, 2000:29).

The argument for taking full account of individual and contextual factors to understand CS, is as strong in the case of children as in that of adults. To achieve this, we should strive to integrate the ethnographic and sociolinguistic richness (as provided, for example, by Zentella or McCormick) with the detailed observation of interaction which characterizes some of the classic case-studies of bilingual child language.

8 Conclusions

8.1 What do we know about code-switching?

A fundamental argument which underlies this book is that we need to distinguish clearly between idiolectal competence – the real locus of language – and abstract or general conceptions of what a language is. Such general conceptions – e.g. the notion of "correct" English, or Japanese – affect the way people speak (to a greater or lesser extent at different times); but idiolectal competence contains many other elements besides. When bilingual speakers code-switch, because they are in informal mode, they are probably less affected by abstract notions of what a language is or should be than in monolingual production. We cannot assume that CS is always to be viewed as a combination of two entities, which, though they can be mixed in various ways, always retain their essential character. Instead, we should adopt a "common sense" approach, which involves looking at the product in its own right and taking account of its internal variability in constructing theories and definitions.

Studies described in this book highlight various characteristics of CS.

(1) CS is highly variable between communities and between individuals. This variability gives the linguist an insight into how bilinguals' linguistic competence is *actually* organized, as opposed to how the "languages" which they officially "speak" might, in theory, mesh together. However, up to now, much of the research has been based on an a priori approach. I have suggested that despite the many advances in the study of bilingualism, this is connected with a persistent, if perhaps subconscious, view of monolingualism as the natural state of humans among many linguists. One example of this is the widespread acceptance of the idea that it is meaningful, and even necessary, to talk of a "base language" in bilingual speech (Gardner-Chloros and Edwards, 2004).

(2) CS is an abstraction derived by linguists from the behaviour of bi/plurilingual speakers. It takes its place within a range or continuum of manifestations of bilinguality, and should be investigated and analysed in relation to other such manifestations, such as borrowing, convergence and creolization. Over twenty years ago, Gumperz had already moved on his definition from the co-occurrence of two languages or varieties and described it as

"the juxtaposition within the same speech exchange of passages of speech belonging to two grammatical systems or subsystems" (1982:56). As evidence continues to accumulate concerning intermediate and compromise phenomena in CS, there is a need to relativize even this definition. There is also a strong argument for the use of a more apposite term, such as "language interaction", to include all manifestations of language contact without prejudging whether the varieties involved are held to belong to discrete systems (LIPPS Group, 2000).

(3) CS shows considerable internal variation. It is particularly apt to show the influence of sociolinguistic factors (broadly defined as all the characteristics which situate speakers within their social groupings) on speakers' production. Second, there are significant effects related to the characteristics of the contributing varieties and the combination of more or less closely related languages – different pairings provide different opportunities and difficulties at a linguistic, and in particular at a syntactic, level (Muysken, 2000). From the comparisons available so far, it appears that sociolinguistic factors are extremely powerful and can *override* considerations arising from apparent incompatibilities of the varieties involved. Such a conclusion, which is likely to be further confirmed by future studies, has far-reaching theoretical consequences.

(4) Various aspects of CS are controversial. For example, conversation analysts argue that CS creates "local effects", i.e. brings about meanings thanks to its structural role in conversation, such as the use of contrasts, framing/footing, showing cooperativeness or the lack of it (preference organization) (Li Wei, 2002). Others, such as Myers-Scotton and Bolonyai (2001), have argued that the varieties' external connotations (e.g. *we code/they code*) are brought to bear in code-switched conversations and add a dimension of meaning going beyond the overt message, for which a knowledge of factors outside the conversation itself is necessary. Although one theory is always more attractive than two, the simultaneous operation of both types of motivation is increasingly being recognized (Milroy and Gordon, 2003; Sebba and Wootton, 1998). Similarly, quantitative approaches contrast with qualitative, ethnographic descriptions, and grammatical descriptions operate largely independently of sociolinguistic ones. Such different approaches are not necessarily incompatible, but their potential complementarity is scarcely discussed in the literature. Linguists studying CS from different perspectives commonly present their results as self-sufficient, and this lack of interdisciplinarity is regrettable. This may also be true of other fields, but that is not a reason not to address the problem in this one.

(5) CS requires an interdisciplinary approach for several important reasons. For example, adult CS often develops out of child bilingualism, yet the development of bilingual skills in children is rarely studied in relation to the

behaviour of adults in the same community (although see the recent work on bilingual socialization, e.g. Badequano-López and Kattan, 2007). CS is natural, unmonitored speech par excellence, yet psycholinguistic studies generally do not use the real CS data collected by sociolinguists and instead investigate bilingual speech in a laboratory setting. Sociolinguists in turn tend not to feed in to their studies the results of historical studies of language contact, although these can throw light on the long-term effect of different sociolinguistic factors – and so it goes on. Formal linguists, who traditionally use introspective data as evidence, are prepared to continue using such data even in the face of the extreme variability with which CS presents them (MacSwan, 1999; 2005). Since their enterprise is based on the reliability of native speakers' intuitions about their mother tongue, the fact that neither "native speaker" nor "mother tongue" can reliably be defined in many cases of CS would seem to constitute a fairly fundamental challenge. As Wasow (1985) somewhat roguishly put it, in basing theories on the selection or rejection of introspectively derived sentences, they have only their own "asterisk".

8.2   Acknowledging fuzziness

One simple reason why CS is so often conceptualized as alternation between discrete systems is, doubtless, that dealing with fuzziness appears less glamorous than findings based on a supposed clarity. Researchers who think "outside the box" do not coalesce into a clear "school", like those, for example, working within Myers-Scotton's Matrix Language Frame (Myers-Scotton and Jake 1995/2000). Such people, however, not only exist but have carried out highly innovative work on CS. Many have been discussed at different points in this book, but they are listed briefly again here, in order to illustrate the range of arguments in favour of the "fuzzy school", which places the complex nature of CS in the centre stage rather than at the periphery.

Michael Clyne is one major scholar who has avoided bandwagons in favour of a pragmatic appreciation of his data's implications. His 1987 paper remains one of the best-formulated challenges to the idea that CS is characterized by universal constraints. Clyne prefers to talk in terms of some aspects of different language combinations being "facilitators" of CS rather than in terms of constraints. His 2003 book contains a wealth of evidence on the complexity of interlingual phenomena in relation to the languages of different immigrant groups in Australia. He considers in detail the linguistic mechanisms of what he terms "transversion" – basically non-insertional CS and other loans, etc. which allow the speaker to move over from one language to another – in the speech of these various groups, and shows how both linguistic (typological) and sociolinguistic factors affect the linguistic outcomes. In so doing, he provides precisely the type of comparative data which, it has been argued, is particularly revealing of the mechanisms of CS.

Auer (1999; 2000) has stressed the difficulty, for an outsider, to determine "the language of interaction" in a bilingual conversation – something which the participants themselves are constantly negotiating. He describes the fluid transition from an interactionally founded phenomenon to a structural one in which individual switches may have no interactional significance. As we saw, he reserves the term "code-switching" for the pragmatically motivated pole of the continuum, pointing out that, in time, the frequency of juxtaposition of the two varieties weakens the contextualization value of this cue.

Alvarez-Cáccamo (1998) pointed to the need to distinguish between the linguistic material present in utterances (linguistic varieties) and the associative mechanisms which underlie their production. He described CS as an "alloy"; in his own data involving Galizan–Portuguese–Spanish, for example, the prosodic patterns of one language sometimes overlap with a stretch of discourse from another; he describes lexical, syntactic and prosodic materials from each as being "fused into an amalgam" (p. 37).

Gafaranga and Torras (2001; 2002) and Gafaranga (2005) challenged the idea that bilingual speakers can always be said to be speaking a particular "language", and pointed out that it makes more sense to think of them using a "medium" which may be composed of several internally mixed varieties. Switches which carry meaning for speakers and their interlocutors might not be easily identifiable by outsiders who do not share the various hybrid "media"/ codes which form the repertoire of the particular community.

Meeuwis and Blommaert (1998) provided a "monolectal" view of CS, emphasizing that, to the speakers, differences between "languages" may be less salient than the differences between dialects, sociolects or speech styles. For example, in the Zairian community in Belgium, all the national languages of Zaire are learned as CS varieties peppered with French, which is both the official language in the homeland and, of course, one of the official languages in Belgium. The apparently chaotic set of combinations available can in practice be reduced to a set of linguistic *practices* allowing communication through different layers of society, but these cannot be distinguished along the lines of the different standard languages which they include.

Rampton (1995) pointed to the need to distinguish notions of *code* and *speech variety*. The use of particular markers, such as [d] for [ð] could represent entire social styles. Similarly, Sebba drew attention to the minimal linguistic changes needed to represent a switch from London English to London Jamaican (1993).

Li Wei's work shows how individuals create personal communities which provide them with meaningful frameworks for solving problems in their daily lives. One of the ways in which they do this is by building social networks, within which characteristic uses of CS develop. The structural contrast between English and Chinese does not provide an adequate explanation of the switching patterns, since these vary according to the group/network that people belong to (1998a; 2000). Li Wei also points to the need for a greater appreciation of variation between individuals in a group, confirming the idiolectal aspect of CS which has so far been neglected (2002).

Woolard (1999) described what she called "bivalent" elements, i.e. elements which could belong to either or both varieties. She claimed these should not be viewed as a category to be identified, put in a box and subsequently ignored. They are likely to be among the most revealing elements in CS speech since they embody the underlying techniques used by bilinguals to combine their languages. Tracy (2000) considered, from a psycholinguist's point of view, that the coactivation of dual systems represented by CS was nothing unusual in itself, and that an aspect of bilingual ability was being able to suspend the requirements of monolingual grammars. Both Romaine (1995) and Winford (2003), who remark that neither insertional nor alternational models of CS can cope with some of the characteristic phenomena which arise in CS (such as operator–verb constructions and bare forms), lend support to the idea that bilinguals have meta-skills of this nature.

Boeschoten (1998) shows how the use of CS encourages a preference for structures which show a high degree of congruence between the varieties and emphasizes that, as a result of CS, new norms can develop at all linguistic levels even within small (e.g. immigrant) communities. Sebba (1998) identifies various processes through which bilingual speakers "construct equivalence" between structures in the two varieties so as to permit CS – such equivalence is not assumed to be a "given" within the languages themselves.

Important insights along these lines also arise in monographs describing particular plurilingual settings. To give just two examples, Agnihotri (1987) and McCormick (2002) both describe linguistic practices lying in a "grey area" not identifiable with any given language.

The above are just a sample from the research which challenges the notion of CS as a series of black and white changes from one variety to another. By contrast, other researchers aim instead, through their descriptions of CS, to reinforce belief in the structural integrity of linguistic systems. These include those who promote the idea of universally valid constraints on where CS can occur – even though, so far, no-one has succeeded in finding any; those who assume the existence of a "Matrix Language"; and psycholinguists who claim to be describing "code-switching" although their evidence all relates to subjects placed in situations of categorical alternation between two standard languages.

A third category of researchers could be said to hold an intermediate position. They are more concerned than the first group not to topple the linguistic edifice – the idea that linguistic production can be explained on the basis of a reasonably consistent set of grammatical principles (leaving aside the question of how these translate into surface rules). Yet they acknowledge a degree of variation between speakers and within practices which defies both constraint (alternational) and matrix-based (insertional) explanations, and requires that sociolinguistic factors be taken seriously. Among these one can count Muysken (2000), Treffers-Daller (1998), Nortier (1990) and Backus (2003). Halmari (1997) provides an example of such a compromise. When she found violations of the principles of UG, as instantiated by the Government constraint, which was compatible with most of her data, and substantial interspeaker variation, she suggested that such violations could be explained on pragmatic/sociolinguistic grounds. Alternatively, she proposed that they could be explained by a deterioration in the speakers' Finnish-speaking skills (1997:216–217). She referred to the accompanying evidence of repair in their speech, such as hesitation, pausing, backtracking, etc. as "physical symptoms of something gone awry" (p. 215).

To some extent at least, these different approaches can be correlated with the different types of data on which these conclusions are based. Muysken (2000) showed that grammatical models of CS could be related to characteristics of the corpora which had inspired them (see section 5.3.4.4). But the authors mentioned above are all aware of variations in CS patterns going well beyond their own personal data-sets. So their convictions must also be influenced by their linguistic background and training. In the same way, the ideas in this book show indebtedness to the model provided by Le Page and Tabouret-Keller (both their 1985 book and more generally to its authors). There may also be a question of temperament at play – psychologists have pointed out the differences between those who like to work towards a single "right answer" and those who prefer problems where there are many possible "right answers" (Hudson, 1966).

8.3   The story so far

Regardless of our sympathies with different linguistic traditions, we should be able to agree on what we now know, with reasonable certainty, about CS, and what remains to be investigated. As a contribution to future research, a short summary of the previous chapters, followed by an attempt to integrate the findings detailed there, may be useful.

(1) It is by no means easy to define CS clearly at a linguistic level – one person's "code-switching" is another person's borrowing, or community

bilingual choices (Chapter 2). Methodological matters to do with selection, transcription and analysis of the linguistic material all play a significant role. For example, Moyer (1998) pointed out that our view of which language is dominant will vary depending on whether we are considering a sentence, a conversation or a whole data-set. CS can arise as a result of a variety of bilingual configurations in the community, including both situations of rapid shift and of relative bilingual stability. Although it can be symptomatic of declining competence in a variety down through the generations, its creative use (for example in rap music) can also reinforce the vitality, and therefore extend the life, of varieties which would otherwise be threatened.

At a linguistic level, CS can include a variety of phenomena. Confusingly, whereas in some cases it appears to be closely tied up with linguistic convergence between varieties (e.g. borrowing at all linguistic levels), in other cases it can be a way to preserve linguistic distinctiveness, while simultaneously allowing the resources of several varieties to be used. There are clear differences between, say, pidginization or convergence and CS, but there are also many grey areas where similar phenomena are found, and CS is often an aspect of these other processes. CS helps us to articulate linguistic aspects of contact situations with the social background, which Thomason and Kaufman (1988) showed to play such an important role in language change.

(2) CS is found in a wide variety of situations (Chapters 3 and 4). It can develop into different forms within a community. Some of it may reflect an imbalance in the competence of different generations, but other instances embody different patterns of identification with the home country, the host country and the community itself (Chapter 3). CS can be studied – and can be relevant – both at a macrolinguistic and a microlinguistic level. At the macrolinguistic level, it is closely related to questions of diglossia and interwoven with the differential values of the different varieties in the linguistic market-place (Heller, 1998a; 1992; Bourdieu, 1997). Both Markedness Theory, the idea that certain varieties carry a particular significance when used in certain contexts, and Network Theory, which seeks to explain behavioural choices with reference to the relationships and bonds which people enter into, are helpful in explaining certain instances of CS. Gumperz's (1982) distinction between situational CS, which arises when the setting, topic or the participants change, and conversational CS, where all those factors are unchanged, is still useful, though the two often co-exist within the same groups and even within the same conversations. Comparisons between communities provide the best opportunity for assessing the relative significance of the different contributing factors.

In Chapter 4, the role of CS in structuring conversation was discussed. This goes beyond the use of connotations and the association of different varieties with different spheres of life, as for example when one variety is associated with the in-group and the home, and the other with the world of officialdom outside. Even where such connotations *are* relevant, speakers may use the contrast between the varieties in their repertoire as a discourse-structuring device in itself. CS marks various conversational moves, such as asides and quotations – the fact that the latter are not always in the language which the original speaker used is particularly instructive. Using a different language to that of one's interlocutor may be a sign of rebellion or at least disagreement. Such "verbal action" may be doubly marked, for example by pausing as well as switching languages, or by other linguistic or paralinguistic means also available to monolinguals. CS also has functions within Speech and Language Accommodation. It allows various "cocktails" to be produced which may constitute a compromise between the interlocutors' differing linguistic competences, preferences and desires to converge to, or diverge from, one another.

Despite the many uses of CS for the bilingual speaker, studies of attitudes towards it generally show it to be a stigmatized form of speech. This is, however, less true among the younger generations, and a positive fashion for CS has even be identified in some groups (Rampton, 1995; Gardner-Chloros, McEntee-Atalianis and Finnis, 2005). Finally, although CS is a non-standard form of speech, it fails to show the traditional gender pattern with respect to non-standardness, i.e. it is not systematically more frequent in men's speech than in women's. Gender differences in the use of CS depend on the functions of CS in the particular community, as well as on the many factors which affect the use of the contributing varieties. Although we can identify "communities of practice" and sub-groups within communities with respect to the use of CS, these are rarely simply definable along gender lines.

(3) At a grammatical level, there is evidence of an identifiable relationship between the grammatical patterns found within CS discourse and the characteristics of the two contributing languages. It is also clear that CS patterns vary according to a number of factors in the non-linguistic environment. There is no evidence that CS between any particular pair of languages is impossible (contrary to the proposals in Sankoff and Mainville, 1986), or that either linguistic or sociolinguistic parameters constitute any sort of absolute constraint on what bilinguals can do. Within given language combinations and given sets of sociolinguistic circumstances, a variety of patterns can be found, sometimes right down to the level of idiolectal variation.

Both *insertional* and *alternational* models of the grammar of CS seek to describe data in terms of the interaction of two discrete systems of linguistic rules. The notion of *constraints* and the notion of *base* or *Matrix Language* imply that these systems are equated with an "external" notion of what a language is, e.g. a variety which, if it does not have a name such as Japanese, Russian or Swahili, is at least identifiable and reasonably consistent. It implies that a whole bundle of features, grammatical, lexical, phonological, etc. are stored and employed as an integrated unit.

The alternative view, which is espoused here, is that individuals construct their own systems from the input and the models to which they are exposed. These systems overlap, but do not necessarily coincide, with officially designated "languages" or even with varieties used by others in their community. The notion of idiolect has so far rarely been applied specifically to bilinguals, yet it is just as relevant as it is to monolinguals. The number of combinations across different linguistic levels which poly-idiolectal competence permits is potentially huge, though it is held in check by the same urges to identify with particular groups which encourage focusing in monolingual speakers, and perhaps by some universal processing constraints (both productive and receptive) relating to the rate of switching between relatively stable sub-systems. To describe CS as if it were made up of the combination of two systems outside the individual is to fail to take account of its highly variable and personal nature. In particular the notion of *base* or *Matrix* Language – even a composite one – has been put in question. Although in some cases individuals may be simply grafting elements from one language onto the underlying structures of another, the combinations which they create are their own and cannot necessarily be predicted by studying the potential interaction of two externally defined systems.

(4) Psycholinguistic research on bilinguals often relies on a restricted definition of bilinguality (Chapter 6). The subjects of experiments are often "elite bilinguals", i.e. students whose mother tongue is a standard language and who have learned another standard language in an academic setting. Moreover, the experiments used often encourage an awareness of the need to separate languages. Psycholinguistic models of language production were originally based on monolinguals, and those which seek to account for bilingual production often represent adaptations of the original ones. The question of CS itself is quite rarely addressed directly in this literature, although several topics studied by psycholinguists interested in bilingualism are relevant. These include bilingual aphasia, where the linguistic recovery patterns of patients having suffered a tumour or lesion help

to reveal how their different languages are stored and separated, and the localization of different languages in the brain, including the issue of whether both languages are *lateralized* in the same way or whether the right hemisphere comes more into play in bilinguals. Explanations of language separation based on the localization of languages in the brain have thus far proved unsatisfactory; and no specific switching *mechanism* has been identified, though there may be a locus where switching behaviour is controlled in the brain (Meuter, 2005). The models available describe the mechanisms of production at a level where the complex and changing nature of CS cannot easily be accommodated.

In the absence of clear anatomical explanations for bilingual ability, psycholinguists such as Green (1986/2000) turned to more abstract "models" of bilingual functioning. Relying on the notions of *activation* of a given language and its opposite, *inhibition*, Green convincingly suggests that CS arises when neither language is inhibited or suppressed and so words can "reach threshold" on the basis of their availability to the speaker, their appropriateness, etc., regardless of which language they are in. He considers that grammatical constraints play a role in production, but the effect of sociolinguistic factors is outside his remit.

De Bot (1992/2000) adapted Levelt's (1989) model of speech production to cover bilingual production and, in particular, codeswitching. He argued that macro-planning, which takes place in the "conceptualizer", is not language-specific, but that as the "preverbal message" advances through the various production stages, the relevant language-specific "formulator" is activated for different parts of the utterance. The relatively abstract nature of such a model is implicitly recognised by De Bot, who says that there is no obvious way to put the proposals through an empirical test.

Grosjean (2000) suggested that bilinguals function within a more or less monolingual or bilingual "mode", depending on the context, interlocutor, etc. By artificially manipulating the context, he was able to show that the amount of CS produced by subjects did indeed vary accordingly. However, this does not tell us how these subjects would behave in real situations where the relevant factors were both more varied and beyond anyone's control. Grosjean also attempted to measure the "base-language effect", or carry-over from one language – supposedly dominant – to the other. Placing bilinguals in mixed-language conditions could not be said to have a clear effect overall – in some cases it seemed to increase the difficulty of their task, in others to make it easier. The lack of clear results indicates that the base language concept needs further refinement, especially since it fails to account for some of the experimental evidence

(Dijkstra and van Hell, 2003) – though it could potentially be combined with the sociolinguistic notions of accommodation and audience design. All in all, the psycholinguistic evidence (including the evidence from the newer brain scanning techniques) casts only limited light on natural CS. It is suggested that in future, psycholinguists might think of ways of making use of the abundant naturally collected data on CS rather than relying purely on experimentation.

(5i) Research on children's CS and that of adult language learners has been, on the whole, contingent on a range of other relevant, but slightly tangential concerns. As regards bilingual children, there has been ongoing controversy as to whether they have a single linguistic system at the outset which gradually differentiates and becomes dual, or whether they can keep the environmental varieties distinct from the outset, at the receptive and the productive level. Many experiments have shown that, from the earliest age, children are able to distinguish, at the receptive level, between linguistic features associated with different languages. The productive level is harder to study. While it is unsurprising to find that young children's CS does not serve the full range of conversational and other functions which are found in sophisticated adult CS, there is evidence that even very young children can address speakers of different languages in their immediate environment in the appropriate "language". But the "mixtures" which they produce require careful interpretation. For example, Deuchar and Quay (2000) point out that it is pointless to describe the child as mixing elements from two systems before they have acquired the full set of translation equivalents – in fact the whole notion of separate language systems may be quite inappropriate (De Houwer 2009). CS as such in children develops in an individual way, depending partly on parental and other input and the tolerance for it in the environment.

(5ii) Relatively little work has been done so far on CS by second language learners. It has been shown, however, that learners use words from their L1 to fill lexical gaps in their target language when this does not render them incomprehensible to their interlocutors. In practice it is not always easy to draw a line between such CS born of necessity and more discourse-oriented CS, which develops as soon as a greater level of fluency is achieved.

We should retain from all these findings regarding CS that the variety and multifariousness which has been described is its outstanding feature, not an incidental aspect. It is precisely because it can be used to fulfil so many different conversational needs that it is so widely exploited. Therefore, in trying to analyse the ways in which people alternate between varieties, we are gaining some understanding of a whole range of characteristics of speaking itself. From the psycholinguistic work we have looked at, it becomes clearer why studying utterances isolated from their context is likely to lead to an incomplete view of their characteristics and meaning. It will never be possible to place CS under a microscope and so it will never satisfy the requirements for the object of a scientific study in the narrow sense. Equally, it will never be possible to capture it through a grammatical or a pragmatic approach alone. Dewaele (2005) has argued cogently that the same is true of L2 acquisition, and has similarly called for a "triangulated" approach combining qualitative and quantitative methods. Psycholinguistic research could usefully be extended to take in questions where CS is studied in its own right as opposed to being studied as a by-product of bilinguality, e.g. through such questions as the relationship between CS and literacy (Gardner-Chloros, 2004), or between spoken and sign language CS (Berent, 2004).

8.4   Code-switching as an instance of a more wide-ranging "switching" skill

As we saw in the Introduction, the term "code-switching" originated in the world of electronics. Applying the term to human behaviour, we should bear in mind that many of the things we do with language are instances of more general cognitive abilities. We can make people laugh, express anger, joy and other emotions both through linguistic and non-linguistic means. The ability to switch between different sets of behaviour also has a more general application. For example, Benoit, Randolph, Dualap and Johnson (2003) applied the term "code-switching" to alternation between different sets of values. Young drug dealers in New York are described as alternating between the culture they were brought up in – their parents were drug users and had often been in trouble with the law – and a code of conduct which involved strictly rejecting the use of all drugs for themselves, except marijuana, in the interests of educational and professional success. Von Raffler Engel (1976) looked at CS in relation to switching between gesture-systems, but found no one-to-one correspondence between language used and gestures.

   Plurilingual CS is a particular instance of a more general ability; in particular, what people do through CS is also done by a variety of means in monolingual discourse. Stroud's term "double-voicedness" to describe CS was discussed in section 4.2.4. Some authors have gone as far as to argue that all speech is made up, in a broad sense, of quotation. Cheshire (2004) showed how much of spoken language is made up of unanalysed "chunks", as did Backus in a bilingual context (2003). Bakhtin (1986:87) writes that it is the concurrence of word and context which creates "the spark of expression". "These words of others carry with them their own expression, their own evaluative tone, which we assimilate, re-work and re-accentuate" (p. 89). Tannen shows how much of what we say is in fact "constructed dialogue". She claims that the term "reported speech" is misleading as (1) most of what is referred to thus has never in fact been spoken, and (2) even if someone's else's discourse is reported word for word, those words exist "primarily, if not only, as an element of the reporting context" (1989:101). Mayes points out that "Many direct quotes are not based on previous utterances at all" (1990:331), and Coulmas (1986), also writing on reported speech, concludes that there is no clear-cut distinction between direct and indirect reported speech. He identifies a hybrid form which he calls "quasi-direct speech". In CS, even the use of a single word in another variety can introduce the sense of quotation, of momentarily invoking another persona or identity. We saw this clearly in the case of the young Greek Cypriot women whose use of Greek "legitimized" humorous or direct interventions, which were not part of their normal English-speaking self-presentation.

Along with the use of language, it is human beings' flexibility/adaptability which distinguishes them from other members of the animal world. They can live in very hot climates and very cold ones. They can be meat-eaters or vegetarians. The ability of many of them to alternate between different linguistic varieties at the drop of a hat, and to make use of several simultaneously when it suits them to do so, is part of the adaptability which has ensured their survival.

8.5   Some directions for future research

Several priorities for future research have emerged during the course of this discussion:

- From the point of view of grammar and sociolinguistics, the priority is to set up comparative studies which will allow us to gauge the effect of the different types of variable which have been found to affect CS, both linguistic and sociolinguistic. As Deuchar wrote with respect to child language, rather than asking whether the child has one system or two, one should look at the *processes of differentiation* – how and when they occur. A methodological framework for analysing data comparatively has been proposed in the LIPPS coding manual (2000), which is outlined in the Appendix.
- At a psycholinguistic level, there is a need to study CS as it occurs in more realistic contexts than the rarified atmosphere of the laboratory. Sociolinguists are aware of the Observer's Paradox, but psycholinguists seem less aware of the paradox involved in studying unregulated, spontaneous and creative social

behaviour in a controlled setting with limited parameters. In so doing one may be studying something *relevant* to CS, but not CS itself. One suggestion as to how this might be done is to carry out analyses of authentic recordings of spontaneous CS, for example by measuring pausing, VOT and other aspects of speech production in CS and monolingual conditions. Any loss in scientific precision would be more than made up for by increased relevance.

- Phonological studies of CS are under-represented in the CS literature (Botero, Bullock, Davis and Toribio, 2004). Yet borrowing and CS can occur at all linguistic levels. Clyne (2003) describes phonological aspects of "transversion" as being intimately bound up with lexical, structural, etc. ones. The fact that "accent" in many people's speech carries over from one language to another is an integrating factor, lending unity or "equivalence" to elements from what could otherwise be termed separate languages. The role of idiolectal "accent" is rarely mentioned as a factor when discussing whether or not items are phonologically integrated, yet this in turn has been used as a criterion to distinguish borrowing and CS – another example of the individual being left out of the account. Woolard's (1999) injunction to pay more attention to "bridge" or "bivalent" elements, rather than simply cataloguing them and then leaving them outside the main analytical framework, is an important one.

8.6   The past and future of code-switching

In a chapter of his book *Imagined Communities*, about the origins of national consciousness and nationalism, Anderson (1991) remarks that the development of printing gradually led to a marginalization of those dialects which did not correspond with the printed varieties. In the nineteenth century, this led to a complex relationship between national "print-languages", national consciousness and nation-states (1991:48–49). The idea of "One Language One Nation" arose at that time, along with notions of linguistic purity and exclusiveness. This ideal contrasts with the laissez faire in earlier historical periods, when several varieties could be used in the same stretch of discourse – even in written records and literature destined for serious purposes. CS was common in writing as well as speech in various historical periods; it is found in the Acts of the Apostles, in medieval literature and political texts, in the writings of Luther and the songs of the troubadours.

At the beginning of the twenty-first century, we are still deeply affected, at institutional and other levels, and particularly in the educational sphere, by ideas originating in the nineteenth, and in particular by the notion of monolingualism. Furthermore, economic transformations in the twentieth century, notably the rise to dominance on the world scene of a basically monolingual (or assimilative) country, the United States, combined to encourage a negative mindset towards hybridity, "half-castes" and cultural fusion. Fishman's work (1968) on the correlation between multilingualism and poor economic status represents a confirmation, for linguists, of this unpalatable truth.

However there are signs that the tide is changing. There has been an increasing empowerment of certain multicultural and multilingual groups, e.g. Hispanics in the USA. There are fashions for what is known as "fusion" in many areas of life. Westerners have adopted elements of traditional dress and decoration from far-flung countries instead of dismissing them, as they would once, as folklore; Italians make their own homegrown version of sushi and rappers rap in multiple codes. "Crossing", as described by Rampton (1995), is the linguistic embodiment of this trend, which looks set to continue. We should not, however, trivialize CS by considering it merely a matter of fashion. Perhaps particularly in young people, it embodies a range of conflicts, ideologies, oppositions to authority and positionings with regard to gender and ethnicity which should give us more wide-ranging food for thought (Pujolar, 2001).

Even the educational establishment has not remained unmoved. In Chapter 3 we saw that schools in many countries of the world tolerate, and sometimes even encourage CS. Amherst College, in Massachusetts, has a professor of *Espanglish*, the Spanish–English mixed code of Hispanic immigrants, who has written a dictionary of Espanglish of six thousand words. Students are set translations. The first two sentences of a translation of Don Quixote into Espanglish run as follows:

Example 1
In a **placete** *de la Mancha* of which *nombre non quiero* **remembrearme**, *vivía*, not so long ago, *uno de eses* gentlemen who always *tienen una lanza* in the rack, *í una* buckler *antigua*, a skinny *caballo y un* greyhound *para el* chase. A *cazuela* with *más* beef than *mutón, carne* **choppeada** *para la* dinner, *un* omlet *pa los sábados*, lentil *pa los viernes, y algún* pigeon *como* delicacy *especial pa los domingos, consumían très cuarers de su* income.

 '*In a* **place** *in La Mancha the name of which I do not wish* **to remember***, there lived, not so long ago, one of those gentlemen who always have a spear in the rack, and an antique buckler, a skinny horse and a greyhound for the chase. A casserole with more beef than mutton, meat* **chopped** *up for dinner, an omelette for Saturdays, lentils on Fridays and some pigeon as a special delicacy for Sundays, consumed three quarters of his income*' (my translation). The words in bold are English words adapted to Spanish morphology. (Mangruel, 2004:178)

As defined here, Espanglish is a code-switched variety incorporating English loans adapted to Spanish morphology.

Naturally, the growing strength of Hispanics in the USA is unusual, and only a small proportion of linguistic minorities is gaining ground to that extent. But it does seem likely that CS will become increasingly acceptable in many contexts. Many would argue that developments like that exemplified above, the acceptance and institutionalization of CS, are retrograde and even harmful. We should be clear that such judgements are political, aesthetic and cultural – not linguistic. The weight of evidence is that bilingualism is beneficial rather than harmful at the individual level, and that learning to code-switch is no different from learning any of the other "rules of use" of any other variety. Nor can any easy conclusions be drawn as to whether such developments will precipitate the impoverishment of particular languages. They are more likely to be a symptom than a cause, and in many cases the alternative may be total death. CS may even keep some languages alive, perhaps for long enough so that the next generation is intrigued enough to revive and teach them. Zentella writes of her Spanish–English code-switching subjects on *el bloque* in New York: "They were competent in Spanish, but insisting that English has not influenced the community's Spanish is akin to maintaining that the experience of being born and/or raised in the US has had no impact on second generation Puerto Ricans, *as if the young passively inherited instead of actively created their culture*" [my italics] (1997:271).

Code-switching can be likened to a linguistic barometer, and we should continue to investigate the pressures and fluctuations which it records and embodies, which arise in different contexts all over the world. It is a goldmine for linguists, because it highlights so many important questions about the relationship of languages to language. A full understanding of CS requires us to take account of all aspects of linguistic enquiry, including grammar, sociolinguistics, psycholinguistics and more. Its study should contribute to putting interdisciplinarity on the linguists' map at last, and in the process, let us hope, to a small and much-needed methodological revolution.

Appendix
Coding and analysing multilingual data: the LIDES Project[1]

A.1   Introduction

Over the last few decades, data on bilingual and multilingual talk has been collected through projects, large and small, in many countries and involving many different languages and dialects. It has become a source of frustration for many who work in this area that there is no basic standard for transcribing data of this kind, nor any central resource to enable researchers to share their data with each other. Meanwhile, researchers in some fields have begun to take advantage of new technological developments to enable data to be shared. Researchers in language acquisition, for example, have both standard ways of transcribing and coding data, and international databases to which they can contribute and on which they can draw for comparative data.

The purpose of the LIPPS initiative is to provide support and propose a system for transcribing and coding bilingual data that takes into account research questions specifically related to multilingual communities and individuals. Researchers in the field may benefit from the LIPPS initiative in two ways:

(1) By following the step-by-step guidelines to carry out the transcription and coding which make it possible to use already existing computer-based analytical tools.

(2) The existence of a set of basic standards for transcribing and coding bilingual data should encourage research on language interaction from an

---

[1] LIDES = *Language Interaction Data Exchange System*. LIPPS = *Language Interaction in Plurilingual and Plurilectal Speakers*. This Appendix is an abridged version of the chapter "Coding and Analysing Multilingual data: the LIDES Project" by Penelope Gardner-Chloros, Melissa Moyer and Mark Sebba (2007), which was itself derived from a longer description of the system in a special issue of the *International Journal of Bilingualism*, 4, 2, June 2000. However, this did not include various developments to the system which have been made since then. The authors of that volume were the LIPPS Group and included (in alphabetical order) Ruthanna Barnett, Eva Codó, Eva Eppler, Montse Forcadell, Penelope Gardner-Chloros, Roeland van Hout, Melissa Moyer, Maria Carme Torras, Maria Teresa Turell, Mark Sebba, Marianne Starren and Sietse Wensing. Permission from Jill Lake of Palgrave publishers to abridge the chapter here is gratefully acknowledged, as is permission from the editor of *IJB*, Li Wei, to reprint the glossary from the special issue of *IJB*.

interdisciplinary perspective. Thus, a special effort is made to cater for the needs of researchers working in very different disciplines within the field. The proposals made here are equally intended to help those who are interested in quantitative and qualitative research. Useful guidelines are provided so that solutions may be found for problems that may arise in the processes of transcription and coding. In addition, some user-friendly computational tools are discussed which provide support in exploring and analysing language interaction data.

We have adopted the term *language interaction* rather than the more commonly used terms "code-switching" and "language contact" in order to include all manifestations of language contact, whether or not the varieties under study are held to belong to two discrete systems.

A.2   The goals of LIDES

In spite of the high level of interest in language contact, no coordinated system has yet been developed for researchers to make use of one another's data. The data is only available, if at all, in widely disparate forms, and coding and transcription practices vary significantly. It is even rarer that anyone except the original researcher gains access to the original data (usually audio recordings).

The LIDES project is modelled on the CHILDES enterprise established by Brian MacWhinney. It consists of a set of standards and computational tools for analysing language acquisition data, and a collection of data-sets contributed by diverse researchers (MacWhinney, 1995; MacWhinney & Snow, 1990), and shows the advantages of being able to access a database in research fields where data on spoken, spontaneous language is essential. Each researcher works independently on his/her own data-set, but a common set of overall goals is kept in mind.

The reasons why it is desirable to achieve a coordinated approach go beyond the advantages of simple data sharing. What researchers typically want to know about patterns of language interaction is to what extent these patterns are dictated by the particular language combination and/or the context and circumstances which are relevant in their study, and to what extent they are universal or at least common to similar language sets or similar combinations of sociolinguistic circumstances. For example, one major strand of research on code-switching focuses on grammatical constraints on where a switch can occur within the sentence. Time after time, constraints proposed on the basis of one data-set (and often put forward as potentially universal) have been disproved when new data-sets have emerged (Muysken, 2000). Furthermore it is not possible, without making comparisons of the kind we propose, to establish the relative role of linguistic features as such and sociolinguistic, psycholinguistic and/or contextual factors in the language interaction patterns that are observed. Both of these are fundamental problems with approaches based on a single data-set.

In this section, we discuss the rationale for basing LIDES on the CHILDES system and the CHAT coding protocol. Section 3 is devoted to the basic steps for preparing language interaction data for analysis. Special attention is dedicated to the steps involved in the preparation and organization of the data and to the minimal requirements for transcription and tagging. Section 4 runs through the essential elements of a CHAT data file. Section 5 takes the reader through the transcription process step by step. In Section 6 we mention some ways of coding data for specific research interests. Section 7 describes some of the programs that automate data analysis. Finally, Section 8 contains practical information about contact addresses and obtaining the LIDES programs and datasets.

A.2.1   Why use CHILDES?

CHILDES has been successfully used for fifteen years and is equipped with an institutional support base,[2] specific detailed guidelines for transcribing and coding data (the CHILDES coding manual) within an existing format (CHAT) and a set of software, the CLAN programs, which researchers can use to carry out a large range of automated analyses of the data in the database. The programs for analysis of bilingual data can be obtained by contacting Brian MacWhinney.

On the other hand, CHILDES was not designed for adult, multilingual, speech data. It was set up to provide a database of conversations involving mainly monolingual adult–child interactions. Therefore, the CHAT format was not initially the most appropriate one for the type of data researchers in this area were collecting, and the CLAN programs were not designed to answer the type of questions that researchers working in the field of multilingualism would want to ask. However, the CHAT coding scheme and the CLAN tools in CHILDES were adopted precisely because they are open to further elaborations and additions. In fact, some adaptations, necessary to cope with multilingual data, can already be found in CHILDES and others have been developed by the LIPPS group. Even greater possibilities are offered by the development of a framework based on XML for CHILDES and TALKBANK (MacWhinney, 2007). The CHILDES database contains data from many different languages, and the way transcription problems have been solved for these different languages can be of help when transcribing language interaction data.

---

[2] The CHILDES system is maintained by Brian MacWhinney at Carnegie Mellon University, Pittsburgh, USA and the University of Antwerp, Belgium; email: macw@cmu.edu; internet: <http://childes.psy.cmu.edu>.

More important in this respect, though, are the bilingual data already available. A separate chapter of the CHILDES manual (MacWhinney, 1995) is devoted to data available on bilingual acquisition, which is becoming an important field of research. In the CHILDES system different types of information are coded on a series of "dependent tiers" linked to the "main tier" which carries the transcription. A separate dependent tier is proposed to code information on the language of the utterance on the main tier (see below), the language of the preceding speaker and the dominant language of the speaker (see MacWhinney, 1995: 63; De Houwer, 1990, for a good example of this type of system). There is also a separate subsection on code-switching in the CHILDES manual (MacWhinney, 1995: subsection 9.4) in which some useful coding options are proposed.

Another point in favour of the CHILDES system is the formal way in which the system is set up. One development is an interface between CHAT and XML formats. XML is a markup metalanguage of the World Wide Web with powerful tools for analysing data on the web. It is a standard way of marking up texts (both spoken and written), which is independent of any word processor or computer system. One of the present tasks of the LIPPS group is to offer a universal set of codes for language interaction data in XML. The new system will also offer user-friendly interfaces which will allow researchers to encode numerous different scripts and have a choice of how to present the transcribed and encoded data in print and on the computer screen. A program for converting CHAT files to XML can be downloaded from the CHILDES web page. This prospect matches the view of MacWhinney (1995:437): "As our work in database development proceeds, we want to think in terms of a more general database of all the varieties of spoken human language."

Another recent innovation to CHILDES that has also been incorporated by LIDES is the adoption of the Unicode encoding system. CLAN programs presently recognize this new system. Unicode is important for research on multilingual data because it allows language interaction researchers to use their computer keyboard to represent a character from any language including Arabic, Chinese or IPA that have different script types. A further advantage to using Unicode is that it permits researchers working in the field of discourse and conversation analysis to use the CA-CLAN programs developed to analyse utterances, turns, overlaps as well as other conversation phenomena used in the transcription conventions put forth by Atkinson and Heritage (1984).

A far-reaching expansion that has also been developed in recent years is the linking of original digitized audio and digitized video–audio recordings to transcribed files. Linking can also be done at the same time one carries out the transcription. New avenues for spoken language analysis and possibilities for checking and revising transcriptions can easily be carried out. More detailed information on linking is provided with the CHILDES programs. A computer program called PRAAT, with which it is possible to analyse, synthesize and manipulate speech, has been developed by Paul Boersma and David Weenik. This program is especially useful for splicing short audio files into a single large file. The CHILDES project is currently developing further CLAN support for this program.

A.2.2   Why use CHAT?

The existing CHAT transcribing and coding conventions are very flexible, making it possible for the researcher to reflect many kinds of phenomena that occur in natural speech data. We give some examples of existing CHAT transcription and coding options below. Furthermore, you can add any type of code you want, as long as you use it consistently and define it properly, which is what you would have to do anyway, be it in a more traditional format or the CHAT format.

You can see from examples one and two that transcribing in CHAT is not that different from the traditional way of transcribing, and that the basic transcribing and coding conventions are not that difficult.

(1) A "traditional" transcription (Moyer, 1992)
The participants in this conversation are Yvonne and Natalie, both housewives. The languages used are Spanish and English. English is given in plain typeface, Spanish in italic typeface.

YVO: Excuse me could we have two coffees and some scones please?

NAT: Yvonne *para mí no vayas a pedir* scones *de esos*
          Yvonne for me not go to ask scones of these
          que ahora me estoy tratando de controlar un poquito antes de Pascua
          that now me are trying to control a little-bit before of Christmas
          "Yvonne, don't order these scones for me because now I am
          trying not to put on weight before Christmas."

YVO: *sí* Christmas *ya está* round the corner *mujer*
          yes Christmas already is round the corner woman
          "Mind you, Christmas is already round the corner."

In this traditional transcription we can see:
● there is a short introduction giving details of speakers and languages used;
● each speaker's turn is put in a separate paragraph following an indication of who is speaking;
● normal and italic fonts are used to indicate the language of each word/phrase;
● the literal gloss for each word is placed on the line beneath; and
● there is a free translation of the conversation provided.
  In the following example the same data is given in CHAT format:

(2) a CHAT transcription (Moyer, 1992)

N.B. Changes are constantly being made to the system. At the time of writing, a new presentation has just been adopted for the bilingual data in Talkbank, whereby only one of the languages is overtly coded. The appropriacy of this for code-switched data in which the dominant language is constantly shifting, or indeterminate, is under discussion in the LIPPS Group.

```
@Begin
@Participants:   YVO housewife1, NAT housewife2
@Languages:      English (1), Spanish (2)
```

*YVO: excuse@1 me@1 could@1 we@1 have@1 two@1 coffees@1 and@1
        some@1 scones@1 please@1?

*NAT: Yvonne@1 para@2 mí@2 no@ vayas@2 a@2 pedir@2 scones@1
        de@2 esos@2 que@2 ahora@2 me@2 estoy@2 tratando@2 de@2
        controlar@2 un@2 poquito@2 antes@2 de@2 Pascua@2.

%glo: Yvonne for me not go to ask scones of these that now me are trying to
        control a little-bit before of Christmas.

%tra: Yvonne, don't order these scones for me because now I am trying not to
        put on weight before Christmas.

*YVO: sí@2 Christmas@1 ya@2 está@2 round@1 the@1 corner@1mujer@2.

%glo: yes Christmas already is round the corner woman

%tra: mind you, Christmas is already round the corner

```
@End
```

Transcription (2) uses the coding system recommended by LIDES, and as you can see, the data looks somewhat different. However, the same information is present:

- there is a set of "headers" giving details of speakers and languages used (@Participants, @Languages);
- each utterance is put on a separate line (the "main tier") following an indication of who is speaking;
- language tags (@1 and @2) are used to indicate the language of each word/phrase;
- there is a separate line or "dependent tier" following the main tier for the literal gloss, the %glo tier; and
- there is a dependent tier for a free translation of each utterance, the %tra tier.

    From the above examples, it is clear that the CHAT transcription is actually very similar to the traditional one. Some extra work is inevitable, for example, tagging each word with a language code, though word processors or "editors" are currently being developed to help do this task automatically.[3] However, once you have done this work, the benefits are substantial. To name a few, you can add as many dependent tiers as you need. You can create additional headers

---

[3] For example, you can use a macro to build up a lexicon of words to be coded by language.

which provide information such as the socio-economic status or age of the participants, the name of the transcriber and the date of the recording. You can create additional dependent tiers on which you can provide a gloss (%glo), a translation (%tra), or code grammatical, pragmatic or other information. You can devise codes to label problematic words which do not clearly belong to one language or another, such as *in* when dealing with English, Dutch and a range of Germanic languages. Once your transcription is complete, you can print it, selecting just those tiers you want to appear on the page, from among all those you have included in your transcription.

An enormous benefit, obvious to every researcher who has done frequency counts using pen and paper on a relatively large set of data, is the fact that you can use the CLAN programs to search your data for patterns or provide certain statistics. This is because all LIDES transcriptions can use either Unicode characters and a common set of transcription and coding guidelines. The latter also makes it easier to exchange and compare data with other researchers, inside or outside the LIDES database.

Finally, although the LIDES system recommends the use of a transcription system based on CHAT to transcribe data, existing data in different formats is not excluded from LIDES. Such data can still be used productively by other language interaction researchers if included in the database. One of our aims is to develop adequate tools to convert these data sets into the transcription format utilized by the CLAN automatic analysis programs.

A.3   The basics of transcription

Transcription is not pre-theoretical, but is a form of interpretation of the data, as discussed by Ochs (1979). For any set of spoken data, there is no single "correct" method of transcription, but a variety of theory-dependent options. The problems, both theoretical and practical, which are inherent in the transcription of monolingual discourse, are multiplied when two or more language varieties are present. Where plurilingual data is involved, most researchers want a transcription system which provides a way of differentiating between the languages (or language varieties) found in the data. One solution may be to use the conventional writing system of the languages concerned, if there is one. If the researcher chooses a "language-neutral" alphabet such as the International Phonetic Alphabet (IPA), they will need some method of indicating which stretches of transcription are in which language. There will still be problems, however. For some utterances it will not be easy to assign them to either language: for example, fillers like *er* and *um* and word fragments of various sorts which are not necessarily language-specific.

What to do in these cases involves theoretical decisions being made by the individual researcher. It is not simply a matter of choosing a method. Assigning a word, by means of some transcription convention, to either L1 or L2, may have consequences later for the outcome of the investigation. The researcher must have a principled basis on which to make these decisions, and may have to take into account aspects of syntax, phonology and pragmatics. Where more than two languages or related varieties are involved, things are even more complicated.

If researchers are to be able to establish large usable machine-readable corpora of code language interaction data, then a *standard format* is needed for transcribing and coding the data that fulfils at least the following requirements:

- It should allow information contained in transcriptions (for example, language labels) to be stored in a format which is not word-processor dependent. This involves using a system-independent format such as Unicode along with a standard markup language such as XML. This enables data transcribed by one researcher to be compared easily with data from another, as well as promoting a more universal software to carry out rapid searches and analyses of data.
- It should encourage researchers to include in their transcriptions, for their own benefit as well as for that of other researchers, information which is relevant to the analysis of language interaction data. This is desirable as a way of helping researchers new to the transcription of language interaction data to include features which will be useful for their own analysis at the time, and to others who may want to use their data later for another purpose.
- It should be flexible enough to accommodate the present and (as far as is predictable) future needs of researchers in terms of what needs to be represented in a transcription. Researchers should feel in control of the transcription process rather than being forced into a straitjacket. The guidelines have no value if researchers do not find them suitable for their own needs.

CHAT allows researchers to include all the information needed for the analysis of their data. Since language interaction data differ according to the language pairs involved, researchers also may ask very different questions regarding their data and thus will want to codify different types of information in order to carry out an analysis. CHAT has the advantage of being adaptable to individual research needs. We give some examples below of language interaction data transcribed and coded in CHAT, including some of the proposed LIDES adaptations.

In the following example a tier (% add) has been inserted to indicate the addressee. From this it is possible to see that the speaker changes the language according to the person he/she speaks to:[4]

---

[4] This example contains a number of non-ASCII characters (ñ, é, à). It is good practice to replace these with sets of Unicode symbols, making clear the mapping between these and the orthographic characters they represent.

(3) **Catalan/Castilian: Torras (1998)**

@Begin
@Participants: OWN owner stall_owner, CU1 customer_one customer, CU2
                 customer_two customer
@Languages: Catalan (1), Castilian (2), unintelligible (0)

*OWN: digui'm@1.
%tra: can I help?
*CU2:   esa@2 xxx@0 de@2 la@2 paletilla@2 de@2 aquella@2 la@2
        màs@2 chiquita@2 que@2 tengas@2.
%tra: that xxx of the shoulder over there the smallest you have.
*OWN: ahora@2 mismo@2 te@2 lo@2 miro@2.
%tra: I'll have a look for you right now.
%add: CU2
*OWN: qué@2 me@2 da@2 señora@2?
%tra: what are you giving me madam?
%add: CU1
*OWN: dos@1 centes@1 setanta@1 dos@1.
%tra: two hundred and seventy two.
%add: CU1
*OWN: molt@1 bé@1 gràcies@1 xxx@0 reina@1.
%tra: very good thanks xxx love.
%add: CU1
@End

A more complicated example is the following. In this example, codes for *speech acts* are added on the speech act coding line (%spa:) to show how a positive answer was given in the same language as the question was (B answers her mother's question twice, first in English, second in Cantonese, both times using the same language as her mother used), whereas a negative answer is given in another language than that in which the question was put (when A asks C in English whether he wants some spring rolls, the answer is 'I don't want' in Cantonese):

(4) **Cantonese / English: Milroy and Li Wei (1995:149), adapted to CHAT conventions:**

@Begin
@Participants: MOT mother, DAU daughter, SON son
@Languages: Cantonese (1), English (2), undetermined (0)
@Age of B: 9
@Age of C: 11
*MOT: who@2 want@2 some@2?

```
%add:       DAU, SON
*MOT:       <crispy@2 a@1 > [>].
%spa:       $i:yq
*DAU:       <yes@2> [<].
%spa:       $i:aa
*MOT:       yiu@1 me@1?
%spa:       $i:yq
%glo:       want some?
*DAU:       hai@1 a@1.
%spa:       $i:aa
%glo:       yes.
%add:       SON
%spa:       $i:yq $i:cl
*SON:       ngaw@1 m@1 yiu@1.
%spa:       $i:an
%glo:       I don't want.
*MOT:       m@1 yiu@1 a@1?
%spa:       $i:yq
%glo:       Don't want?
*MOT:       crispy@2 la@1
*SON:       mm@0
%gpx:       shaking head
%spa:       $i:an
@End
```

Key to symbols

<...>	scope of phenomenon
[>]	overlap follows
[<]	overlap precedes
%glo:	gloss; LIDES recommendation
%spa:	speech act coding tier
%act:	activity
%gpx:	gestural and proxemic activity coding tier

Speech act codes (MacWhinney, 1995:101–103):

$i:	illocutionary force code follows
yq	yes/no question
aa	answer in the affirmative to yes/no question
an	answer in the negative to yes/no question
cl	call attention to hearer by name or by substitute exclamations.

Other interesting features in this example are the way overlaps are transcribed (using <>, [<], [>]), and how various non-linguistic activities are rendered in CHAT (%act:, %gpx:).

A.4   The essentials of a CHAT data file

Once the researcher has completed transcribing and encoding the data, his/her data set will contain three or four files: the CHAT *data file*, the *depfile*, a *read me* file and possibly a *depadd file*.

A.4.1   The CHAT data file

A CHAT data file typically consists of three components: *file headers*, *main tiers*, and *dependent tiers*. For all of these components the following general requirements obtain (MacWhinney, 1995:8):
(a) every character in the file must be in the basic Unicode character set;
(b) every line must end with a carriage return (= enter).
   Other requirements obtain only for a specific component, and will be given where the component in question is discussed.

A.4.1.1   File headers   File headers are lines of text which provide information about the file and they appear at the beginning of any transcript. They all begin with the sign @ followed by the name of the header. Some headers require nothing more; these are the "bare" headers (for example, @Begin). Other headers must be followed by information regarding the participants, the situation and so on. This information is called the entry. Headers that require an entry are followed by a colon and a tab after which the entry is given. For example:

(5) @Participants: SHO shopkeeper, RES researcher, SEA seamstress
[Besides the distinction between bare headers and headers requiring an entry, CHAT makes a distinction between obligatory and optional file headers. *Obligatory file headers* (MacWhinney, 1995:13–14) are required for the CLAN automatic analysis programs to work. These are the following:]

@Begin   The first line of any transcription file. This is a bare header.
@Participants: This header states who the participants of the conversation are. It requires an entry which may consist of two or three parts: a speaker ID (obligatory) which is composed of one to three characters (letters in capitals and/or numbers), for example, MAR, or S09; the speakers' names (optional); and the speakers' role (obligatory), for example, Interviewer. A role which is not included in the depfile must be added in the depadd file (see Glossary and Section A.4.3). The latter two

	parts may consist of multiple elements, but they must be connected with an underscore, for example, Penelope_ Gardner_Chloros or sister_in_law
@End	The last line of any transcription file. @End is a bare header.

There are two types of optional headers: constant and changeable. *Constant headers* contain useful information that does not change throughout the file.[5] They must be placed at the beginning of the file before any of the actual spoken utterances. Because of the interaction of different languages in LIDES files, the following two file headers are recommended to be used consistently:

@Languages:	This header indicates what the main language or languages of the transcription files are.
@Language of XXX:	This header can be used to indicate the primary language(s) of a given participant, if there is any.[6]

Changeable headers contain information that can change within the file, for example, showing how the conversation can be divided into several stages each associated with a different activity. These headers appear, then, at the point within the file where the information changes. Besides these headers, new headers may be created to fulfil specific needs as long as they are added to the *depadd* file located in the same directory as your data files.

A.4.1.2 The main tier   The actual utterances are transcribed on what is known as the *main* (speaker) *tier*. This is the line that reproduces in written form what each one of the participants says. Requirements for the main speaker tiers are as follows (MacWhinney, 1995:8–9):

- Main lines indicate what was actually said and begin with an asterisk*. Each main line should contain one and only one utterance[7] (but can extend over several computer lines).
- After the asterisk * on the main line comes a code (the speaker ID, see the Participant header) for the participant who was the speaker of the utterance being coded. After the speaker ID comes a colon and then a tab; for example, *MAR: I'm tired.

---

[5] Some headers may be considered either constant or changeable, for example, date, location, situations and so on.

[6] There are different views as to whether it is possible, always or even sometimes, to decide which is the primary language, and if so how this should be done. The reader is referred to discussions surrounding the "Matrix Language" as defined by Myers-Scotton (see for example, Gardner-Chloros and Edwards 2004: 117–120).

[7] The notion of utterance may vary from one researcher to another depending on specific research interests. LIDES purposely does not provide a single definition of utterance. Some criteria for distinguishing an utterance can be a single word, an intonation unit, a long pause and so on. Because of the possibility of sound linking to the transcripts the issue of where to put boundaries on an utterance may become somewhat less arbitrary, but we do not expect it will solve the segmentation problem completely.

- Continuations of main tiers over several computer lines begin with a tab.
- Utterances must end with an utterance terminator, that is full stop (.), exclamation mark (!) or question mark (?).

A.4.1.3 Dependent tiers   Dependent tiers are lines typed below the main tier containing codes, comments and descriptions of interest to the researcher. It is important to have all this information on separate lines because the use of complex codes on the main tier would make it unreadable. Though all dependent tiers are optional, we recommend having at least a *gloss* tier (%glo) and a tier in which a *free translation* of the utterance is given (%tra). Requirements for dependent tiers are the following (MacWhinney, 1995:8–9):

- Dependent tiers typically include codes and/or commentary on what is said and begin with the symbol %.
- After the % symbol comes a three-letter code in lower case letters for the type of dependent tier, a colon, and then a tab; for example, %glo: I am tired.
- Continuations of dependent tiers over several computer lines begin with a tab.

Dependent tiers do not require ending punctuation. The researcher's interests determine the number and nature of dependent tiers in a transcript. In the examples above, we saw the following dependent tiers:

%add: specifies the addressee(s) of the utterance.

%glo: gives a word-by-word or even morpheme-by-morpheme gloss of the utterance.

%spa: this tier is for coding speech acts. Any sort of speech act can be used to describe the utterance on the main tier. A proposal for codes to be used on this line can be found in MacWhinney 1995: Chapter 13.

%tra: tier where a free translation (in English or some other widely known language) of the utterance is given. We propose to use %tra instead of the %eng tier in the CHILDES manual, %tra being more language neutral.

Other useful tiers include:

%gpx: gestural and proxemic activity coding line, for example:

%gpx: shaking head

%mor: coding of morphological information for the words on the main tier. Codes used on the %mor tier can be found in MacWhinney 1995: Chapter 14.

In order to make it possible to exchange all the data coming from different researchers using different computer systems (Mac, PC, UNIX and so on) and printers, we strongly recommend that data be transcribed in Unicode format, by using a true Unicode editor. In the CHILDES manual (1995), you can find the description of a Unicode editor specially created for the transcription (and coding) of CHAT files: the so-called CED editor. This allows the user to link a full digitized audio recording of the interaction directly to the script. Furthermore, the CED editor supports the display of non-ASCII Roman-based characters such as á, ñ or ç, as well as non-Roman characters from Cyrillic, Japanese, Chinese and other languages. In all cases, CED displays these fonts correctly, but the underlying file is saved in Unicode characters. The CED editor is included in the CLAN package, which can be downloaded from the internet site (see Section A.8.3).

A.4.2   *The readme file*

All data sets should be accompanied by a *readme* document (00readme.doc), which is aimed at providing general information about them. Information which is specific about a particular file in this set should not be included here but in the header of the specific file. Below is a checklist of information that the readme file should specify:
- acknowledgements;
- researcher (name, institution, history of the project, etc.);
- characteristics of the community to which informants belong;
- informants (age, sex, class);
- sampling techniques;
- number of hours recorded;
- number of hours transcribed;
- special transcription and coding practices;
- interaction type;
- working definitions used to identify given language interaction phenomena;
- warnings about limitations on the use of the data (that is, what has been transcribed and coded and what has not);
- list of files;
- instruments used for data collection;
- changes made in the 00depaddfile.

This list is not meant to be exhaustive. Contributors may add whatever they consider useful for future users. It may be helpful to comment on a particular aspect of a language or variety so that readers unfamiliar with it have a better understanding of the data. For example, a researcher dealing with Swahili data may want to provide an outline of the null prefix system of this language because he/she thinks this is relevant to the study of his/her corpus.

A.4.3   *depfile and depadd files*

These are files which list the codes used in the data file and are needed by the CLAN programs for them to be able to check your transcription and carry out analyses. Depfile.cut is a standard file that is delivered with the CLAN programs. The 00depadd file is a file you make yourself. For more information on the contents of the CHILDES depfile, and their meaning, see MacWhinney (1995:62–164).

For analysing language interaction data, it is possible to extend the CHAT depfile by creating an additional file, a "depadd file" called "00depadd.cut", which you should place into the same directory as the files being checked. All new codes must be included in this corpus-specific LIDES depadd file: new header codes, new dependent tiers and the possible strings that may occur on those tiers. The LIDES depadd file (changed only if necessary) should also remain with the data files as a form of documentation of the particular divergence from the standard CHAT depfile and the standard LIDES depadd file. In the *readme* file, you should describe any changes you made in the standard LIDES depadd file.

A.5   A step-by-step outline of the minimal transcription process

This section gives a step-by-step outline of the basic information a data file should contain in order to enable researchers to carry out the analysis of switches between languages. You can find the details of various steps in the sections referred to at these steps. There are eight steps (data from Moyer, 1992):

● Step 1. Transcription

Y: Excuse me, could we have two coffees and some scones, please?
N: Yvonne, Para mí no vayas a pedir scones de esos que ahora me estoy
     tratando de controlar un poquito antes de Pascua.
Y: Sí Christmas ya está round the corner, mujer.

● Step 2. Obligatory File Format

@Begin
@Participants: YVO housewife1, NAT housewife2

*YVO: Excuse me, could we have two coffees and some scones, please?
*NAT: Yvonne, para mí no vayas a pedir scones de esos que ahora me estoy
         tratando de controlar un poquito antes de Pascua.
*YVO: Sí Christmas ya está round the corner, mujer.
*YVO: Yo ya no hago dieta hasta por lo menos enero, febrero y eso con suerte
@End

● Step 3. Run the CHECK programs
  In order to check the overall structure, the CHILDES system provides special CHECK programs which runs twice over the files. In the first pass, CHECK searches for errors by comparing the files to the prescribed format. If errors

are found (for example, no @Begin and @End markers at the beginning and end of files) the offending line is printed, followed by a description of the problem. On the second pass it checks if the used symbols and codes are declared in either "depfile.cut", or in "00depadd.cut".

Run the CHECK programs now to check if the basic format is correct.

- Step 4. Language tagging

@Begin
@Participants: YVO housewife1, NAT housewife2
@Languages: English (1), Spanish (2)

*YVO: Excuse@1 me@1 could@1 we@1 have@1 two@1 coffees@1 and
        @1 some@1 scones@1 please@1?
*NAT: Yvonne@1 para@2 mí@2 no@2 vayas@2 a@2 pedir@2 scones@1
        de@2 esos@2 que@2 ahora@2 me@2 estoy@2 tratando@2 de@2
        controlar@2 un@2 poquito@2 antes@2 de@2 Pascua@2.
*YVO: Sí@2 Christmas@1 y@2 está@2 round@1 the@1 corner@1
        mujer@2.
*YVO: Yo@2 ya@2 no@2 hago@2 dieta@2 hasta@2 por@2 lo@2
        menos@2 enero@2 febrero@2 y@2 eso@2 con@2 suerte@2.
@End

- Step 5. Insert the %glo and the %tra dependent tiers

@Begin
@Participants: YVO housewife1, NAT housewife2
@Languages: English (1), Spanish (2)

*YVO: excuse@1 me@1 could@1 we@1 have@1 two@1 coffees@1
        and@1 some@1 scones@1 please@1?
*NAT: Yvonne@1 para@2 mí@2 no@2 vayas@2 a@2 pedir@2 scones@1
        de@2 esos@2 que@2 ahora@2 me@2 estoy@2 tratando@2 de@2
        controlar@2 un@2 poquito@2 antes@2 de@2 Pascua@2.
%glo: Yvonne for me not go to ask scones of these that now me are trying to
        control a little-bit before of Christmas
%tra: Yvonne, don't order these scones for me because now I am trying not
        to put on weight before Christmas
*YVO: sí@2 Christmas@1 ya@2 está@2 round@1 the@1 corner@1
        mujer@2.
%glo: yes Christmas already is round the corner woman
%tra: mind you, Christmas is already round the corner
*YVO: yo@2 ya@2 no@2 hago@2 dieta@2 hasta@2 por@2 lo@2 menos@2
        enero@2 o@2 febrero@2 y@2 eso@2 con@2 suerte@2.

%glo: I already not make diet until for the less January or February and that
          with luck
%tra: I am not going on a diet until at least January or February and even
          then with a bit of luck
@End

- Step 6. Run the CHECK Programs again.
  Once the transcription and tagging is completed, the next stage is to check
  again the overall structure of the files, and the symbols and codes used in the
  main and dependent tiers as declared in the CHILDES depfile and the LIDES
  depadd file.
- Step 7. Make changes in the depadd file.
  Eventually, it may be necessary to add symbols to the LIDES depadd file for
  your own special data-set of files. In this case the depadd file must be
  changed using an ASCII editor and then you can run the CHECK programs
  once again.
- Step 8. Create a *readme* document to accompany the transcription file.

A.6.   Using CHAT for language interaction data

The transcription and coding requirements of language interaction data differ
according to whether the language pairs under study are genetically related,
typologically similar or whether the mixed pairs are isolating, agglutinative,
inflective or incorporative languages. This section presents some suggestions as
to how to deal with specific transcription issues faced by researchers studying
language interaction.

A.6.1   Expanding the language tags

The language tag can be expanded, by using more numbers. You could, for
example, use the language tag not only to signal the languages used, but also to
assign a tag to mixed words. You could also use the language tag to code single-
word calques, borrowings and so on. Aside from expanding the language tag for
language interaction types, and/or mixed words, you can also expand the language tag to a two (or more) digit system, where, for example, the first digit
denotes the language of the word, and the second digit word class, or vice versa.

A.6.2   Coding at morpheme level

For some research in language interaction data it is necessary to look not only at
words, but also at smaller morpheme units. There are two ways in CHAT to
dissect words into morphemes. The first is to code morphemes on the main tier.

Alternatively, you can use the %mor tier for more extensive morphological coding. For more information on coding on the %mor tier we refer the reader to MacWhinney (1995).

A.6.3   Coding turns

Turns are not basic units in CHAT, and without adaptations (like separately coding for turns) the CLAN programs cannot make analyses pertaining to turns. There are, however, various options for representing turns in a transcription file, for example, by representing turns as a main tier.

A.7   Automated data analysis

The CLAN tools provide many possibilities for automatic analysis, although they are not a substitute for the researcher's efforts in analysing and interpreting the data. They are especially helpful when large amounts of language data have to be processed. Following we present a few of the most obvious applications of the CLAN tools to multilingual data. There is extensive information on this in the CHILDES manual. Three of the most useful analytical tools are FREQ, COMBO and FLO.

A.7.1   FREQ frequency counts

The FREQ program makes frequency counts, which are useful for many different purposes. FREQ has properties which make this tool effective in handling multilingual files for other types of counts as well, but we will start with straightforward word counts.

A.7.2   COMBO pattern matching

COMBO is a CLAN tool which provides the user with ways of composing complex search strings. The strings or patterns defined are used to find matches of letters, words or groups of words in the data files specified. With the COMBO tool the language tags on the main tier can be used, for example, for capturing switches within utterances.

A.7.3   FLO output for other programs

There are sometimes advantages in looking at the data in their "pure" form, particularly when a large amount of information and coding is added through the dependent tiers. By applying the FLO tool all coding and other information on the dependent tiers is left out. This output file can be made the input file for the statistical package SPSS.

Table A.1. *Switched phrasal categories by language in oral and written texts, in percentages*

Switched phrasal categories:	Texts:		
	Oral texts	Written texts	Percentage of Total
Sentence:			36
English	32	8.7	16
Spanish	21	19	20
Noun phrase:			35
English	18	11	13
Spanish	9.9	27	22
Verb phrase:			4.0
English	–	2.4	1.7
Spanish	–	3.4	2.4
Adjective phrase:			6.1
English	7.7	0.5	2.7
Spanish	–	4.8	3.4
Prepositional phrase:			16
English	10	6.8	7.7
Spanish	2.2	11	8.4
Adverbial phrase:			3.0
English	–	1.0	0.7
Spanish	–	3.4	2.4
Total	100%	100%	100%
(Absolute number):	(91)	(206)	(297)

Source: Moyer (2000)

A comparison of the Gibraltar oral corpus with the Gibraltar written corpus (Moyer, 2000) illustrates how FREQ and COMBO, two of the most useful CLAN programs, yield quantified information on the major differences between oral and written code-switching styles.[8] Prior classification and codification of the data following the LIDES recommendations according to major structural and conversational units (that is, word, phrasal constituents, utterances and turns) by language is needed for running the CLAN programs.

---

[8] The Gibraltar oral corpus is made up of sixteen recordings from eight different contexts in Gibraltar. A total of 6,765 words have been transcribed. The written corpus is made up of sixteen written constructions of oral speech used by two speakers. The size of this corpus is 5,049 words.

Table A.2. *Turns by language in oral and written texts, in percentages of turns*

Language of turns:	Oral texts	Written texts	Percentage of Total
English	21	13	18
English-Spanish	8.3	56	23
Spanish	40	4.8	29
Spanish-English	15	22	17
Equal number[*]	0.5	3.6	1.5
Unknown	15	0.4	10
Total	100%	100%	100%
(Absolute number)	(531)	(250)	(781)

[*] "Equal number" refers to turns that have the same number of words in both English and Spanish.
Source: Moyer (2000)

The FREQ program can tell us about: (a) the language that dominates in each corpus; (b) the number and type of syntactic constituent in each language; (c) the number of utterances by speaker (and language); and (d) the number of turns by speaker (and language). Table A.1 shows the output of a FREQ program showing in percentages the language of switched phrases in the oral and the written corpora.

The COMBO program allows for more complex searches such as the combination of language switches within an utterance or turn of a given speaker. Table A.2 illustrates the results in percentages for the combination of language and turn in oral and written code-switching styles.

Corpus-based studies and quantitative information about code-switching patterns provide important empirical support for formal and interpretative claims. Furthermore, the LIDES project offers data sets from a variety of language pairs as well as the necessary tools for carrying out the analysis.

A.8   Practical information

A.8.1   *Datasets currently available in the LIDES database*

The LIDES database contains sample corpora with the following language combinations: Dutch–Turkish, Dutch–French, Alsatian German–French, Catalan–Spanish, Catalan–Spanish–English, English–Spanish, English–German, English–Punjabi, English–Greek Cypriot Dialect, English–Jamaican Creole.

These corpora vary widely in their size and their degree of development. For more up to date and detailed information, please consult the LIPPS website indicated below.

A.8.2   Research contacts

Researchers interested in participating in the LIPPS group and the LIDES database are advised to contact the steering committee. A list of email addresses is provided below.

> Penelope Gardner-Chloros: p.gardner-chloros@bbk.ac.uk
> Roeland van Hout: roeland.vanhout@kub.nl
> Melissa G. Moyer: melissa.moyer@uab.es
> Mark Sebba: m.sebba@lancaster.ac.uk
> More information can be found on the LIPPS homepage on the World Wide Web. The URL for the LIPPS homepage is: www.ling.lancs. ac.uk/staff/mark/lipps/lipps.htm

A.8.3   How to obtain the CLAN programs

You can download the CLAN tools together with a CHAT depfile from the CHILDES Internet pages: http://childes.psy.cmu.edu

A.9   Glossary of terms

(This glossary is adapted from the LIDES Coding Manual, *International Journal of Bilingualism* (2000) 4(2):131–270)

alternation   A concept introduced by Muysken (1995) to characterize code-switching from a psycholinguistic perspective within a sentence or between sentences. It involves the use of stretches of language from different systems which do not necessarily make up a syntactic constituent. Alternation contrasts with *insertion* and *congruent lexicalization*. In *insertion*, the grammar of a single language predominates, incorporating a word or larger syntactic constituent from another language. In *congruent lexicalization*, the syntax of the two languages in the sentence is the same, thus allowing the lexical items from either language to be used.

borrowing   In language interaction research lexical borrowing typically refers to the linguistic forms being taken over by one language or language variety from another. A crucial methodological issue is the distinction between borrowing and code-switching. Difficulties involved in this distinction include estimating, and deciding the relevance of, the degree of morphological, phonological and syntactic integration of the borrowed item.

changeable headers   A CHAT data file may contain information which changes within the file (for example, a change in the activity being carried out by the participants). Changeable headers may be placed within the body of the transcription file and they are preceded by the symbol @ (for example, @Activities: PAT tries to get CHI to put on her coat). Changeable headers should be distinguished from constant and obligatory file headers which are preceded by the same symbol @. Obligatory file headers are essential if a researcher wants to use the CLAN automatic analysis programs (see 4.1.1).

CHAT   The transcription system created by MacWhinney (1991, 1995) for the CHILDES project. This transcription scheme has been adapted and elaborated further by LIDES to deal more precisely with the theoretical and practical problems raised by language interaction data.

CLAN programs   The analytical tools developed by MacWhinney (1991, 1995) for the CHILDES project, which can be used by researchers to carry out automated analyses of their data files.

code-switching   This is a general term which refers to the alternate use of two or more languages or language varieties by bilinguals for communicative purposes. Code-switching embraces various types of bilingual behavior such as switching within and between utterances, turns and sentences. A theoretically neutral and less confusing term adopted for code-switching is *language interaction*.

COMBO program   The main use of this CLAN program is to search transcription files for specific expressions, words or strings. The COMBO search command is constructed with a set of Boolean operators (AND, OR, NOT, etc.) which are used to define the parameters of the search string, which may be some aspect of the coding (that is language tags) or words or utterances from the text data file. Searches may be carried out on main or dependent tiers. An example of a COMBO search command to find all lexical items which cannot be assigned to a given language and which are coded on the main tier as @0 is: *combo +s *\ @0^*^* gibraltar.doc* OJO

constant headers   A CHAT data file may contain non-obligatory constant headers at the beginning of the file in order to specify information relevant to the conversation text transcribed.

Such information may include gender or age of participants, level of education, social economic status, information about coders and transcribers, and languages spoken by each of the participants. As with the case of *obligatory* and *changeable* headers, constant headers are preceded by the symbol @ such as: *@Gender of participants: CHI female, PAT male*

depadd file The file where a researcher using CHAT incorporates the list of their newly created symbols or coding schemes used in their transcription. Adding symbols to the depadd file is easy and it gives flexibility to the researcher to develop his/her own system of coding. The depadd file, like the depfile, is used by the CHECK program to verify the syntax and structure of data files.

dependent tier The CHAT transcription scheme makes use of dependent tiers to include information or additional coding (that is syntactic, morphological, speech acts, general comments and so on) which refer to the preceding main tier. It is possible to have any number of dependent tiers at the same time which make reference to a single main tier. All dependent tiers should be preceded by the symbol % followed by a three letter code among those already defined in the depfile or a newly created code which should be added to the depadd file. An example of a dependent tier code for a gloss of the main tier utterance is: *%glo*.

file headers One of the main components of a CHAT transcript are the file headers. These are lines of text preceded by the symbol @ (for example, @Participants). Headers can be obligatory (such as @Begin, or @End) or optional (such as @Participants, or @Coder). Different types of headers can be inserted in different places in a CHAT transcription.

gloss A morpheme by morpheme translation of one or more utterances on the main tier. This gloss is strongly recommended for researchers contributing their data to the database and it should be incorporated on a specific dependent tier (*%glo*).

main tier This is the line in a CHAT transcription which includes a person's speech transcribed in written form. It is preceded by an asterisk, the speaker's initials or other three-letter code (for example, *PAM:). Each turn of the conversation may

	be divided into several entries or the speech may be transcribed in a single entry
meta-character	May also be referred to as a meta-symbol. A meta-character is a symbol used in coding a transcription in CHAT (for example, %, *). Meta-symbols or characters are used for various types of coding in the headers, the main tier and dependent tiers. Any non-letter character is a meta character.
readme file	Provides important background information about the files belonging to a data-set. This information is crucial for other researchers working with this data. The original researcher may include any comment which is important for understanding the particular data set or the particular way it has been transcribed and coded. The readme file is a separate document or file which is included with all data contributed to the LIDES database.
SGML	This acronym stands for *Standard Generalized Mark-up Language*. It is a meta-language which is used as a standard way of marking up a text (both spoken and written), and is independent of any word processor or computer system.
XML (Extensible Markup Language)	This language is a flexible text format derived from SGML (see above). XML is a metalanguage written in SGML which allows a user to design customized markup languages. XML now provides the framework for the CHILDES and TALKBANK databases. See http://www.w3.org/XML/ for more information.

Bibliography

Aaho, T. 1999. Code-switching in the Greek Cypriot community in London. Unpublished MA thesis, University of Helsinki, Dept. of English.

Adams, J. N. 2003. *Bilingualism and the Latin Language*. Cambridge: Cambridge University Press.

Adams, J. N., Janse, M. & Swain, S. (eds) 2002. *Bilingualism in Ancient Society: language contact and the written text*. Oxford: Oxford University Press.

Adone, D. 1994. *The Acquisition of Mauritian Creole*. Amsterdam: John Benjamins.

Agnihotri, R. K. 1987. *Crisis of Identity: The Sikhs in England*. New Delhi: Bahri.

Aikhenvald, A. Y. 2002. *Language Contact in Amazonia*. Oxford: Oxford University Press.

Aitchison, J. 1994. *Words in the Mind*, 2nd ed. Oxford: Blackwell.

2000. *Language Change: Progress or Decay?* 3rd ed. Cambridge: Cambridge University Press.

Aitsiselmi, F. 2003. L'alternance codique sur Beur FM. Talk given at French Linguistics Day, London Metropolitan University, 15 March 2003.

Albert, M. L. & Obler, L. K. 1978. *The Bilingual Brain: neuropsychological and neurolinguistic aspects of bilingualism*. New York: Academic Press.

Alfonzetti, G. 1998. The conversational dimension in code-switching between Italian and dialect in Sicily. In P. Auer 1998b (ed.), 180–214.

Alvarez-Cáccamo, C. 1998. From 'switching code' to 'code-switching': towards a reconceptualization of communicative codes. In P. Auer (ed.) 1998c, 29–50.

Anderson, B. 1991. *Imagined Communities: Reflections on the Origins and Spread of Nationalism*. London and New York: Verso.

Angermeyer, P. S. 2005. Spelling bilingualism: script choice in Russian American classified ads and signage. *Language in Society* 34(4): 493–531.

Ann, J. 2001. Bilingualism and language contact. In C. Lucas (ed.), *The Sociolinguistics of Sign Languages*. Cambridge: Cambridge University Press.

Anthias, F. 1992. *Ethnicity, Class, Gender and Migration*. Aldershot: Avebury.

Appel, R. & Muysken. P. 1987. *Language Contact and Bilingualism*. London: Edward Arnold.

Arnberg, L. N. & Arnberg, P. W. 1992. Language awareness and language separation in the young bilingual child. In R. J. Harris (ed.), *Cognitive Processes in Bilinguals*. Oxford: Elsevier, 475–500.

Aslanov, C. 2000. Interpreting the language-mixing in terms of codeswitching: The case of the Franco-Italian interface in the Middle Ages. *Journal of Pragmatics* 32, 1273–1281.

Atkinson, J. M. & Heritage, J. 1984. *Structures of Social Action: studies in conversation analysis*. Cambridge: Cambridge University Press.

Auer, P. 1984. *Bilingual Conversation*. Amsterdam/Philadelphia: John Benjamins.

1995. The pragmatics of code-switching: a sequential approach. In Milroy & Muysken, 1995, 115–135.

1998a. 'Bilingual Conversation' revisited. In Auer, P. 1998c, 1–25.

1998b (ed.). *Code-switching in Conversation: Language, Interaction and Identity*. London: Routledge.

1999. From codeswitching via language mixing to fused lects: toward a dynamic typology of bilingual speech. *International Journal of Bilingualism*, 3(4), 309–332.

2000. Why should we and how can we determine the 'base language' of a bilingual conversation? *Estudios de Sociolingüística*, 1(1), 129–144.

2005. A postscript: code-switching and social identity. *Journal of Pragmatics* 37, 403–410.

Azuma, S. 1996. Speech production units among bilinguals. *Journal of Psycholinguistic Research* 25(3), 397–416.

1997. Lexical categories and code-switching: a study of Japanese–English code-switching in Japan. *Journal of the Association of Teachers of Japanese*, 31(2), 1–24.

1998. Meaning and form in code-switching. In R. Jacobson, 1998a, 109–125.

Backus, A. 1992. *Patterns of Language Mixing: a study of Turkish–Dutch bilingualism*. Wiesbaden: Harrassowitz.

1996. *Two in One: bilingual speech of Turkish immigrants in the Netherlands*. Tilburg: Tilburg University Press.

1999. The intergenerational codeswitching continuum in an immigrant community. In Extra & Verhoeven, 1999, 261–279.

2003. Units in codeswitching: evidence for multimorphemic elements in the lexicon. *Linguistics* 41(1), 83–132.

2004. Convergence as a mechanism of language change. *Bilingualism, Language and Cognition* 7(2), 179–181.

2005. Codeswitching and language change: one thing leads to another? *International Journal of Bilingualism* 9(3/4), 307–341.

Backus, A. & van Hout, R. 1995. Distribution of code-switches in bilingual conversations. In *Proceedings of the Summer School on Codeswitching and Language Contact*. Leeuwaarden: Fryske Akademy, pp. 16–28.

Badequano-López, P. & Kattan, S. 2007. Growing up in a multilingual community: insights from language socialization. In P. Auer & Li Wei (eds), *Handbook of Multilingualism and Multilingual Communication*. Berlin: Mouton de Gruyter, 69–99.

Bader, Y. & Minnis, D. D. 2000. Morphological and syntactic code-switching in the speech of an Arabic–English bilingual child. *Multilingua* 19(4), 383–403.

Baetens Beardsmore, H. 1986. *Bilingualism: basic principles*, 2nd ed. Clevedon: Multilingual Matters.

Baetens Beardsmore, H. & Anselmi, G. 1991. Code-switching in a heterogeneous, unstable, multilingual speech community. In *Papers for the Symposium on Code-switching in Bilingual Studies: theory, significance and perspectives*, March, 1991. Barcelona: European Science Foundation, 405–436.

Baker, C. & Prys Jones, S. 1998. *Encyclopedia of Bilingualism and Bilingual Education*. Clevedon: Multilingual Matters.

Bakhtin, M. 1986. The problem of speech genres. In C. Emerson & M. Homquist (eds), *Speech Genres and Other Late Essays*. Austin: University of Texas Press, 60–101.

Bakker, P. 1997. *A Language of Our Own: the genesis of Michif, the mixed Cree–French language of the Canadian Metis*. Oxford: Oxford University Press.

Bakker, P. & Mous, M. 1994 (eds). *Mixed Languages: fifteen case studies in language intertwining*. Studies in Language and Language Use, 13. Amsterdam: Institute for Functional Research into Language and Language Use.

Barrett, R. 1998. Markedness and styleswitching in performances by African American Drag Queens. In Myers-Scotton, 1998, 139–167.

Barron-Hauwert, S. 2004. *Language Strategies for Bilingual Families: the one-parent-one-language approach*. Clevedon: Multilingual Matters.

Bauer, E. B., Hall, K. J. & Kruth, K. 2002. The pragmatic role of codeswitching in play contexts. *International Journal of Bilingualism* 6(1), 53–74.

Baugh, A. C. 1951. *A History of the English Language*. London: Routledge.

Belazi, H. M., Ruben, J. R. & Toribio, A. J. 1994. Code-switching and X-bar theory: the functional head constraint. *Linguistic Enquiry* 25, 221–237.

Bell, A. 1984. Language style as audience design. *Language in Society* 13, 145–204.

  1997. Language style as audience design. In N. Coupland & A. Jaworski (eds)1997, *Sociolinguistics: a reader*. New York: St Martin's Press, 240–250.

  2001. Back in style: reworking audience design. In Eckert & Rickford, 2001, 139–169.

Benoit, E., Randolph, D., Dunlap, E. & Johnson, B. 2003. Code-switching and inverse imitation among marijuana-using crack sellers. *British Journal of Criminology* 43, 506–525.

Benson, E. J. 2001. The neglected early history of codeswitching research in the United States. *Language and Communication* 21(1), 23–36.

Bentahila, A. 1983. *Language Attitudes Among Arabic–French Bilinguals in Morocco*. Clevedon: Multilingual Matters.

Bentahila, A. & Davies, E. E. 1983. The syntax of Arabic–French code-switching. *Lingua* 59, 301–330.

  1991. Constraints on code-switching: a look beyond grammar. *Papers for the Symposium on Code-switching in Bilingual Studies: theory, significance and perspectives*. March, 1991. Barcelona: European Science Foundation, 369–405.

  1998. Codeswitching: an unequal partnership? In Jacobson, 1998a, 25–51.

  2002. Language mixing in rai music: localization or globalization? *Language and Communication* 22, 187–207.

Berent, G. P. 2004. Sign language–spoken language bilingualism: code-mixing and mode-mixing by ASL–English bilinguals. In Bhatia & Ritchie 2004, 312–336.

Besnier, N. 2003. Crossing genders, mixing languages: the linguistic construction of transgenderism in Tonga. In J. Holmes & M. Meyerhoff (eds), *The Handbook of Language and Gender*. Oxford: Blackwell, 279–301.

Bhatia, T. K. 1992. Discourse functions and pragmatics of mixing: advertising across cultures. *World Englishes* 11 (2/3), 195–215.

Bhatia, T. K. & Ritchie, W. C. 1996. Bilingual language mixing, Universal Grammar, and second language acquisition. In W. C. Ritchie & T. K. Bhatia (eds), *The Handbook of Second Language Acquisition*. San Diego/London: Academic Press, 627–688.

    2004 (eds). *Handbook of Bilingualism*. Oxford: Blackwell.

Bialystok, E. 1991 (ed.). *Language Processing in Bilingual Children*. Cambridge: Cambridge University Press.

Biber, D. & Finegan, E. 1993 (eds). *Sociolinguistic Perspectives on Register*. New York: Oxford University Press.

Biber, D., Johansson, S., Leech, G., Conrad, S. & Finegan, E. 1999. *Longman Grammar of Spoken and Written English*. Harlow: Longman.

Bickerton, D. 1981. *Roots of Language*. Ann Arbor: Karoma.

Bister-Broosen, H. 2002. Alsace. In J. Treffers-Daller & R. Willemyns (eds), *Language Contact at the Romance–Germanic Language Border*. Clevedon: Multilingual Matters, 98–111.

Blom, J. P. & Gumperz, J. J. 1972. Social meaning in linguistic structures: code-switching in Norway. In Gumperz & Hymes, 1972, 407–434. Reprinted in Li Wei, 2000, 111–136.

Boeschoten, H. 1994. L2 influence on L1 development: the case of Turkish children in Germany. In G. Extra & L. Verhoeven 1994 (eds), *The Cross-Linguistic Study of Bilingual Development*. Amsterdam: North-Holland, 253–264.

    1998. Codeswitching, codemixing, and code alternation: what a difference. In Jacobson, 1998a, 15–24.

Boeschoten, H. E. & Verhoeven, L. T. 1987. Language mixing in children's speech: Dutch language use in Turkish discourse. *Language Learning* 37(2), 191–217.

Bokamba, E. 1988. Code-mixing, language variation and linguistic theory: evidence from Bantu languages. *Lingua* 76, 21–62.

Bolonyai, A. 1998. In-between languages: language shift/maintenance in childhood bilingualism. *International Journal of Bilingualism* 2(1), 21–43.

Bosch, L. & Sebastián-Gallés, N. 2001. Early language differentiation in bilingual infants. In Cenoz & Genesee, 2001, 71–94.

Botero, C., Bullock, B., Davis, K. & Toribio, J. A. 2004. Perseverative phonetic effects in bilingual code-switching. Paper presented at the 34th Linguistic Symposium on Romance Languages, University of Utah, March.

Bourdieu, P. 1997. *Language and Symbolic Power*. Oxford: Polity Press.

Brazil, D. 1995. *A Grammar of Speech*. Oxford: Oxford University Press.

Breitborde, L. B. 1982. Levels of analysis in sociolinguistic explanation: bilingual codeswitching, social relations and domain theory. *International Journal of the Sociology of Language* 39, 4–45.

Broca, P. 1861. Remarques sur le siège de la faculté du langage articulé, suivies d'une observation d'aphémie (perte de la parole). *Bulletin de la Société Anatomique* 6, 330–357.

Broeder, P. & Extra, G. 1995. *Minderheldsgroepen en Minderheidstalen*. Den Haag: Günther Narr Verlag.

Broersma, M. & de Bot, K. 2006. Triggered codeswitching: a corpus-based evaluation of the original triggering hypothesis and a new alternative. *Bilingualism, Language and Cognition* 9(1), 1–13.

Brown, P. 1994. Gender, politeness, and confrontation in Tenejapa. In D. Tannen (ed.), *Gender and Conversational Interaction*. New York: Oxford University Press, 144–161.

Brown, P. & Levinson, S. 1987. *Politeness: some universals in language use*. Cambridge/New York: Cambridge University Press.

Brown, R. & Gilman, A. 1960. The pronouns of power and solidarity. In P. Giglioli (ed.), *Language and Social Context: Selected Readings*, Harmondsworth: Penguin, 252–282.

Brulard, I. & Carr, P. 2003. French–English bilingual acquisition of phonology: one production system or two? *International Journal of Bilingualism* 7(2), 177–202.

Bullock, B. & Toribio, A. J. 2004. Introduction: convergence as an emergent property in bilingual speech. *Bilingualism, Language and Cognition* 7(2), 91–93.

Burt, S. M. 2002. Maxim confluence. *Journal of Pragmatics* 34, 993–1001.

Bynon, T. 1977. *Historical Linguistics*. Cambridge: Cambridge University Press.

Cameron, D. 1992. *Feminism and Linguistic Theory*. London: Macmillan/New York: St Martin's.

1995. *Verbal Hygiene*. London/New York: Routledge.

1997. Demythologizing sociolinguistics. In Coupland & Jaworski, 1997, 55–68.

Camilleri, A. 1996. Language values and identities: code-switching in secondary classrooms in Malta. *Linguistics and Education* 8(1), 85–103.

Canut, C. & Caubet, D. 2001. *Comment les langues se mélangent: codeswitching en francophonie*. Paris: L'Harmattan.

Cashman, H. 2005. Identities at play: language preference and group membership in bilingual talk in interaction. *Journal of Pragmatics* 37, 301–315.

Caubet, D. 2001. Comment apprehender le code-switching? In Canut & Caubet, 2001, 21–33.

Cenoz, J. & Genesee, F. 2001 (eds). *Trends in Bilingual Acquisition*. Amsterdam: Benjamins.

Cenoz, J., Hufeisen, B. & Jessner, U. 2001 (eds). *Cross-linguistic Influences in Trilingualism and Third Language Acquisition*. Clevedon: Multilingual Matters.

Cenoz, J. & Jessner, U. 2000 (eds). *English in Europe: The Acquisition of a Third Language*. Clevedon: Multilingual Matters.

Chambers, J. K. 2003. *Sociolinguistic Theory*, 2nd ed. Oxford: Blackwell.

Chambers, J. K., & Trudgill, P. 1999. *Dialectology*, 2nd ed. Cambridge: Cambridge University Press.

Chan, B. 1999. Aspects of the syntax, production and pragmatics of code-switching with special reference to Cantonese–English. Unpublished PhD thesis, Department of Linguistics, University College London.

Chana, U. & Romaine, S. 1984. Evaluative reactions to Panjabi–English code-switching. *Journal of Multilingual and Multicultural Development* 5, 447–453.

Charles, R. 1995. Code-switching in the Punjabi–English community in Britain: a mixed code. Unpublished MA dissertation, Department of Applied Linguistics, Birkbeck College, London.

Cheng, Karen Kow Yip 2003. Code-switching for a purpose: focus on pre-school Malaysian children. *Multilingua* 22(1), 59–77.

Cheshire, J. 2004. Old and new cultures in contact: approaches to the study of syntactic variation and change. Paper given at Sociolinguistics Symposium 15, University of Newcastle, 1–4 April, 2004.

Cheshire, J. & Gardner-Chloros, P. 1997. Communicating gender in two languages. In H. Kothoff & R. Wodak (eds), *Communicating Gender in Context*. Amsterdam: Benjamins, 249–283.

1998. Code-switching and the sociolinguistic gender pattern. *International Journal of the Sociology of Language* 129, 5–34.

Cheshire, J. & Moser, L. 1994. English as a cultural symbol: the case of advertisements in French-speaking Switzerland. *Journal of Multilingual and Multicultural Development* 15, 451–469.

Chomsky, N. 1965. *Aspects of the Theory of Syntax*. Cambridge, MA: MIT Press.

1981. *Lectures on Government and Binding*. Dordrecht: Foris.

1986. *Knowledge of Language: its nature, origin and use*. New York: Praeger.

1995. *The Minimalist Program*. Cambridge, MA: MIT Press.

Christodoulou-Pipis, I. 1991. *Greek Outside Greece III. Research Findings: language use by Greek-Cypriots in Britain*. Nicosia: Diaspora Books, Greek Language Research Group.

Cicero, Marcus Tullius 1999. *Letters to Atticus*. Edited and translated by D. R. Shackleton Bailey. Cambridge, MA/London: Harvard University Press.

Clark, H. H. & Clark, E. V. 1977. *Psychology and Language: an introduction to psycholinguistics*. New York: Harcourt Brace Jovanovich.

Cleghorn, A. 1992. Primary level science in Kenya: constructing meaning through English and indigenous languages. *International Journal of Qualitative Studies in Education* 5(4), 311–323.

Clyne, M. 1967. *Transference and Triggering: observations on the language assimilation of postwar German-speaking migrants in Australia*. The Hague: Martinus Nijhoff.

1972. *Perspectives on Language Contact: a study of German in Australia*. Melbourne: Hawthorn.

1987. Constraints on code switching: how universal are they? *Linguistics* 25, 739–764.

1991a. Structural and typological aspects of community languages. In Clyne, 1991b, 157–212.

1991b. *Community Languages: the Australian experience*. Cambridge: Cambridge University Press.

2003. *Dynamics of Language Contact: English and immigrant languages*. Cambridge: Cambridge University Press.

Coates J. 1993. *Women, Men and Language*. London: Longman.

1996. *Women's Talk: conversations between women friends*. Oxford: Blackwell.

Colina, S. & MacSwan, J. 2005. Language Mixing at the Interface: How Does Phonology Affect the Syntax of Codeswitching? Paper presented at the 5th International Symposium on Bilingualism (ISB5), Barcelona, Spain.

Comeau, L., Genesee, F. & Lapaquette, L. 2003. The modelling hypothesis and child bilingual codemixing. *International Journal of Bilingualism* 7(2), 113–126.

Coulmas, F. 1986. Reported speech: some general issues. In F. Coulmas (ed.), *Direct and Indirect Speech*. Berlin: Mouton de Gruyter, 59–77.

1997 (ed.). *The Handbook of Sociolinguistics*. Oxford: Blackwell.

Coupland, N. 1985. Hark hark the lark: social motivations for phonological style-shifting. *Language and Communication* 5, 153–171.

2001. Language, situation and the relational self: Theorizing dialect-style in sociolinguistics. In P. Eckert & J. R. Rickford (eds), 185–211.

2007. Style: *Language variation and identity*. Cambridge: Cambridge University Press.

Coupland, N. & Jaworski, A. 1997. *Sociolinguistics: a reader and coursebook*. Basingstoke/London: Macmillan.

Cowie, F. 1999. *What's within? Nativism Reconsidered*. Oxford: Oxford University Press.

Cromdal, J. 2001. Overlap in bilingual play: some implications of code-switching for overlap resolution. *Research on Language and Social Interaction* 34(4), 421–451.

Crowley, T. 1990. *Beach-la-Mar to Bislama: emergence of a national language in Vanuatu*. Oxford: Oxford University Press.

Crystal, D. 2000. *Language Death*. Cambridge: Cambridge University Press.

Cummins, J. 2003. Bilingual education: basic principles. In Dewaele, Housen & Li Wei, 2003, 56–67.

Dabène, L. & Moore, D. 1995. Bilingual speech of migrant people. In Milroy & Muysken, 1995, 17–44.

Davis, J. 1989. Distinguishing language contact phenomena in ASL interpretation. In C. Lucas (ed.), *The Sociolinguistics of the Deaf Community*. New York: Academic Press/Harcourt Brace Jovanovich, 85–103.

De Bose, C. 1992. Codeswitching: black English and Standard English in the African–American linguistic repertoire. *Journal of Multilingual and Multicultural Development* 13, 157–167.

De Bot, K. 1992/2000. A bilingual production model: Levelt's 'speaking' model adapted. *Applied Linguistics* 13, 1–24. Reproduced in Li Wei, 2000, 420–442.

2004. The multilingual lexicon: modelling selection and control. *International Journal of Multilingualism*, 1(1), 17–32.

De Bot, K. & Schreuder, R. 1993. Word production and the bilingual lexicon. In Schreuder & Weltens, 1993, 191–214.

De Groot, A. M. B. & Kroll, X. 1997. *Tutorials in Bilingualism: psycholinguistic perspectives*. Mahwah, NJ: Lawrence Erlbaum.

De Houwer, A. 1990. *The Acquisition of Two Languages from Birth: a case study*. Cambridge: Cambridge University Press.

1995. *Bilingual language acquisition*. In Fletcher & MacWhinney, 1995, 219–250.

2009. *Bilingual First Language Acquisition*. Clevedon: Multilingual Matters.

Dell, G. 1986. A spreading activation theory of retrieval in sentence production. *Psychological Review* 93, 283–321.

De Mejía, A.-M. 2002. *Power, Prestige and Bilingualism: international perspectives on elite bilingual education*. Clevedon: Multilingual Matters.

Denison, N. 1972. Some observations on language variety and plurilingualism. In J. B. Pride & J. Holmes (eds), *Sociolinguistics*. Harmondsworth: Penguin, 65–77.

1984. Language acquisition in a plurilingual environment. *Grazer linguistische Studien* 21, 35–64.

1986. Sociolinguistics, linguistic description, language change and language acquisition. In J. Fishman (ed.), *The Fergusonian Impact. Vol. 1: From phonology to society*. Berlin: Mouton de Gruyter, 83–98.

1987. Sauris, a typical 'linguistic island' in the Carnian Alps. In *Isole linguistiche e culturali*, Proceedings of the 24th AIMAV Colloquy, University of Udine, 13–16 May, 65–75.

Deuchar, M. 2006. Welsh–English code-switching and the Matrix Language frame model. *Lingua* 116(11), 1986–2011.

Deuchar, M. & Quay, S. 2000. *Bilingual Acquisition: theoretical implications of a case-study.* Oxford: Oxford University Press.

De Villiers P. A. & De Villiers J. G. 1979. *Early Language.* Fontana Paperbacks.

Dewaele, J.-M. 2001. Activation or inhibition? The interaction of L1, L2 and L3 on the language mode continuum. In U. Jessner, B. Hufeisen & J. Cenoz (eds), *Cross-linguistic Influence in Third Language Acquisition: psycholinguistic perspectives.* Clevedon: Multilingual Matters, 69–89.

2003. Code-switching and emotion talk among multilinguals. Paper presented at the 4th International Symposium on Bilingualism, Phoenix, Arizona.

2004. The emotional force of swearwords and taboo words in the speech of multilinguals. *Journal of Multilingual and Multicultural Development* 25(2/3), 204–222.

2005. Investigating the psychological and emotional dimensions in Instructed Language Learning: obstacles and possibilities. *Modern Language Journal* 89(iii), 367–380.

Dewaele, J.-M. & Edwards, M. 2000. Conversations trilingues (arabe, français, anglais) entre mère et fille: un saute-Mouton Mouton de Gruyter référentiel? In C. Charner (ed.), *Communications référentielles et processus référentiels. Langues, cultures, interprétations.* Série *Le fil du discours.* Publications de Praxiling –Université Paul-Valéry, Montpellier, 193–214.

Dewaele, J.-M., Housen, A. & Li Wei 2003 (eds). *Bilingualism: beyond basic principles. Festschrift in honour of Hugo Baetens Beardsmore.* Clevedon: Multilingual Matters.

Diaz, R. M. 1983. Thought in two languages: the impact of bilingualism on cognitive development. In E. W. Gordon (ed.), *Review of Research in Education.* Vol. X. Washington, DC: AERA.

Dijkstra, T. & van Hell, J. 2003. Testing the Language Mode Hypothesis using trilinguals. *International Journal of Bilingual Education and Bilingualism,* 6(1), 2–16.

D'Introno, F. 1996. Spanish–English code-switching: conditions on movement. In Roca & Jensen, 1996, 187–201.

Di Sciullo, A. M., Muysken, P. & Singh, R. 1986. Government and code-mixing. *Journal of Linguistics* 22, 1–24.

Dolitsky, M. 2000. Codeswitching in a child's monologues. *Journal of Pragmatics* 32, 1387–1403.

Döpke, S. 2000 (ed.). *Cross-linguistic Structures in Simultaneous Bilingualism.* Amsterdam/Philadelphia: Benjamins.

Dorian, N. 1981. *The Life Cycle of a Scottish Gaelic Dialect.* Philadelphia: University of Pennsylvania Press.

Doron, E. 1983. On a formal model of code-switching. *Texas Linguistic Forum* 22, 35–59.

Dressler, W. U. & Wodak-Leodolter, R. 1977. Introduction to: Language death. *International Journal of the Sociology of Language* 12, 5–12.

Duranti, A. 1988. Intentions, language and social action in a Samoan context. *Journal of Pragmatics* 12, 13–33.

Dussias, P. E. 2001. Psycholinguistic complexity in codeswitching. *International Journal of Bilingualism* 5(1), 87–100.

Eastman, C. M. 1992 (ed.). *Codeswitching.* Clevedon: Multilingual Matters.

Eckert, P. 1989. The whole woman: sex and gender differences in variation. *Language Variation and Change* 1(3), 245–268.

1996. (ay) goes to the city: exploring the expressive use of variation. In G. R. Guy, C. Feagin, D. Schiffrin & J. Baugh (eds), *Towards a Social Science of Language. Volume 1. Variation and change in language and society.* Amsterdam: Benjamins, 47–68.

2000. *Linguistic Variation as Social Practice.* Oxford/Malden, MA: Blackwell.

Eckert, P. & Rickford, J. R. 2001 (eds). *Style and Sociolinguistic Variation.* Cambridge: Cambridge University Press.

Edwards, J. 1995. Principles and alternative systems in the transcription, coding and mark-up of spoken discourse. In Leech, Myers & Thomas, 1995, 19–34.

Edwards, M. & Gardner-Chloros, P. 2007. Compound verbs in code-switching: bilinguals making do? *International Journal of Bilingualism*, 11(1), 73–91.

Eilers, R. E., Gavin, W. J. & Oller, D. K. 1982. Cross-linguistic perception in infancy: early effects of linguistic experience. *Journal of Child Language* 9, 289–302.

Eisikovits E. 1991. Variation in subject–verb agreement in Inner Sydney English. In J. Cheshire (ed.), *English Around the World: sociolinguistic perspectives.* Cambridge: Cambridge University Press, 227–234.

Eliasson, S. 1989. English–Maori Language contact: code-switching and the free morpheme constraint. *Reports from Uppsala University Department of Linguistics (RUUL)* 18, 1–28.

1991. Models and constraints in code-switching theory. *Papers from the Workshop on Constraints, Conditions and Models.* Strasbourg: European Science Foundation, 17–50.

Eppler, E. 1999. Word order in German–English mixed discourse. *UCL Working Papers in Linguistics* 11, 285–308.

Epstein, S. P., Groat, E. M., Kawashima, R. & Kitahara, H. 1998. *A Derivational Approach to Syntactic Relations.* Oxford: Oxford University Press.

Ervin-Tripp, S. 2001. Variety, style-shifting, and ideology. In Eckert & Rickford, 2001, 44–56.

Ervinn-Tripp, S. & Reyes, I. 2005. Child codeswitching and adult content contrasts. *International Journal of Bilingualism*, Special Issue on Cognitive Approaches to Bilingualism 9(1), 85–103.

Extra, G. & Verhoeven, L. 1999. *Bilingualism and Migration.* Berlin: Mouton de Gruyter.

Fabbro, F. 1999. *The Neurolinguistics of Bilingualism: an introduction.* Hove: Psychology Press.

Fabbro, F., Skrap, M. & Aglioti, S. 2000. Pathological switching between languages after frontal lesions in a bilingual patient. *Journal of Neurology, Neurosurgery and Psychiatry* 68, 650–652.

Fano, R. M. 1950. The information theory point of view in speech communication. *Journal of the Acoustical Society of America* 22, 691–696.

Fantini, A. E. 1985. *Language Acquisition of a Bilingual Child: a sociolinguistic perspective (to age ten).* Providence, RI: College Hill.

Farrar, K. & Jones, M. C. 2002. Introduction. In M. C. Jones & E. Esch (eds), *Language Change: the interplay of internal, external and extra-linguistic factors.* Berlin/NY: Mouton de Gruyter, 1–19.

Ferguson, C. 1959. Diglossia. *Word* 15, 325–337. Reprinted in Li Wei, 2000, 65–80.

Finlayson. R. & Slabbert, S. 1997. 'I'll meet you halfway with language': code-switching within a South African urban context. In M. Pütz (ed.), *Language Choices: conditions, constraints, and consequences.* Amsterdam/Philadelphia: John Benjamins, 381–423.

Finnis, K. 2006. Language use and socio-pragmatic meaning: code-switching amongst British-born Greek-Cypriots. Unpublished PhD thesis, Birkbeck, University of London.

Fishman, J. 1965. Who speaks what language to whom and when? *La linguistique* 2, 67–87. Reprinted in Li Wei, 2000, 89–06.

1967. Bilingualism with and without diglossia, diglossia with and without bilingualism. *Journal of Social Issues* 23, 29–38.

1968. *Language Problems of Developing Nations.* New York: Wiley.

1972. Domains and the relationship between micro and macro sociolinguistics. In Gumperz & Hymes, 1972, 435–453.

Fletcher, P. & MacWhinney, B. 1995. *A Handbook of Child Language.* Oxford: Blackwell.

Florence, S. 2003. *A Guide to Reading and Writing Japanese: a comprehensive guide to the Japanese writing system.* Boston: Tuttle.

Foley, J. A. 1998. Code-switching and learning among young children in Singapore. *International Journal of the Sociology of Language* 130, 129–150.

Franceschini, R. 1998. Code-switching and the notion of code in linguistics: proposals for a dual focus model. In Auer, 1998c, 51–74.

Fries, C. C. & Pike, K. L. 1949. Coexistent phonemic systems. *Language* 25(1), 29–50.

Gafaranga, J. 2005. Demythologizing language alternation studies: conversational structure vs. social structure in bilingual interaction. *Journal of Pragmatics* 37, 281–300.

Gafaranga, J. & Torras, M.-C. 2001. Do speakers speak a language? Language versus medium in the study of bilingual conversation. *International Journal of Bilingualism* 5(2), 195–219.

2002. Interactional otherness: towards a redefinition of code-switching. *International Journal of Bilingualism* 6(1), 1–22.

Gal, S. 1979. *Language Shift: social determinants of linguistic change in bilingual Austria.* New York: Academic Press.

1988. The political economy of code choice. In M. Heller (ed.) *Codeswitching: anthropological and sociolinguistic perspectives.* Berlin: Mouton de Gruyter, 245–264.

Gardner-Chloros, P. 1987. Code-switching in relation to language contact and convergence. In G. Lüdi (ed.), *Devenir bilingue-parler bilingue; actes du 2ème colloque sur le bilinguisme, 20–22 septembre 1984.* Tübingen: Niemeyer, 99–115.

1991. *Language Selection and Switching in Strasbourg.* Oxford: Oxford University Press.

1992. The sociolinguistics of the Greek-Cypriot Community in London. In M. Karyolemou (ed.), *Plurilinguismes: sociolinguistique du grec et de la Grèce.* No.4, juin. Paris: CERPL, 112–136.

1995. Code-switching in community, regional and national repertoires: the myth of the discreteness of linguistic systems. In Milroy & Muysken, 1995, 68–90.

1997. Code-switching: language selection in three Strasbourg department stores. In Coupland & Jaworski, 1997, 361–376.

1998. Code-switching and the sociolinguistic gender pattern (with J. Cheshire). *International Journal of the Sociology of Language.* Special edition on Women's Languages in Various Parts of the World. 129, 5–34.

2000. The tortoise and the hare: distinguishing processes and end-products in language contact. *Bilingualism, Language and Cognition* 3(2), 112–114.

2004. Code-switching and Literacy: the case of a Brussels French/Dutch illiterate bilingual. Sociolinguistics Symposium 15, University of Newcastle, 1–4 April.

Gardner-Chloros, P. & Charles, R. 2007. Subiko welcome (*Welcome* to everyone): Hindi/ English code-switching in the British-Asian media. *BISAL (Birkbeck Studies in Applied Linguistics)* 2, 89–122. www.bisal.bbk.ac.uk/publications/volume2/pdf/ article5pdf.

Gardner-Chloros, P., Charles, R. & Cheshire, J. 2000. Parallel patterns? A comparison of monolingual speech and bilingual codeswitching discourse. *Journal of Pragmatics. Special Issue on Code-switching*. 32, 1305–1341.

Gardner-Chloros, P. & Edwards, M. 2004. Assumptions behind grammatical approaches to code-switching: when the blueprint is a red herring. *Transactions of the Philological Society* 102(1), 103–129.

Gardner-Chloros. P. & Finnis, K. 2004. How code-switching mediates politeness: gender-related speech among London Greek-Cypriots. *Estudios de Sociolingüística*. Special Issue: Language and Gender: An interdisciplinary perspective. 4(2), 505–533.

Gardner-Chloros, P., McEntee-Atalianis, L. & Finnis, K. 2005. Language attitudes and use in a transplanted setting: Greek Cypriots in London. *International Journal of Multilingualism* 52–80.

Gardner-Chloros, P., Moyer, M. & Sebba, M. 2007. The LIDES Corpus. In J. C. Beal, K. P. Corrigan & H. Moisl (eds), *Models and Methods in the Handling of Unconventional Digital Corpora. Vol. 1: Synchronic Corpora; Vol.2: Diachronic Corpora*. Basingstoke: Palgrave, 91–121.

Gardner-Chloros, P., Moyer, M., Sebba, M. & van Hout, R. 1999. Towards standardizing and sharing bilingual data. *International Journal of Bilingualism* 3(4), 395–424.

Garrett, M. 1980. Levels of processing in sentence production. In B. Butterworth (ed.), *Language Production, Vol. 1*. New York: Academic Press, 170–220.

Garrett, P., Griffiths, Y., James, C. & Scholfield, P. 1994. Use of the mother-tongue in second language classrooms. *Journal of Multilingual and Multicultural Development* 15(5), 371–383.

Gawlitzek-Maiwald, I. 2000. I want a chimney builden; the acquisition of infinitival constructions in bilingual children. In Döpke, 2000, 123–148.

Gawlitzek-Maiwald, I. & Tracy, R. 1996. Bilingual bootstrapping. *Linguistics* 34: 901–26.

Geluykens, R. 1992. *From Discourse Process to Grammatical Construction: on left-dislocation in English*. Amsterdam: John Benjamins.

Genesee, F. 1989. Early bilingual language development: one language or two? *Journal of Child Language* 16, 161–79. Reprinted in Li Wei, 2000, 327–347.

2001. Bilingual first language acquisition: exploring the limits of the language faculty. *Annual review of Applied Linguistics* 21, 153–168.

Genesee, F., Nicoladis, E. & Paradis, M. 1995. Language differentiation in early bilingual development. *Journal of Child Language* 22, 611–631.

George, A. 1990. Whose language is it anyway? Some notes on idiolects. *The Philosophical Quarterly* 40(160), 275–295.

Giacalone Ramat, Anna 1995. Code-switching in the context of dialect-standard language relations. In Milroy & Muysken, 1995, 45–67.

Giancarli, P.-D. 1999. Fonctions de l'alternance des langues chez des enfants bilingues francophones- anglophones. *Langage et société* 88, 59–88.

Gibbons, J. 1987. *Code-mixing and Code-choice: a Hong Kong case study.* Clevedon: Multilingual Matters.

Giesbers, H. 1989. *Code-switching tussen dialect en standaardtaal.* Amsterdam: P. Meertensinstituut.

Giles, H. & Coupland, N. 1991. *Language: contexts and consequences.* Milton Keynes: Open University Press.

Giles, H. & Smith, P. 1979. Accommodation Theory: optimal levels of convergence. In H. Giles & R. St. Clair (eds), *Language and Social Psychology.* Oxford: Blackwell, 45–66.

Goffman, E. 1979. Footing. *Semiotica* 25, 1–29.

Goglia, F. 2006. Communicative strategies in the Italian of Igbo-Nigerian Immigrants in Padova, Italy: a Contact-Linguistic Approach. Unpublished PhD thesis, University of Manchester.

Goodz, N. 1989. Parental language mixing in bilingual families. *Journal of Infant Mental Health* 10(1), 25–44.

1994. Interaction between parents and children in bilingual families. In F. Genesee (ed.), *Educating Second Language Children.* New York: Cambridge University Press, 61–81.

Grammont, M. 1902. *Observations sur le langage des enfants.* Paris: Mélanges Meillet.

Green, D. W. 1986/2000. Control, activation and resource: a framework and a model for the control of speech in bilinguals. *Brain and Language* 27, 210–223. Reprinted in Li Wei, 2000, 407–420.

1993. Towards a model of L2 comprehension and production. In Schreuder & Weltens, 1993, 249–279.

2001 (guest ed.). The cognitive neuroscience of bilingualism. Special Issue, *Bilingualism, Language and Cognition* 4(2).

Greenberg, J. H. 1963. Some universals of grammar with particular reference to the order of meaningful elements. In J. H. Greenberg (ed.), *Universals of Language.* Cambridge: MIT Press, 58–90.

Grice, P. 1989. *Studies in the Way of Words.* Cambridge, MA: Harvard University Press.

Grosjean, F. 1982. *Life with two Languages.* Cambridge, MA: Harvard University Press.

1988. Exploring the recognition of guest words in bilingual speech. *Language and Cognitive Processes* 3(3), 233–274.

1989. Neurolinguists, beware! The bilingual is not two monolinguals in one person. *Brain and Language* 36, 3–15.

1997. Processing mixed language: issues, findings and models. In De Groot & Kroll, 1997, 225–254.

1998. Studying bilinguals: methodological and conceptual issues. *Bilingualism, Language and Cognition* 1(2), 131–149.

2000. Processing mixed language: issues, findings, and models. In Li Wei, 2000, 443–470.

2001. The bilingual's language modes. In Nicol, 2001, 1–23.

Grosjean, F, Li, P., Münte, T. F. & Rodriguez-Fornells, A. 2003. Imaging bilinguals: when the neurosciences meet the language sciences. *Bilingualism, Language and Cognition* 6(2), 159–165.

Grosjean, F. & Miller, J. 1994. Going in and out of languages: an example of bilingual flexibility. *Psychological Science* 5, 201–206.

Grosjean, F. & Soares, C. 1986. Processing mixed language: some preliminary findings. In J. Vaid (ed.), *Language Processing in Bilinguals: psycholinguistic and neuro-linguistic perspectives.* Hillsdale, NJ: Lawrence Erlbaum Associates, 145–179.

Gumperz, J. J. 1964. Hindi–Panjabi code-switching in Delhi. In H. Lunt (ed.), *Proceedings of the Ninth International Congress of Linguists, Boston, MA.* The Hague: Mouton de Gruyter, 1115–1124.

1967. On the linguistic markers of bilingual communication. *Journal of Social Issues* 23(2), 48–57.

1982/1991. *Discourse Strategies,* 2nd ed. Cambridge: Cambridge University Press.

Gumperz, J. & Hernandez, E. 1969. Cognitive aspects of bilingual communication. Working Paper No.28, Language Behavior Research Laboratory, December 1969. Berkeley: University of California Press.

Gumperz, J. J. & Hymes, D. 1972 (eds). *Directions in Sociolinguistics.* New York: Holt Rinehart & Winston.

Gumperz, J. J. & Wilson, R. D. 1971. Convergence and creolization: a case from the Indo-Aryan-Dravidian border. Hymes, 1971, 151–168.

Gut, U. 2000. Cross-linguistic structures in the acquisition of intonational phonology by German–English bilingual children. In Döpke, 2000, 201–225.

Gutierrez, M. J. & Silva-Corvalan, C. 1992. Spanish clitics in a contact situation. In A. Roca & J. Lipski (eds), *Spanish in the United States. Linguistic Contact and Diversity.* Berlin: Mouton de Gruyter, 75–89.

Guttfreund, D. 1990. Effects of language use on the emotional experience of Spanish–English and English–Spanish bilinguals. *Journal of Consulting and Clinical Psychology* 58(5), 604–607.

Halmari, H. 1997. *Government and Codeswitching: explaining American Finnish.* Amsterdam/Philadelphia: John Benjamins.

Halmari, H. & Smith, W. 1994. Code-switching and register shift: evidence from Finnish–English child bilingual conversation. *Journal of Pragmatics* 21, 427–445.

Hamers, J. & Blanc, M. H. A. 2000. *Bilinguality and Bilingualism,* 2nd ed. Cambridge: Cambridge University Press.

Harris, A. C. & Campbell, L. 1995. *Historical Syntax in Cross-Linguistic Perspective.* Cambridge: Cambridge University Press.

Hasselmo, N. 1972. Code-switching as ordered selection. In. E. Scherabon Firchow, K. Grimstad, N. Hasselmo & W. A. O'Neil (eds), *Studies for Einar Haugen.* The Hague: Mouton de Gruyter, 261–280.

Haugen, E. 1950. The analysis of linguistic borrowing. *Language* 26(2), 210–231.

1956. *Bilingualism in the Americas: a Bibliography and Research Guide.* Publications of the American Dialect Society 26, Alabama: University of Alabama Press.

Haust, D. 1995. *Codeswitching in Gambia: eine soziolinguistische Untersuchung von Mandinka, Wolof und Englisch in Kontakt.* Cologne: Köppe Verlag.

Haust, D. & Dittmar, N. 1998. Taxonomic or functional models in the description of codeswitching? Evidence from Mandinka and Wolof in African contact situations. In Jacobson, 1998a, 79–90.

Heath, J. 1989. *From Code-switching to Borrowing: foreign and diglossic mixing in Moroccan Arabic.* London/New York: Kegan Paul International.

Heine, B. & Kuteva, T. 2005. *Language Contact and Grammatical Change*. Cambridge: Cambridge University Press.

Heller, M. 1988a (ed.). *Codeswitching: anthropological and sociolinguistic perspectives*. Berlin: Mouton de Gruyter.

1988b. Strategic ambiguity: code-switching in the management of conflict. In Heller, 1988a, 77–96.

1992. The politics of code-switching and language choice. *Journal of Multilingual and Multicultural Development* 13(1–2), 123–42.

Heller, M. & Martin-Jones, M. 2001 (eds). *Voices of Authority. Education and Linguistic Difference*. Westport, CT: Ablex Publishing.

Herdina, P. & Jessner, J. 2002. *A Dynamic Model of Multilingualism: perspectives of change in psycholinguistics*. Clevedon: Multilingual Matters.

Hewitt, R. 1986. *White Talk Black Talk*. Cambridge: Cambridge University Press.

Hill, J. & Hill, K. 1986. *Speaking Mexicano: dynamics of syncretic language in Central Mexico*. Tucson: University of Arizona Press.

Hinrichs, L. 2006 (ed.). *Codeswitching on the Web: English and Jamaican creole in e-mail communication (Pragmatics and Beyond)*. Amsterdam: John Benjamins.

Hoffmann, C. 1991. *An Introduction to Bilingualism*. London: Longman.

2001. Towards a description of trilingual competence. *International Journal of Bilingualism* 5, 1–17.

Højrup, T. 1983. The concept of life-mode: a form-specifying mode of analysis applied to contemporary Western Europe. *Ethnologia Scandinavica*, 15–50.

Holmes, J. 1995. *Women, Men and Politeness*. Harlow: Longman.

Hudson, L. 1966. *Contrary Imaginations*. Harmondsworth: Penguin.

Hulk, A. and Müller, N. 2000. Bilingual first language acquisition at the interface between syntax and semantics. *Bilingualism: Language and Cognition* 3, 227–244.

Hurtado, N. M. 2003. Code-switching as a communicative and conceptual tool in the classroom discourse of bilingual students. Unpublished University of California at Santa Barbara dissertation. Dissertation Abstracts International, A: the Humanities and Social Sciences, 63, 9, March, 3091-A.

Huwaë, R. 1992. Tweetaligheid in Wierden: het taalgebruik van jongeren uit een Molukse gemeenschap. Unpublished MA thesis in linguistics, Universiteit van Amsterdam.

Hyltenstam, K. and Obler, L. K. 1989 (eds). *Bilingualism across the Lifespan*. Cambridge: Cambridge University Press.

Hyltenstam, K. & Stroud, C. 1989. Bilingualism in Alzheimer's dementia: two case studies. In Hyltenstam & Obler, 1989, 202–227.

Hymes, D. 1971 (ed.). *Pidginization and Creolization of Languages*. Cambridge: Cambridge University Press.

Jackendoff, R. 1997. *The Architecture of the Language Faculty*. Cambridge, MA: MIT Press.

Jacobson, R. 1998a (ed.). *Codeswitching Worldwide*. Berlin: Mouton de Gruyter.

1998b. Conveying a broader message through bilingual discourse. An attempt at contrastive codeswitching research. In Jacobson 1998a, 51–76.

2001 (ed.). *Codeswitching Worldwide II*. Berlin: Mouton de Gruyter.

Jake, J. L. 1998 Constructing Interlanguage: building a composite Matrix Language. *Linguistics* 36, 333–382.

Jake, J. L., Myers-Scotton, C. & Gross, S. 2002. Making a Minimalist approach to codeswitching work: adding the Matrix Language. *Bilingualism, Language and Cognition* 5(1), 69–91.

Jakobson, R., Fant, M. & Halle, M. 1952. *Preliminaries to Speech Analysis: the distinctive features and their correlates*. Cambridge, MA: MIT Press. Reprinted in *Selected Writings of Roman Jakobson. Major Works 1976–1980*. Vol.8. Berlin/ NY/Amsterdam: Mouton de Gruyter, 583–646.

Janički, K. 1990. *Towards Non-essentialist Sociolinguistics*. Berlin: Mouton de Gruyter.

Javier, R. A. & Marcos, L. R. 1989. The role of stress on language-independence and code-switching phenomena. *Journal of Psycholinguistic Research* 18(5), 449–472.

Jespersen, O. 1928. *Growth and Structure of the English Language*, 4th ed. Leipzig: Teubner.

Jisa, H. 2000. Language mixing in the weak language: evidence from two children. *Journal of Pragmatics* 32(9), 1363–1386.

Johanson, L. 2002. *Structural Factors in Turkic Language Contacts*. Richmond: Curzon Press.

Johnson, C. & Lancaster, P. 1998. The development of more than one phonology: a case study of a Norwegian–English bilingual child. *International Journal of Bilingualism* 2(3), 265–300.

Johnson, J. S. & Newport, E. L. 1989. Critical period effects in second language learning: the influence of maturational state on the acquisition of English as a second language. *Cognitive Psychology* 21, 60–99.

Jones, M. 1996. *Foundations of French Syntax*. Cambridge: Cambridge University Press.

1998. *Language Obsolescence and Revitalization: linguistic change in two sociolinguistically contrasting Welsh communities*. Oxford: Oxford University Press.

2005. Some structural and social correlates of single word intrasentential codeswitching in Jersey Norman French. *Journal of French Language Studies* 15, 1–23.

Jörgensen, J. N. 2005. Plurilingual conversations among bilingual adolescents. *Journal of Pragmatics* 37, 391–402.

Joshi, A. K. 1985. Processing of sentences with intrasentential code-switching. In D. R. Dowty, L. Karttunen & A. M. Zwicky (eds), *Natural Language Processing: psychological, computational and theoretical perspectives*. Cambridge: Cambridge University Press, 190–205.

Juan-Garau, M. & Pérez-Vidal, C. 2001. Mixing and pragmatic parental strategies in early bilingual acquisition. *Journal of Child Language* 28, 56–86.

Kamwangamalu, N. & Li, C. 1991. Chinese–English code-mixing: a case of matrix language assignment. *World Englishes* 10, 247–261.

Karousou-Fokas, R. & Garman, M. 2001. A psycholinguistic interpretation of code-switching: evidence from fluent Greek-English bilingual adults. *International Journal of Bilingualism* 5(1), 39–71.

Kecskes, I. & Moyer, M. 2002. An ethno-conceptual approach to codeswitching. Paper presented at Sociolinguistics Symposium 14, University of Ghent, Belgium, April 2002.

Kerswill, P. 1994. *Dialects Converging: rural speech in urban Norway*. Oxford: Oxford University Press.

Kessler, C. 1971. *The Acquisition of Syntax in Bilingual Children*. Washington, DC: Georgetown University Press.

King, R. 2000. *The Lexical Basis of Grammatical Borrowing: a Prince Edward Island French case-study*. Amsterdam/Philadelphia: Benjamins.

Klavans, J. L. 1985. The syntax of code-switching: Spanish and English. *Proceedings of the Linguistic Symposium on Romance Languages*. Amsterdam: Benjamins. 213–231.

Kolers, P. A. 1963. Interlingual word associations. *Journal of Verbal Learning & Verbal Behavior* 2, 291–300.

Köppe, R. & Meisel, J. M. 1995. Code-switching in bilingual first language acquisition. In Milroy & Muysken, 1995, 276–302.

Kroll, J. F. 1993. Accessing conceptual representations for words in a second language. In Schreuder & Weltens, 1993, 53–83.

Labov, W. 1971. The notion of 'system' in creole languages. In Hymes, 1971, 447–472.

  1972. *Sociolinguistic Patterns*. Philadelphia, PA: University of Pennsylvania Press.

Lanvers, U. 2001. Language alternation in infant bilinguals: a developmental approach to codeswitching. *International Journal of Bilingualism* 5(4), 437–464.

Lanza, E. 1992. Can bilingual two-year-olds code-switch? *Journal of Child Language* 19, 633–658.

  1997. *Language Mixing in Infant Bilingualism: a sociolinguistic perspective*. Oxford: Oxford University Press.

  2001. Bilingual first language acquisition: a discourse perspective on language contact in parent–child interaction. In Cenoz & Genesee, 2001, 201–229.

Lavandera, B. 1978. The variable component in bilingual performance. In J. E. Alatis (ed.), *International Dimensions of Bilingual Education*. Washington DC: Georgetown University Press, 391–409.

Lawson-Sako, S. & Sachdev, I. 1996. Ethnolinguistic communication in Tunisian streets. In Y. Suleiman (ed.), *Language and Ethnic Identity in the Middle East and North Africa*. Richmond: Curzon Press, 61–79.

  2000. Codeswitching in Tunisia: attitudinal and behavioural dimensions. *Journal of Pragmatics* 32, 1343–1361.

Lebrun, Y. 1991. Polyglotte Reaktionen. *Neurolinguistik*, 5, 1–9.

Leech, G., Myers, A. & Thomas, J. A. 1995 (eds). *Spoken English on Computer*. London: Longman.

Leopold, W. 1939–1949. *Speech Development of a Bilingual Child: a linguist's record*. 4 vols. Evanston, IL: Northwestern University Press.

Le Page, R. B. 1989. What is a Language? *York Papers in Linguistics* 13, 9–24.

  1997. The evolution of a sociolinguistic theory of language. In Coulmas, 1997, 15–32.

Le Page, R, and Tabouret-Keller, A. 1985. *Acts of Identity*. Cambridge: Cambridge University Press.

Levelt, W. J. M. 1989. *Speaking: from intention to articulation*. Cambridge, MA: MIT Press.

Lin, A. M. Y. 2001. Symbolic domination and bilingual classroom practices in Hong Kong schools. In Heller & Martin-Jones, 2001, 139–168.

Lindholm, K. A. & Padilla, A. M. 1978. Language mixing in bilingual children *Journal of Child Language* 5, 327–335.

LIPPS Group 2000. The LIDES coding manual: a document for preparing and analysing language interaction data. Special Issue, *International Journal of Bilingualism*.

Lipski, J. M. 1978. Code-switching and the problem of bilingual competence. In Paradis, 1978, 250–264.

Lisker, L. & Abramson, A. 1964. A cross-language study of voicing in initial stops. *Word* 20, 384–422.

Li Wei 1994. *Three Generations, Two Languages, One Family: language choice and language shift in a Chinese community in Britain*. Clevedon: Multilingual Matters.

1998a. Banana split? Variations in language choice and code-switching patterns of two groups of British-born Chinese in Tyneside. In Jacobson, 1998a, 153–176.

1998b. The 'why' and 'how' questions in the analysis of conversational code-switching. In Auer, 1998b, 156–180.

2000 (ed.). *The Bilingualism Reader*. London: Routledge.

2002. 'What do you want me to say?' On the Conversation Analysis approach to bilingual interaction. *Language in Society* 31, 159–180.

2005. "How can you tell?" Towards a common sense explanation of conversational code-switching. *Journal of Pragmatics* 37(3), 375–389.

Li Wei, Milroy, L. & Pong Sin Ching 2000. A two-step sociolinguistic analysis of code-switching and language choice: the example of a bilingual Chinese community in Britain. In Li Wei, 2000, 188–209.

Lüdi, G. 1993. Second language acquisition by migrants in Europe. In R. Posner & J. N. Green (eds), *Trends in Romance Linguistics and Philology*. Berlin: Mouton de Gruyter, 495–534.

2003. Code-switching and unbalanced bilingualism. In Dewaele, Housen & Li Wei, 2003, 174–188.

Macnamara, J. 1971. The bilingual's linguistic performance: a psychological overview. *Journal of Social Issues* 23(2), 67–71.

MacSwan, J. 1999. *A Minimalist Approach to Intrasentential Code Switching*. New York: Garland.

2000. The architecture of the bilingual language faculty: evidence from codeswitching. *Bilingualism, Language and Cognition* 3(1), 37–54.

2004. Code switching and linguistic theory. In Bhatia & Ritchie, 2004, 283–312.

2005. Code-switching and generative grammar: a critique of the MLF model and some remarks on 'modified minimalism'. *Bilingualism, Language and Cognition* 8(1), 1–22.

MacWhinney, B. 1995 [1991]. *The CHILDES Project: Tools for Analyzing Talk*. 2nd ed. Hillsdale, NJ: Erlbaum.

2007. The TalkBank Project. In Joan C. Beal, Karen P. Corrigan & Hermann Moisl (eds), *Creating and Digitizing Language Corpora: synchronic databases (Volume 1)*, 163–180. London: Palgrave.

MacWhinney, B. & Snow, C. 1990. The Child Language Data Exchange System: an update. *Journal of Child Language* 17, 457–472.

Maehlum, B. 1990. Codeswitching in Hemnesberget–Myth or Reality? In E. Hakon Jahr & O. Lorentz (eds), *Tromsø Linguistics in the Eighties*. Oslo: Novus Press, 338–355. Reprinted in *Journal of Pragmatics* 1996, 25(6), 749–761.

Mahootian, S. 1993. A null theory of codeswitching. Unpublished doctoral dissertation, Northwestern University.

2005. Written code: the discourse of social change. Talk presented at ISB 5, Barcelona, March 2005.

Maneva, B. & Genesee, F. 2002. Bilingual babbling: evidence for language differentiation in dual language acquisition. In *Proceedings of the 26th Boston University Conference on Language Development*. Somerville, MA: Cascadilla Press.

Mangruel, A. 2004. *Journal d'un lecteur.* Translated from English by Christine Le Boeuf. France: Actes Sud.

Maniakas, T. M. 1991. KANO + INF.: the case of a Greek auxiliary verb in a language contact situation. *Journal of Applied Linguistics* 7, 114–131.

Man-Siu Yau, F. 1997. Code switching and language choice in the Hong Kong Legislative Council. *Journal of Multilingual and Multicultural Development* 18(1), 40–53.

Marantz, A. 1995. The Minimalist Program. In Gert Webelhuth (ed.), *Government and Binding Theory and the Minimalist Program: principles and parameters in syntactic theory.* Oxford: Blackwell, 349–381.

Martin, E. 2002. Mixing English in French advertising. *World Englishes* 10(2), 139–151.

Martin, P. 2003. Bilingual encounters in the classroom. In Dewaele, Housen & Li Wei, 2003, 67–87.

Martin-Jones, M. 1995. Code-switching in the classroom: Two decades of research. In Milroy & Muysken, 1995, 90–112.

    2000. Bilingual classroom interaction: a review of recent research. *Language Teaching* 33, 1–9.

Martin-Jones, M. & Romaine, S. 1986. Semilingualism: a half-baked theory of communicative competence. *Applied Linguistics* 7(1), 26–38.

Marty, S. & Grosjean, F. 1998. Aphasie, bilinguisme et modes de communication. *Aphasie und verwandte Gebiete* 12(1), 8–28.

Maters, K. 1979. An evaluation of syntactic constraints on code-switching and their potential application to Dutch/English. Unpublished MPhil thesis, University of Cambridge.

Matras, Y. 2000a. Mixed languages: a functional-communicative approach. *Bilingualism, Language and Cognition* 3(2), 79–99.

    2000b. Fusion and the cognitive basis for bilingual discourse markers. *Bilingualism, Language and Cognition* 4(4), 505–529.

Matzen, R. 1980. *Dichte isch bichte: Gedichte in Strassburger Mundart.* Kehl: Morstadt Verlag.

Mayes, P. 1990. Quotation in spoken English, *Studies in Language* 14, 325–363.

McClure, E. 1981. Formal and functional aspects of the code switched discourse of bilingual children. In R. P. Duran (ed.), *Latina Language and Communicative Behaviour.* Norwood, NJ: Ablex, 69–94.

    1998. The relationship between form and function in written national language – English codeswitching: evidence from Mexico, Spain and Bulgaria. In Jacobson, 1998a, 125–152.

McClure, E & McClure, M. 1988. Macro- and micro-sociolinguistic dimensions of code-switching in Vingard (Romania). In Heller, 1988a, 25–51.

McConvell, P. 1988. Mix-im-up: Aboriginal code-switching, old and new. In M. Heller (ed.) *Codeswitching: anthropological and sociolinguistic perspectives.* Berlin: Mouton de Gruyter, 97–124.

McCormick, K. 2002. *Language in Cape Town's District Six.* Oxford: Oxford University Press.

McLelland, N. 2004. A historical study of codeswitching in writing: German and Latin in Schottelius' *Ausführliche Arbeit von der Teutschen Haubtsprache* (1663). *International Journal of Bilingualism* 8(4), 499–525.

Meeuwis, M. & Blommaert, J. 1994. The 'markedness model' and the absence of society. *Multilingua* 13, 387–423.

1998. A monolectal view of code-switching: layered code-switching among Zairians in Belgium. In Auer, 1998c, 76–101.

Meisel, J. M. 1989. Early differentiation of languages in bilingual children. In Hyltenstam & Obler, 1989, 13–41. Reprinted in Li Wei, 2000, 344–369.

1994 (ed.). *Bilingual First Language Acquisition: French and German grammatical development*. Amsterdam/Philadelphia: Benjamins.

2000. Early differentiation of languages in bilingual children. In Li Wei, 2000, 336–360.

Merritt, M., Cleghorn, A., Abagi, J. O. & Bunyi, G. 1992. Socializing multilingualism: determinants of codeswitching in Kenyan primary classrooms. *Journal of Multilingual and Multicultural Development* 13 (1/2), 103–122.

Meuter, R. F. I. 2005. Language selection in bilinguals: mechanisms and processes. In J. F. Kroll & A. M. B. de Groot (eds), *The Handbook of Bilingualism: psycholinguistic approaches*. Oxford: Oxford University Press, 349–370.

Michina, S. 1999. The role of parental input and discourse strategies in the early language mixing of a bilingual child. *Multilingua* 18(4), 317–342.

Milroy, J. 1998. Towards a speaker-based account of language change. In E. Håkon Jahr (ed.), *Language Change: advances in historical sociolinguistics*. Berlin: Mouton de Gruyter, 21–36.

Milroy, L. & Gordon, M. 2003. *Sociolinguistics: method and interpretation*. Oxford: Blackwell.

Milroy, L. & Li Wei 1995. A social network approach to code-switching: the example of a bilingual community in Britain. In Milroy & Muysken, 1995, 136–157.

Milroy, L. & Muysken, P. 1995 (eds). *One Speaker, Two Languages: cross-disciplinary perspectives on code-switching*. Cambridge: Cambridge University Press.

Mishina, S. 1999. The role of parental input and discourse strategies in the early language mixing of a bilingual child. *Multilingua* 18(4), 317–342.

Mishoe, M. 1998. Styleswitching in Southern English. In Myers-Scotton, 1998, 162–178.

Mitchell, R. & Miles, F. 2004. *Second Language Learning Theories*, 2nd ed. London: Arnold.

Montes-Alcala, C. 1998. Written codeswitching: powerful bilingual images. In Jacobson, 2001, 193–223.

Moreno, E. M., Federmaier, K. D. & Kutas, M. 2002. Switching languages, switching *palabras* (words): an electrophysiological study of code-switching. *Brain and Language* 80(2), 188–207.

Morita, E. 2003. Children's use of address and reference terms. *Multilingua* 22, 367–395.

Morton, J. 1979. Word recognition. In J. Morton & J. Marshall (eds), *Psycholinguistics: Series 2. Structures and Processes*. London: Elek, 107–156.

Mougeon, R. & Beniak, E. 1991. *Linguistic Consequences of Language Contact and Restriction: The case of French in Ontario, Canada*. Oxford: Oxford University Press.

Moyer, M. G. 1992. Analysis of codeswitching in Gibraltar. Unpublished PhD dissertation, Universitat Autònoma de Barcelona.

1998. Bilingual conversation strategies in Gibraltar. In Auer, 1998c, 215–236.

2000. Gibraltar oral and written corpus 1987–1990. Unpublished.

Muñoz, M. C. 1999. Usages du français et double appartenance: le cas des Portugais en
France. *Education et Sociétés Plurilingues*, 7, December, 21–33.

Muysken, P. 1990. Concepts, methodology and data in language research: ten remarks
from the perspective of grammatical theory. Papers for the workshop on concepts,
methodology and data. European Science Foundation Netword on Code-Switching.

1995. Code-switching and grammatical theory. In Milroy & Muysken, 1995, 177–199.

1997. Accounting for variation in code-mixing patterns. Paper presented at the
Bilingualism Symposium, Newcastle, United Kingdom.

2000. *Bilingual Speech: a typology of code-mixing*. Cambridge: Cambridge
University Press.

Muysken, P., Kook, H. & Vedder, P. 1996. Papiamento/Dutch code-switching in bilingual parent–child reading. *Applied Psycholinguistics* 17, 485–505.

Myers-Scotton, C. 1983. The negotiation of identities in conversation: a theory of
markedness and code choice. *International Journal of the Sociology of Language*
44, 115–136.

1986. Diglossia and code-switching. In J. A. Fishman, A. Tabouret-Keller, M. Clyne,
B. Krishnamurti & M. Abdulaziz (eds), *The Fergusonian Impact*, 2 vols, Berlin:
Mouton de Gruyter, ii, 403–417.

1988. Code-switching as indexical of social negotiations. In Heller, 1988a, 151–186.

1992. Comparing code-switching and borrowing. *Journal of Multilingual and
Multicultural Development* 13(1/2), 19–39.

1993a. *Social Motivations for Code-switching: evidence from Africa*. Oxford: Oxford
University Press.

1993b *Duelling Languages*. Oxford: Oxford University Press.

1997. Codeswitching. In Coulmas, 1997, 217–237.

1998. (ed.) *Codes and Consequences: choosing linguistic varieties*. Oxford: Oxford
University Press.

1999. Explaining the role of norms and rationality in codeswitching. *Journal of
Pragmatics* 32, 1259–1271.

2002a. *Contact Linguistics: bilingual encounters and grammatical outcomes*. Oxford:
Oxford University Press.

2002b. Frequency and intentionality in (un)marked choices in CS: 'This is a 24 hour
country'. *International Journal of Bilingualism* 6(2), 205–219.

2003. Code-switching: evidence of both flexibility and rigidity in language. In
Dewaele, Housen & Li Wei, 2003, 189–203.

Myers-Scotton, C. & Bolonyai, A. 2001. Calculating speakers: codeswitching in a
Rational Choice Model. *Language in Society* 30, 1–28.

Myers-Scotton, C. & Jake, J. L. 1995/2000. Matching lemmas in a bilingual competence and
production model. *Linguistics* 33, 981–1024. Reprinted in Li Wei, 2000, 281–320.

2000. Testing the 4-M model: an introduction. *International Journal of Bilingualism*
4(1), 1–8.

2001. Explaining aspects of code-switching and their implications. In Nicol, 2001,
84–117.

2009. No chaos allowed. In B. Bullock & J. Toribio. (eds), *Handbook of Code-switching*. Cambridge: Cambridge University Press.

Nehrlich, B. & Clarke, D. D. 1994. Language, action and context: linguistic pragmatics in Europe and America (1800–1950). *Journal of Pragmatics* 22, 439–463.

Neufeld, G. G. 1976. The bilingual's lexical store, *International Review of Applied Linguistics* 14(1), 15–35.

Nicol, J. L. 2001. *One Mind, Two Languages: bilingual language processing*. Oxford: Blackwell.

Nicoladis, E. & Secco, G. 2000. The role of a child's productive vocabulary in the language choice of a bilingual family. *First Language* 20, 3–28.

Nilep, C. 2006. 'Code switching' in sociocultural linguistics. *Colorado Research in Linguistics* 19, 1–68.

Nishimura, M. 1997. Japanese/English code-switching: syntax and pragmatics. *Berkeley Insights in Linguistics and Semiotics* 24, New York: Peter Lang.

Nivens, R. J. 2002. *Borrowing versus Code-switching in West Tarangan (Indonesia)*. Dallas, TX: SIL International.

Nortier, J. 1990. *Dutch–Moroccan Arabic Code Switching*. Dordrecht: Foris Publications.

Obler, L. K., Zatorre, R. J., Galloway, L. & Vaid, J. 2000. Cerebral lateralization in bilinguals: methodological issues. In Li Wei, 2000, 381–394.

Ochs, E. 1979. Transcription as theory. In E. Ochs & B. B. Schieffelin (eds), *Developmental Pragmatics*. New York: Academic Press, 43–72.

Oesch-Serra, C. 1998. Discourse connectives in bilingual conversation: the case of an emerging Italian–French mixed code. In Auer, 1998c, 101–124.

Oezguezel, S. 1994. De vitaliteit van het Turks in Nederland. Unpublished PhD dissertation, Tilburg University.

Otheguy, R. 1995. When contact speakers talk, linguistic theory listens. In E. Contini-Mrava & B. Sussman Goldberg (eds), *Advances in Linguistic Sign Theory*. Berlin: Mouton de Gruyter, 213–242.

Pandharipande, R. V. 1998. Is genetic connection relevant in code-switching? Evidence from South Asian languages. In Jacobson, 1998a, 201–220.

Pandit, I. 1990. Grammaticality in code-switching. In R. Jacobson (ed.), *Codeswitching as a Worldwide Phenomenon*. New York: Peter Lang, 33–69.

Paradis, J. 2000. Beyond 'One system or two'? Degrees of separation between the languages of French–English bilingual children. In Döpke, 2000, 175–201.

Paradis, J., Nicoladis, E. & Genesee, F. 2000. Early emergence of structural constraints on code-mixing: evidence from French–English bilingual children. *Bilingualism, Language and Cognition* 3(3), 245–261.

Paradis, M. 1978 (ed.). *Aspects of Bilingualism*. Columbia, SC: Hornbeam Press.

1981. Neurolinguistic organization of a bilingual's two languages. In J. E. Copeland & P. W. Davis (eds), *The 7th LACUS Forum*. Columbia, SC: Hornbeam Press, 486–494.

1987. *The Assessment of Bilingual Aphasia*. Hillsdale, NJ: Lawrence Erlbaum.

1995. Selective deficit in one language is not a demonstration of a different anatomical representation: comments on Gomez-Tortosa et al. *Brain & Language* 54, 170–173.

Paradis, M. & Goldblum, M. C. 1989. Selective crossed aphasia in a trilingual aphasic patient followed by reciprocal antagonism. *Brain & Language* 36, 62–75.

Pavlenko, A. 2004. 'Stop doing that, *ia komu skazala!'*: language choice and emotions in parent–child communication. *Journal of Multilingual & Multicultural Development* 25(2/3), 179–203.

2005. *Emotions and Multilingualism*. Cambridge: Cambridge University Press.

Peal, E. & Lambert, W. 1962. The relationship of bilingualism to intelligence. *Psychological Monographs* 76, 1–23.

Penfield, W. & Roberts, L. 1959. *Speech and Brain Mechanisms*. Princeton, NJ: Princeton University Press.

Perecman, E. 1984. Spontaneous translation and language mixing in a polyglot aphasic. *Brain and Language* 23, 43–63.

1989. Language processing in the bilingual: evidence from language mixing. In Hyltenstam & Obler, 1989, 227–245.

Perrot, M.-E. 2001. Ordre des mots et restructurations dans le *chiac* de Moncton: l'example du syntagme nominal. In Canut & Caubet, 2001, 49–59.

Pfaff, C. 1979. Constraints on language-mixing: intrasentential code-switching and borrowing in Spanish–English. *Language* 55, 291–318.

Pinker, S. 1994. *The Language Instinct*. Harmondsworth: Penguin.

Poplack, S. 1980. Sometimes I'll start a sentence in Spanish Y TERMINO EN ESPAÑOL: toward a typology of code-switching. *Linguistics* 18, 581–618.

1988. Contrasting patterns of code-switching in two communities, in Heller, 1988a, 215–245.

2000. Preface to the reprint of 'Sometimes I'll start a sentence in Spanish Y TERMINO EN ESPAÑOL: toward a typology of code-switching' (see Poplack 1980). In Li Wei, 2000, 221–223.

Poplack, S. & Meechan, M. 1995. Patterns of language mixture: nominal structure in Wolof–French and Fongbe–French bilingual discourse. In Milroy & Muysken, 1995, 199–232.

Poplack, S. & Sankoff, D. 1984. Borrowing: the synchrony of integration. *Linguistics* 22, 99–135.

Poplack, S., Sankoff, D. & Miller, C. 1988. The social correlates and linguistic processes of lexical borrowing and assimilation. *Linguistics* 26, 47–104.

Poplack, S., Wheeler, S. & Westwood, A. 1987. Distinguishing language contact phenomena: evidence from Finnish–English bilingualism. In P. Lilius & M. Saari (eds), *The Nordic Languages and Modern Linguistics*, 6, Helsinki: University of Helsinki Press, 33–56. Reprinted in R. Jacobson (ed.) 1990, *Code-switching as a World-wide Phenomenon*, 170–185. New York: Peter Lang.

Popper, K. 1959. *The Logic of Scientific Discovery*. London: Hutchinson.

Pötzl, O. 1925. Über die parietal bedingte Aphasie und ihren Einfluss auf das Sprechen mehrerer Sprachen [On aphasia of parietal origin and its influence on the speaking of several languages]. *Zeitshrift für die gesamte Neurologie und Psychiatrie* 96, 100–124. Translated in M. Paradis (ed.), 1983, *Readings on Aphasia in Bilinguals and Polyglots*. Montreal; Marcel Didier, 176–198.

Poulisse, N. 1997. Language production in bilinguals. In De Groot & Kroll, 1997, 201–225.

Poulisse, N. & Bongaerts, T. 1994. First language use in second language production. *Applied Linguistics* 15, 36–57.

Pujadas, J., Pujol Berché, M. & Turell, M. T. 1988–1992. Catalan–Spanish database. Unpublished.

Pujolar i Cos, J. 2001. *Gender, Heteroglossia and Power. A sociolinguistic study of youth culture*. Berlin/New York: Mouton de Gruyter.

Radford, A. 1996. Towards a structure-building model of acquisition. In H. Clahsen (ed.), *Generative Perspectives on Language Acquisition*. Amsterdam/Philadelphia: John Benjamins, 43–91.

Ramat, A. G. 1995. Code-switching in the context of dialect/standard language relations. Milroy & Muysken, 1995, 45–67.

Rampton, B. 1995. *Crossing: language and ethnicity among adolescents*. London: Longman.

Redlinger, W. E. & Park, T. 1980. Language mixing in young bilinguals. *Journal of Child Language* 7, 337–352.

Rindler-Schjerve, R. 1998. Code-switching as an indicator for language shift? Evidence from Sardinian–Italian bilingualism. In Jacobson, 1998a, 221–248.

Robinson, W. P. & Giles, H. 2001. *The New Handbook of Language and Social Psychology*. Chichester, NY/ Weinheim/Brisbane/Singapore/Toronto: John Wiley & Sons.

Roca, A. & Jensen, J. B. 1996. *Spanish in Contact: issues in bilingualism*. Somerville, MA: Cascadilla Press.

Romaine, S. 1986. The syntax and semantics of the code-mixed compound verb in Panjabi–English bilingual biscourse. In D. Tannen & J. Alatis (eds), *Language and Linguistics. The Interdependence of Theory, Data and Application*. Washington DC: Georgetown University Press, 35–49.

1989. *Bilingualism*. Oxford: Basil Blackwell.

1995. *Bilingualism*, 2nd ed. Oxford: Blackwell.

1992. *Language, Education and Development: urban and rural Tok Pisin in Papua New Guinea*. Oxford: Oxford University Press.

Ronjat, J. 1913. *Le développement du langage observé chez un enfant bilingue*. Paris: Champion.

Rozensky, R. H. & Gomez, M. Y. 1983. Language switching in psychotherapy with bilinguals: two problems, two models and some case examples. *Psychotherapy Theory, Research and Practice* 20, 152–160.

Rubagumya, C. M. 1994 (ed.). *Teaching and Researching Language in African Classrooms: a Tanzanian perspective*. Clevedon: Multilingual Matters.

Rubin, E. J. & Toribio, A. J. 1995. Feature-checking and the syntax of language contact. In J. Amastae, G. Goodall, M. Montalbetti & M. Phinney (eds), *Contemporary Research in Romance Linguistics*. Amsterdam: Benjamins, 177–185.

Sachdev, I. & Bourhis, R. Y. 1990. Bi- and multilingual communication. In H. Giles and P. Robinson (eds), *The Handbook of Language and Social Psychology*, Chichester, NY/Weinheim/Brisbane/Singapore/Toronto: John Wiley & Sons, 293–308.

2001. Multilingual communication. In Robinson & Giles, 2001, 407–429.

Sachdev, I. & Giles, H. 2004. Bilingual accommodation. In Bhatia & Ritchie, 2004, 353–378.

Sankoff, D. 1998. A formal production-based explanation of the facts of code-switching. *Bilingualism, Language and Cognition* 1(1), 39–50.

Sankoff, D. & Mainville, S. 1986. Code-switching and context-free grammars. *Theoretical Linguistics* 13, 75–90.

Sankoff, D. & Poplack, S. 1981. A formal grammar for code-switching. *Papers in Linguistics* 14(1), 3–46.

Sankoff, D., Poplack, S. & Vanniarajan, S. 1990. The case of the nonce loan in Tamil. *Language Variation and Change* 2(1), 71–101.

Sankoff, G. 2001. Linguistic outcomes of language contact. In J. Chambers, P. Trudgill & N. Schilling-Estes (eds), *The Handbook of Language Variation and Change*. Oxford: Blackwell, 638–668.

Sarkar, M. & Winer, L. 2006. Multilingual codeswitching in Quebec rap: poetry, pragmatics and performativity. *International Journal of Multilingualism* 3(3), 173–192.

Saunders, G. 1982. *Bilingual Children: guidance for the family*. Clevedon: Multilingual Matters.

Saville-Troike, M. 1982. *The Ethnography of Communication: an introduction*. Oxford: Blackwell.

Schelletter, C. 2000. Negation as a crosslinguistic structure in a German–English bilingual child. In Döpke, 2000, 105–121.

Schendl, H. 2002. Linguistic aspects of code-switching in medieval English texts. In Trotter, 2002, 77–93.

Schmidt, A. 1985. *Young People's Djirbal*. Cambridge: Cambridge University Press.

Schreuder, R. & Weltens, B. 1993 (eds). *The Bilingual Lexicon*. Amsterdam: Benjamins.

Schuffenecker, G. 1981. Mode de vie en Alsace. Institut national de la statistique et des études économiques. Dernières Nouvelles d'Alsace, 6–15 February.

Schütze, C. T. 1996. *The Empirical Basis of Linguistics: grammaticality judgments and linguistic methodology*. Chicago: University of Chicago Press.

Scotton C. M. 1976. Strategies of neutrality: language choice in uncertain situations. *Language* 52(4): 919–941.

Seaman, P. D. 1972. *Modern Greek and American English*. The Hague: Mouton de Gruyter.

Sebba, M. 1993. *London Jamaican: Language Systems in Interaction*. London/New York: Longman.

1995a. Code-switching: a problem for transcription and text encoding. In Leech, Myers & Thomas, 1995, 144–148.

1995b. Towards a bilingual corpus of code-switching data. Network on codeswitching and language contact: Proceedings of the ESF Summer School on codeswitching and language contact, Ljouwert/Leeuwaarden, the Netherlands, 14–17 September, 1994, Fryske Akademy, 229–241.

1998. A congruence approach to the syntax of code-switching. *International Journal of Bilingualism* 2, 1–20.

2005. Towards a typology and analytical framework for mixed language texts. Talk delivered at ISB5, Barcelona, March.

Sebba, M. & Wootton, T. 1998. We, they and identity: sequential v. identity-related explanation in CS. In Auer, 1998c, 262–290.

Sella-Mazi, E. 1997. Language contact today: the case of the Muslim minority in north-eastern Greece. *International Journal of the Sociology of Language* 126, 83–103.

1999. *La minorité musulmane turcophone de Grèce: approche sociolinguistique d'une communauté bilingue*. Athens: Trohalia.

Selting, M., Auer, P. Barden, B., Bergmann, J., Cer-Kuhlen, E., Günthner, S., Meier, C., Quasthoff, U., Schlobinski, P. & Uhmann. S. 1998. Gesprächsanalystisches Transkriptionssystem (GAT). *Linguistische Berichte* 173, 91–122.

Shepard, C. A., Giles, H. & Le Poire, B. A. 2001. Communication Accommodation Theory. In Robinson & Giles, 2001, 33–56.

Shin, S. J. & Milroy, L. 2000. Conversational code-switching among Korean–English bilingual children. *International Journal of Bilingualism* 4(3), 351–383.

Siegel, J. 1994. Review of S. Romaine 'Language, education and development'. *Language in Society* 23, 144–149.

Sifianou, M. 1992. *Politeness Phenomena in England and Greece. A cross-cultural perspective*, Oxford: Oxford University Press.

Singh, R. 1983. We, they and us: a note on code-switching and stratification in North India. *Language in Society* 12(1), 71–73.

Sinka, I. 2000. The search for cross-linguistic influences in the language of young Latvian–English bilinguals. In Döpke, 2000, 149–175.

Smith, N. 1989. *The Twitter Machine: reflections on language*. Oxford: Blackwell.

Smith, Z. 2000. *White Teeth*. Penguin Books.

Sokolov, J. & Snow, C. 1994 (eds). *Handbook of Research in Language Development Using CHILDES*. Hillsdale NJ: Erlbaum.

Spolsky, B. & Cooper, R. L. 1991. *The Languages of Jerusalem*. Oxford: Oxford University Press.

Sridhar, S. & Sridhar, K. 1980. The syntax and psycholinguistics of bilingual code-switching. *Canadian Journal of Psychology* 34, 407–416.

Stolt, B. 1964 *Die Sprachmischung in Luthers Tischreden: Studien zum Problem der Zweisprachigkeit* (Acta Universitatis Stockholmiensis, Stockholmer germanistische Forshungen 4). Stockholm: Almquist & Wiksell.

Stroud, C. 1992. The problem of definition and meaning in code-switching. *Text* 12(1), 127–155.

1998. Perspectives on cultural variability of discourse and some implications for code-switching. In Auer, 1998c, 321–348.

Swain, S. 2002. Bilingualism in Cicero? The evidence of code-switching. In Adams & Swain, 2002, 128–168.

Swigart, L. 1991. Women and language choice in Dakar: a case of unconscious innovation. *Women and Language* 15(1), 11–20.

Tabouret-Keller, A. 1969. Le bilinguisme de l'enfant avant 6 ans: étude en milieu alsacien. Thèse lettres, Université de Strasbourg.

1995. Conclusion. Code-switching as a theoretical challenge. In Milroy & Muysken, 1995, 344–355.

1997. Language and identity. In Coulmas, 1997, 315–326.

Tabouret-Keller, A. & Luckel, F. 1981a. La dynamique sociale du changement linguistique: quelques aspects de la situation rurale en Alsace. *International Journal of the Sociology of Language* 29, 51–66.

1981b. Maintien de l'alsacien et adoption du français; éléments de la situation linguistique en milieu rural en Alsace. *Langages* 61, 39–62.

Taeschner, T. 1983. *The Sun is Feminine: a study on language acquisition in bilingual children*. Berlin: Springer.

Takashi, K. 1990. A sociolinguistic analysis of English borrowings in Japanese advertising texts. *World Englishes* 9(3), 327–341.

Tamis, A. 1986. The state of the Modern Greek language as spoken in Victoria. Unpublished PhD thesis, University of Melbourne.

Tannen D. 1989. *Talking Voices: repetition, dialogue, and imagery in conversational discourse*. Cambridge/New York: Cambridge University Press.

Thomason, S. G. 1997. Introduction. In S. G. Thomason (ed.), *Contact Languages: a wider perspective*. Amsterdam/Philadelphia: Benjamins, 1–9.

2001. *Language Contact: an introduction*. Edinburgh: Edinburgh University Press.

Thomason, S. G. & Kaufman, T. 1988. *Language Contact, Creolization and Genetic Linguistics*. Berkeley: University of California Press.

Timm, L. 1975. Spanish–English code-switching: el porqué y how-not-to. *Romance Philology* 28(4), 473–482.

1978. Code-switching in war and peace. In Paradis, 1978, 302–315.

Toribio, A. J. 2004. Convergence as an optimization strategy in bilingual speech: evidence from code-switching. *Bilingualism: Language and Cognition* 7(2), 165–173.

Toribio, A. J. & Rubin, E. J. 1996. Code-switching in generative grammar. In Roca & Jensen, 1996, 203–226.

Torras, M. C. 1998. Code negotiation and code alternation in service encounters in Catalonia. Unpublished MA dissertation, Lancaster University.

Tosi, A. 1984. *Immigration and Bilingual Education: a case study of movement of population, language change and education within the EEC*. Oxford: Pergamon Press.

Tracy, R. 1995. Child language in contact: bilingual language acquisition (English/German) in early childhood. Habilitationsschrift, University of Tübingen.

2000. Language mixing as a challenge for Linguistics. In Döpke, 2000, 11–36.

Treffers-Daller, J. 1990. Towards a uniform approach to code-switching and borrowing. Papers for the Workshop on Constraints, Conditions and Models, European Science Foundation Network on Code-switching in Language Contact. Strasbourg: ESF, 259–277.

1992. Switching between French and Dutch: (dis)similarities in the switching patterns of men and women. Paper presented at the International Conference on Code-Switching, Nijmegen, Holland, June 1992.

1994. *Mixing Two Languages, French–Dutch contact in a comparative perspective*. Berlin: Mouton de Gruyter.

1998. Variability in code-switching styles: Turkish–German code-switching patterns. In Jacobson, 1998a, 177–198.

1999. Borrowing and shift-induced interference: contrasting patterns in French–Germanic contact in Brussels and Strasbourg. *Bilingualism, Language and Cognition* 2, 77–80.

Trotter, D. A. 2002 (ed.). *Multilingualism in Later Medieval Britain*. Cambridge: D.S. Brewer.

Trudgill, P. 1972. Sex, covert prestige and linguistic change in the urban British English of Norwich. *Language in Society* 1(2), 179–195.

1974. *The Social Differentiation of English in Norwich*. Cambridge: Cambridge University Press.

1977. Creolization in reverse: reduction and simplification in the Albanian Dialects of Greece. *Transactions of the Philological Society* 7, 32–50.

1986. *Dialects in Contact*. Oxford: Blackwell.

1997. Acts of conflicting identity: the sociolinguistics of British pop songs pronunciation. In Coupland & Jaworski, 1997, 251–267.

Tsitsipis, L. D. 1998. *A Linguistic Anthropology of Praxis and Language Shift: Arvanitika (Albanian) and Greek in contact*. Oxford: Oxford University Press.

Turell, M. T. & Forcadell, M. 1992. Catalan/Spanish/English Corpus. Unpublished.

1996. Transcription and coding proposal for LIDES based on La Canonja Corpus. Paper presented at LIPPS meeting III, Nijmegen, Max Planck Institute, April 1996.

1997. Transcription, tagging and coding of bilingual corpora via LIDES. *Papers de l'IULA (Working Paper)*. Barcelona: Institut Universitari de Lingüística Aplicada, Universitat Pompeu Fabra.

Vaid, J. & Hull, R. 2002. Re-envisioning the bilingual brain using functional neuro-imaging: methodological and interpretative issues. In F. Fabbro (ed.), *Advances in the Neurolinguistics of Bilingualism: essays in honor of Michel Paradis*. University of Udine: Forum, 315–357.

Valdès-Fallis, G. 1977. Code-switching among bilingual Mexican–American women: towards an understanding of sex-related language alternation. *International Journal of the Sociology of Language* 7, 65–72.

Van der Linden, E. 2000. Non-selective access in child bilingualism activation: the lexicon. In Döpke, 2000, 37–57.

Vihman, M. M. 1985. Language differentiation by the bilingual infant. *Journal of Child Language* 12, 297–324.

1998. A developmental perspective on code-switching: conversations between a pair of bilingual siblings. *International Journal of Bilingualism* 2(1), 45–84.

Volterra, V. & Taeschner, T. 1978. The acquisition and development of language by bilingual children. *Journal of Child Language* 5, 311–326.

Von Raffler Engel, W. 1976. Linguistic and kinesic correlates in code-switching. In W. C. McCormack & S. A. Wurm (eds), *Language and Man: anthropological issues*. The Hague/Paris: Mouton de Gruyter, 229–239.

Vygotsky, L. 1934/1962/1986. *Thought and Language* (first translation into English 1962; new edition 1986). Cambridge, MA: MIT Press.

Wasow, T. 1985. Topic...comment: the wizards of ling. *Natural Language and Linguistic Theory* 3(4), 485–491.

Weinreich, U. 1953. *Languages in Contact: findings and problems*. New York: Linguistic Circle of New York. Reprinted as 1964, *Languages in Contact*. The Hague, Mouton de Gruyter.

Wei Zhang 2005. Code-choice in bidialectal interaction: the choice between Putonghua and Cantonese in a radio phone-in program in Shenzhen. *Journal of Pragmatics* 37(iii), 355–375.

Wernicke, C. 1874/1977. Der aphasische symptomencomplex: Eine psychologische studie auf anatomischer basis. In G. H. Eggert (ed.), *Wernicke's Works on Aphasia: a sourcebook and review*. The Hague: Mouton de Gruyter, 91–145.

Williams, G. 1992. *Sociolinguistics: a sociological critique*. London: Routledge.

Winford, D. 2003. *An Introduction to Contact Linguistics*. Oxford: Blackwell.

Winter, J. & Pauwels, A. 2000. Gender and language contact research in the Australian context. *Journal of Multilingual and Multicultural Development* 21(6), 508–522.

Woolard, K. A. 1988. Code-switching and comedy in Catalonia. In Heller, 1988a, 53–76.

1997. Between friends: gender, peer group structure and bilingualism in urban Catalonia. *Language in Society* 26, 533–560.

1999. Simultaneity and bivalency as strategies in bilingualism. *Journal of Linguistic Anthropology* 8(1), 3–29.

Woolard, K. & Genovese, N. 2007. Strategic bivalency in Latin and Spanish in Early Modern Spain. *Language in Society* 36(4), 487–509.

Woolford, E. 1983. Bilingual code-switching and syntactic theory. *Linguistic Inquiry* 14, 520–536.

Yip, V. & Matthews, S. 2000. Syntactic transfer in a Cantonese–English bilingual child. *Bilingualism, Language and Cognition* 3(3), 193–208.

Zentella, A. C. 1997. *Growing up Bilingual: Puerto Rican children in New York*. Oxford/ Malden, MA: Blackwell.

Zimman, L. 1993. Spanish–English code-switching. Unpublished MA dissertation, Birkbeck, University of London.

Index